Financing Water Security and Green Growth

Financing Water Security and Green Growth

Robert C. Brears

OXFORD
UNIVERSITY PRESS

OXFORD
UNIVERSITY PRESS

Great Clarendon Street, Oxford, OX2 6DP,
United Kingdom

Oxford University Press is a department of the University of Oxford.
It furthers the University's objective of excellence in research, scholarship,
and education by publishing worldwide. Oxford is a registered trade mark of
Oxford University Press in the UK and in certain other countries

Published in the United States of America by Oxford University Press
198 Madison Avenue, New York, NY 10016, United States of America

British Library Cataloguing in Publication Data
Data available

Library of Congress Control Number: 2023930620

ISBN 978–0–19–284784–3

DOI: 10.1093/oso/9780192847843.001.0001

Printed and bound in the UK by
Clays Ltd, Elcograf S.p.A.

Acknowledgement

First, I wish to thank Adam Swallow for being a visionary who enables books like mine to come to fruition. Second, I wish to thank Mum, who has a great interest in the environment and has supported me in this journey of writing the book.

Contents

List of Tables   ix

1. Introduction   1

2. Water Security and Green Growth   7

3. Innovative Policies and Technologies to Achieve Water
   Security and Green Growth   21

4. Financing Water Security and Green Growth   37

5. Green Bonds, Environmental Impact Bonds, and Green
   Loans Financing Water Security and Green Growth   53

6. Debt-for-Nature Swaps Financing Water Security and
   Green Growth   73

7. Payments for Watershed Services Financing Water
   Security and Green Growth   89

8. Market-based Instruments Financing Water Security
   and Green Growth   105

9. Public–Private Partnerships Financing Water Security
   and Green Growth   127

10. Biodiversity Offsets Financing Water Security and
    Green Growth   145

11. Tradable Permits Financing Water Security and Green Growth   165

12. Best Practices and Conclusion   187

Bibliography   203
Index   219

List of Tables

2.1 Synergies between water security and green growth   9

2.2 Interlinkages between the sustainable development goals and water   10

2.3 Urbanization and water quality   14

3.1 Types of demand management tools   23

3.2 Benefits of smart digital water management   25

3.3 Water reuse and water recycling benefits   27

3.4 Types of nature-based solutions   29

3.5 Benefits of renewable energy   33

4.1 Barriers to financing water security and green growth   39

4.2 Collaboration to achieve water security and green growth   40

4.3 Costs from failing to implement environmental corporate social responsibility   44

4.4 Blended finance instruments   45

4.5 Potential roles of blended finance   46

4.6 Principles for fostering investment in water security and green growth   49

5.1 Types of bond issuers   54

5.2 Green bond principle's indicators for sustainable water and wastewater Management Projects   58

5.3 Categories of eligibility for green projects   68

5.4 Malaysia's green technology financing scheme   70

5.5 Criteria for water sector   70

6.1 Benefits of debt-for-nature swaps   76

6.2 General elements of a debt-for-nature swap   77

6.3 Guidelines for domestic financial facilities   82

7.1 Benefits of payments for ecosystem services schemes   91

7.2 Role of intermediaries in payments for ecosystem services schemes   93

8.1 Benefits of environmental taxes and environmental charges   107

8.2 Residential charges for customers in the greater western water area   112

8.3 Various stormwater fee methods   114

8.4 Stormwater credit categories   123

9.1 Benefits of water service public–private partnerships   136

9.2 Considerations for successful water service public–private partnerships   137

9.3 Aspects of community-based public–private partnerships   142

10.1 Principles for ensuring success of biodiversity offsets   149

10.2 Common metrics used by biodiversity offset schemes   150

10.3 Benefits of aggregated biodiversity offsets   151

10.4 Options for meeting recurrent cost needs of biodiversity offsets   154

11.1 Types of tradable permit schemes   166

11.2 Types of water rights   168

11.3 Public policy benefits of water trading   169

11.4 Water entitlements, water allocations, and water usage definitions   171

11.5 Conditions for successful water quality trading schemes   172

11.6 Credit verification timelines for alternative best management practices   174

11.7 Groundwater trading structures   180

1
Introduction

Introduction

Water security and green growth worldwide are at risk from various climatic and non-climatic trends, including rapid population growth and urbanization, economic growth and rising income levels, ageing infrastructure, and increased demand for energy and food, impacting water quantity and water quality.[1,2,3,4,5,6,7,8,9,10,11,12,13,14] As such, there is an expectation that demand for innovative water management solutions will increase, in particular, solutions that enable the more efficient use of available water resources, enhance the quality of water for humans and nature, improve water resource planning, enhance resilience to extreme weather events, and mitigate carbon emissions.[15,16]

Demand management involves balancing rising demand with limited, and often variable, supplies of water to achieve water security for both humans and nature by making better use of existing water supplies before plans are made to further increase supply. Smart digital water management can facilitate demand management by increasing water efficiency, detecting leaks promptly, and monitoring droughts. Nevertheless, even with successful demand management measures, some locations will require alternative water sources, namely water reuse and water recycling initiatives. Water reuse and water recycling systems can provide a reliable, climate-resilient, and economically sound water source for non-potable and potable uses. Various water reuse and water recycling systems are available to meet non-potable and potable needs across different user groups, including urban and agricultural.[17]

Traditionally, the most common means of mitigating the risks from climatic extremes has been increasing investment in conventional—or 'grey'—infrastructure, such as dams and levees. However, engineers and decision-makers have realized the extent of the economic and environmental costs of these solutions. For example, grey infrastructure is often capital-intensive in building, operation, maintenance, and replacement. Furthermore, as it is mainly built to address a specific water management problem, it can amplify

Financing Water Security and Green Growth. Robert C. Brears, Oxford University Press. © Robert C. Brears (2023). DOI: 10.1093/oso/9780192847843.003.0001

risks downstream. Environmentally, grey infrastructure often degrades the quality and quantity of water supply, resulting in ecosystem degradation. As such, there has been a turn toward more long-term economically and environmentally sustainable solutions that provide equivalent or similar benefits to grey infrastructure.[18,19]

Nature-based solutions involve the use of natural or semi-natural systems that utilize nature's ecosystem services in the management of water resources and associated risks. For example, green infrastructure can help purify polluted water, while the equivalent grey infrastructure solution is wastewater treatment plants. To reduce the impacts of floods, green infrastructure solutions increase the water infiltration and storage capacity of wetlands and soils. Water managers can also mitigate droughts by releasing water from natural storage features such as lakes and aquifers for human and natural use. Finally, unlike grey infrastructure, the value of green infrastructure solutions can appreciate over time with the regeneration of nature and its associated ecosystem services.[20,21,22]

Regarding climate change mitigation and circular economy thinking, the facilities and infrastructure of water and wastewater treatment plants provide opportunities to generate renewable energy and recover resources from wastewater. Energy derived from wastewater treatment is a renewable energy resource. In particular, water utilities can implement traditional renewable energy activities on facility-owned buildings and surrounding land. At the same time, numerous resources can be recovered from wastewater to generate new revenue streams for water utilities.[23]

Nonetheless, despite knowledge of the multiple benefits that demand management, smart digital water management, nature-based solutions, and renewable energy and resource recovery from wastewater provide, a key barrier to their widespread adoption is a lack of understanding of their financing such as: how can demand management strategies be financed sustainably?, what are the best practices for blended finance projects?, and who should pay for green infrastructure solutions? For instance, water is generally an under-valued resource that is not properly accounted for by investors that depend on it; water services are generally under-priced, resulting in limited resources for upgrading ageing infrastructure; and often the benefits of green infrastructure can accrue to multiple stakeholders, making it difficult to determine who should pay and which funding structure to use. Furthermore, there are no one-size-fits-all solutions for financing water infrastructure and services as they are highly context-specific regarding, for example, climatic risks and ecosystems, geographical scale, level of implementation, governance structures, socio-economic beneficiaries, and time scales.[24,25]

Financing Water Security and Green Growth provides a comprehensive overview of innovative financial instruments and approaches available to implement, as well as mainstream water security and green growth initiatives at various scales and in different contexts. In particular, the book provides readers with knowledge of how the water sector is applying a range of financial instruments and approaches to create climate-resilient water supplies, reduce water–energy–food nexus pressures, encourage water conservation and efficiency, increase water reliability, decrease the costs and pollution associated with wastewater disposal, utilize natural processes to improve water quality, manage water quantity by restoring the hydrologic function of the landscape, and improve overall water governance. Furthermore, the book provides in-depth case studies of the innovative application of financing tools to achieve water security and green growth in various locations of differing climates, lifestyles, and income levels, with best practices identified.

The synopsis of the book is as follows.

Chapter 2: Water Security and Green Growth: This chapter first provides an overview of the concept of water security before discussing it in the context of green growth. Finally, the chapter will review the various climatic and non-climatic challenges to achieving water security and green growth.

Chapter 3: Innovative Policies and Technologies to Achieve Water Security and Green Growth: This chapter first defines the concept of innovative water management before discussing the various innovative policies and technologies available to achieve water security and green growth, including demand management, smart digital water management, alternative water supplies, nature-based solutions, renewable energy, and resource recovery.

Chapter 4: Financing Water Security and Green Growth: This chapter first defines the concept of innovative financing to achieve water security and green growth. The chapter then reviews the various sources of finance available. Finally, the chapter provides a series of principles for fostering investment in water security and green growth projects.

Chapter 5: Green Bonds, Environmental Impact Bonds, and Green Loans Financing Water Security and Green Growth: This chapter first reviews the differences between green bonds and regular bonds. The chapter then discusses how environmental impact bonds are a form of debt characterized by a pay for success component that determines the amount that investors are repaid based on environmental performance. Finally, the chapter discusses how green loans support various green projects, including those focusing on achieving water security and green growth.

Chapter 6: Debt-for-Nature Swaps Financing Water Security and Green Growth: This chapter first discusses the concept of debt-for-nature (DFN) swaps before discussing how they can be operationalized and administered. The chapter then provides an overview of best practices for DFN swaps. Finally, the chapter provides case studies of DFN swaps implemented to achieve water security and green growth.

Chapter 7: Payments for Watershed Services to Achieve Water Security and Green Growth: This chapter first discusses the concept of Payments for Ecosystem Services, the benefits they provide, and the various design considerations that should be addressed. The chapter then discusses the concept of Payments for Watershed Services, the various benefits these schemes provide, and a guideline to ensure a scheme's success.

Chapter 8: Market-based Instruments Financing Water Security and Green Growth: This chapter discusses the various market-based instruments available for locations to finance water security and green growth, particularly water pollution taxes, various water pricing structures, subsidies, and incentives.

Chapter 9: Public-Private Partnerships Financing Water Security and Green Growth: This chapter first discusses the concept of public–private partnerships (PPPs) and their financing. The chapter then discusses PPPs in the context of water resources management. Finally, the chapter reviews irrigation-specific and community-based PPPs for green infrastructure.

Chapter 10: Biodiversity Offsets Financing Water Security and Green Growth: This chapter first defines the concept of biodiversity offsets. The chapter then reviews how their performance and success can be enhanced, followed by a review on how to ensure their financial sustainability. Finally, the chapter provides a framework for preparing and implementing biodiversity offsets on the ground or in the water.

Chapter 11: Tradable Permits Financing Water Security and Green Growth: This chapter first discusses the concept of tradable permit schemes before discussing tradable water rights and water quality trading. The chapter then reviews the concept of urban water trading and stormwater volume credit trading. Following this, the chapter discusses groundwater trading and the acquiring of water for the environment.

Chapter 12: Best Practices and Conclusion

Notes

1. Nigel W. Arnell et al., 'The Implications of Climate Change for the Water Environment in England', *Progress in Physical Geography: Earth and Environment* 39, no. 1 (2015).

2. R.C. Brears, *Urban Water Security* (Chichester, UK; Hoboken, NJ: John Wiley & Sons, 2016).

3. R.C. Brears, *Blue and Green Cities: The Role of Blue-Green Infrastructure in Managing Urban Water Resources* (Palgrave Macmillan UK, 2018).

4. Robert I. McDonald et al., 'Water on an Urban Planet: Urbanization and the Reach of Urban Water Infrastructure', *Global Environmental Change* 27 (2014).

5. PwC, 'The World in 2050: Will the Shift in Global Economic Power Continue?' (2015), http://www.pwc.com/gx/en/issues/the-economy/assets/world-in-2050-february-2015.pdf.

6. Sharon L. Harlan et al., 'Household Water Consumption in an Arid City: Affluence, Affordance, and Attitudes', *Society & Natural Resources* 22, no. 8 (2009).

7. UN-Water, 'Partnerships for Improving Water and Energy Access, Efficiency and Sustainability' (2014), http://www.un.org/waterforlifedecade/water_and_energy_2014/pdf/water_and_energy_2014_final_report.pdf.

8. John Kearney, 'Food Consumption Trends and Drivers', *Philosophical Transactions of the Royal Society of London. Series B, Biological sciences* 365, no. 1554 (2010).

9. UNESCO, 'Managing Water under Uncertainty and Risk' (2012), http://www.unesco.org/new/fileadmin/MULTIMEDIA/HQ/SC/pdf/WWDR4%20Volume%201-Managing%20Water%20under%20Uncertainty%20and%20Risk.pdf.

10. McDonald et al., 'Water on an Urban Planet: Urbanization and the Reach of Urban Water Infrastructure'.

11. Sam Fox et al., 'Experimental Quantification of Contaminant Ingress into a Buried Leaking Pipe During Transient Events', *Journal of Hydraulic Engineering* 142, no. 1 (2016).

12. Melle Säve-Söderbergh et al., 'Gastrointestinal Illness Linked to Incidents in Drinking Water Distribution Networks in Sweden', *Water Research* 122 (2017).

13. IEA, 'Weo-2016 Special Report: Water-Energy Nexus' (2016), https://webstore.iea.org/weo-2016-special-report-water-energy-nexus.

14. FAO, 'Towards a Water and Food Secure Future: Critical Perspectives for Policy-Makers' (2015), http://www.fao.org/3/a-i4560e.pdf.

15. Uta Wehn and Carlos Montalvo, 'Exploring the Dynamics of Water Innovation: Foundations for Water Innovation Studies', *Journal of Cleaner Production* 171 (2018).

16. R.C. Brears, *Climate Resilient Water Resources Management* (Cham, Switzerland: Palgrave Macmillan, 2018).

17. Brears, *Urban Water Security*.

18. Brears, *Blue and Green Cities*.

19. *Nature-Based Solutions to 21st Century Challenges* (Oxfordshire, UK: Routledge, 2020).

20. *Blue and Green Cities: The Role of Blue-Green Infrastructure in Managing Urban Water Resources*.

21. *Regional Water Security* (Wiley, 2021).

22. *Water Resources Management: Innovative and Green Solutions* (De Gruyter, 2021).

23. *Developing the Circular Water Economy* (Cham, Switzerland: Palgrave Macmillan, 2020).

24. J. Guy Alaerts, 'Financing for Water—Water for Financing: A Global Review of Policy and Practice', *Sustainability* 11, no. 3 (2019).

25. Robert Schmitt, 'Pursuing Innovative Finance Models to Enable Beneficial Energy and Water Infrastructure and Systems', *The Electricity Journal* 33, no. 1 (2020).

2
Water Security and Green Growth

Introduction

The concept of water security has received increased attention over the past couple of decades since it emerged in the 1990s, with multiple definitions of its concept existing, promoted by a range of international organizations.[1,2,3] The term has transitioned over time from being used to express a general vision to it being used to explicitly state the goals we wish to achieve with better management, such as protecting water quality, ensuring equitable access, and protecting environmental flows, for instance.[4,5] Furthermore, multilateral agencies and national governments, among others, are calling for the development of the green economy where investments and innovation underpin sustainable growth and new economic opportunities.[6] According to the Global Water Partnership, water security and green growth are inextricably linked. Water touches every aspect of society and the environment, is essential for human well-being, is embedded in energy and other productive activities, and is vital for sustaining ecosystems on which everything depends. Therefore, innovative thinking and effective solutions are required to enhance water security and green growth synergies.[7] This chapter will first provide an overview of the concept of water security before discussing it in the context of green growth. Finally, the chapter will review the various climatic and non-climatic challenges to achieving water security and green growth.

Water Security

UN-Water defines water security as 'the capacity of a population to safeguard sustainable access to adequate quantities of acceptable quality water for sustaining livelihoods, human well-being, and socio-economic development, for ensuring protection against water-borne pollution and water-related disasters, and for preserving ecosystems in a climate of peace and political

Financing Water Security and Green Growth. Robert C. Brears, Oxford University Press. © Robert C. Brears (2023).
DOI: 10.1093/oso/9780192847843.003.0002

stability'.[8] Furthering this concept, the Asian Development Bank developed a water security framework with five interdependent key dimensions:

1. *Household water security*: The foundation of water security is what happens at the household level. Providing all people with reliable, safe water, and sanitation services should be the main priority of all decision-makers. Efforts need to eradicate poverty and support economic development.
2. *Economic water security*: Water is used in all economic activities, such as powering industry and cooling energy-generating plants. Economic water security is concerned with the productive use of water to sustain economic growth in various sectors of the economy, including food production, industry, and energy.
3. *Urban water security*: Cities have become important drivers of the global economy. As such, urban water security is concerned with the better management of water and related services and supporting vibrant and liveable cities.
4. *Environmental water security*: The environment and natural resources have suffered from neglect as governments have prioritized economic growth over environmental objectives. However, sustainable development and improved lives depend on healthy water bodies and ecosystems.
5. *Resilience to water-related disasters*: Communities need to be resilient to water-related disasters. Resilient communities can adapt to change and are able to reduce risk from natural disasters related to water.[9]

Water Security and Green Growth

The United Nations Environment Programme defines the green economy as one that results in 'improved human well-being and social equity, while significantly reducing environmental risks and ecological scarcities'. In the green economy, green growth is defined by the OECD as 'fostering economic growth and development, while ensuring that natural assets continue to provide the resources and environmental services on which our well-being relies'. Green growth is relevant to all countries, irrespective of the level of development, as high-income countries will need to retrofit their resource-consuming industries and lifestyles, while lower-income countries can avoid copying damaging development paths and instead leapfrog old

Table 2.1 Synergies between water security and green growth

Characteristics of green growth	Characteristics of water security
Effective use of natural resources in economic growth	Enough water for social and economic development
Valuing ecosystems	Ensuring adequate water for ecosystems
Inter-generational economic policies	Sustainable availability of water for future generations
Increased use of renewable sources of energy	Harnessing the productive power of water
Protection of vital assets from climatic extremes	Minimizing the destructive power of water
Reducing waste of resources	Maintaining water quality and avoiding pollution and degradation

solutions and adopt new technologies and ideas without incurring extra costs.[10] Overall, innovative thinking and effective solutions are required to enhance synergies between water security and green growth, as outlined in Table 2.1.[11]

Water Security, Ecosystems, and the Sustainable Development Goals

The relationship between water security and ecosystems is one of mutual benefit and support. Ensuring sufficient, good quality freshwater is crucial for ecosystem health. A healthy ecosystem provides many benefits, including clean water supplies, water for agricultural production, habitat for biodiversity, recreation, and tourism, and greater resilience to climatic extremes.[12,13] Therefore, maintaining the integrity of ecosystems before they become compromised is crucial in achieving water security. Furthermore, if ecosystems are not protected, then the success of achieving each Sustainable Development Goal (SDG) is jeopardized as every SDG has an interlinkage with water (Table 2.2).[14]

Table 2.2 Interlinkages between the sustainable development goals and water

Sustainable development goal	Interlinkage with water
No poverty	Consistent access to clean water and the buffering of water-related extreme events by ecosystems are key to reducing poverty worldwide
Zero hunger	Sustainable and efficient use of water in agriculture can meet the growing demand for food from the increasing world population
Good health and well-being	Well-functioning ecosystems support high levels of water quality, improving various aspects of quality of life, such as reduced exposure to water-borne diseases in addition to cultural and spiritual well-being
Quality education	Educating the next generation of environmental stewards focuses the education system on twenty-first-century problem solutions
Gender equality	Improved water services can reduce gender inequality in household water collection and management, which in low-income countries typically fall to women and girls
Clean water and sanitation	Upstream healthy ecosystems have an essential role in providing drinking water to downstream users
Affordable and clean energy	Efficient water use in both renewable and non-renewable energy systems reduces costs, enhances the resilience of energy systems to climate change, and mitigates emissions
Decent work and economic growth	Ecosystem-based water systems support long-term economic growth. New investment in water-related technologies creates employment opportunities
Industrial innovation and infrastructure	Innovation in water technology can enhance efficiency and economic development
Reduced inequalities	Rectifying imbalances in water services and sanitation, now unequally distributed among high-income and low-income countries, is a significant step towards equality generally
Sustainable cities and communities	Efficient use of water in cities can enhance resilience to climate change
Responsible consumption and production	Reducing water needs in production and consumption reduces threats to human water security and biodiversity
Climate action	Efficient use of water mitigates climate change and enhances adaptation to extreme water-related events
Life below water	Improving water quality will reduce ocean pollution and sustain fisheries
Life on land	Upstream water source protection promotes forest conservation and restoration measures
Peace, justice, and strong institutions	Well-managed river basins can reduce conflicts over scarce water resources within and across national borders
Partnerships for the goals	Water's role in government, civil society, and the private sector means partnerships can be formed to achieve broader development agendas

Challenges to Water Security and Green Growth

Water security and green growth worldwide is at risk from various climatic and non-climatic trends, and so achieving it has become one of the highest priorities of governments and policymakers globally.[15] The challenges include the following.

Climate Change

Human activities have caused around 1.0 degrees Celsius of global warming above pre-industrial levels, with global warming likely to reach 1.5 degrees Celsius between 2030 and 2052 if we continue a business-as-usual approach. Extreme precipitation events are increasing as the climate warms and the atmosphere's capacity to hold water increases. At the same time, warmer temperatures increase the frequency of heatwaves and droughts. The result is that some areas will have wetter climates and others drier. In addition to the increased intensification of extreme events, climate change is resulting in extended periods of rainfall and longer heatwaves and droughts.[16,17,18] Climate change is impacting water quantity and water quality as well as freshwater biodiversity. Climate change impacts the volume and timing of river flows, inflows to lakes, transitional waters, and the coastal zone, and groundwater recharge. Groundwater is typically recharged during winter when soil moisture deficits are minimal. Warmer temperatures will reduce the recharge season (starting later and finishing earlier). Climate change impacts surface water quality, resulting in the degradation of drinking water quality, particularly during extreme meteorological events. Among water quality parameters, dissolved organic matter, micropollutants, and pathogens from a range of agricultural, domestic, industrial, and transport activities rise in concentration or number in waterways during heavy rainfall events. During dry periods, pollutant concentrations in waterways increase due to lower flow volumes. Sea level rise can lead to saline intrusion into coastal aquifers; however, the exact effect is dependent on local hydraulic gradients and the amount of abstraction from the aquifer. Finally, climate change impacts freshwater biodiversity from eutrophication, organic enrichment, pollution, changes in water temperature, and changes in the volume and timing of river flows and lake water levels. For instance, many species have thermal limits that determine the success of spawning, migration, and survival.[19,20,21,22]

Water-related Disasters

Floods and droughts are the two main water-related disasters. Over the period 2009–2019, floods resulted in nearly 55,000 deaths and affected another 103 million people. They also caused nearly $80 billion in economic losses. Over the same period, droughts resulted in the deaths of over 2,000 people while affecting another 100 million people. Furthermore, droughts directly resulted in over $10 billion in economic losses.[23] Climate change is increasing the frequency and intensity of floods and droughts in all climate regions.[24] For example, in the United States, the current likelihood of a megadrought (a drought lasting more than three decades) in the Southwest and Central Plains is 12 per cent. If greenhouse gas emissions continue an upward trajectory, there is an 80 per cent likelihood of a decades-long megadrought in the region between 2050 and 2099.[25] In north-western Europe, climate change is increasing the risk of flooding. In some local hotspots, flows have increased by nearly 18 per cent every decade, and a 100-year-flood discharge in 1960 has now typically become a 50–80-year flood discharge: potentially reducing the levels of protection provided by existing flood defence structures.[26]

Population Growth

The world's population is projected to increase from around 7.7 billion in 2019 to around 8.5 billion in 2030, 9.7 billion in 2050, and 10.9 billion in 2100. Population growth will challenge sustainable development, with the 47 least developed countries among the world's fastest-growing, some of which are projected to double in population between 2019 and 2050.[27] Around a quarter of the world's population lives in potential severely water-scarce areas, and by 2050 this will increase by 42 to 95 per cent.[28] A growing global population and a shift towards more resource-intensive consumption patterns have resulted in global freshwater withdrawals for agriculture, industry, and municipal uses increasing nearly six-fold since 1900. Global demand for water has more than doubled since the 1960s. Domestic water demand has increased 600 per cent from 1960 to 2014, significantly faster than any other sector.

Meanwhile, 12 per cent of the world's population drinks water from unimproved or unsafe sources. In addition, more than 30 per cent of the world's population lives without any form of sanitation—this lack of sanitation results in water pollution. Currently, 90 per cent of sewage in developing countries is discharged into the water untreated.[29]

Rapid Urbanization

In 2018, 55 per cent of the world's population lived in urban areas, and by 2050, it is estimated to be 68 per cent. The world's urban population reached 4.2 billion in 2018, and the combination of an increase in population growth and urbanization will see the world add 2.5 billion to the world's urban population by 2050. Finally, megacities (cities with 10 million inhabitants or more) will increase from 33 in 2018 to 43 in 2030.[30] As a result, urban water demand is projected to increase by 50–80 per cent by 2050, often in regions that experience irrigation development.[31] Water reallocation from rural to urban regions is one of the main responses to meeting the rising demand for water in cities and addressing the impacts of climate change and water quality problems. In a review of 69 urban centres receiving water through 103 reallocation projects, around 16 billion cubic metres of water was transferred per annum over 13,000 kilometres to urban recipients in regions with a total estimated 2015 population of 383 million.[32] Therefore, there is a high potential for conflict between the urban and agricultural sectors as climate change and urbanization intensify.[33] Urbanization impacts water quality within urban boundaries, with Table 2.3 detailing the slow changes in land and water use when urbanization occurs and the possible effect on the local water system.[34] Urbanization also impacts urban source watersheds. Most watersheds that cities rely on for drinking water have some level of degradation from sedimentation and phosphorous and nitrogen pollution, resulting in rising water treatment costs.[35]

Global Material Usage

From 1970 to 2017, the annual global extraction of materials grew from 27 billion tonnes to 92 billion tonnes. At the same time, gross domestic product (GDP) quadrupled. The material footprint includes the volumes of biomass, metals, non-metallic metals, and fossil fuels extracted to achieve socio-economic goals. Most growth in resource extraction has occurred in upper-middle-income countries, which increased their global share of domestic material consumption from 33 per cent in 1970 to 56 per cent in 2017. On a per-capita basis, the material footprint consumption in high-income countries is 60 per cent higher than in upper-middle-income countries and 13 times the level of low-income countries. It is estimated that natural resource extraction and processing accounts for more than 90 per cent of global biodiversity loss and water stress, in addition to half of global

Table 2.3 Urbanization and water quality

Stage of urbanization	Change in land use	Water quality impact
Beginning of urbanization	• Removal of trees and vegetation • Houses being built, some with sewer and others with septic tanks	• More stormwater runoff and erosion due to less vegetation as it runs downhill • More sediment is washed into streams • Flooding can occur due to water-drainage pattern changes
Continuing urbanization	• Urbanization is finished by the addition of more roads, houses, and commercial and industrial buildings • More wastewater is discharged into local waterways • New water supply and distribution systems are built to supply the growing population • Stream channels are changed to accommodate building construction	• More impervious surfaces lower the water table. The runoff flows into storm sewers which then flow into streams, polluting water and causing flooding • Changing of stream channels can increase flooding and erosion • More sewage is discharged into streams • The use of large wells can lower the water table, potentially causing saltwater to be drawn into drinking-water wells

greenhouse gas emissions. Since 2000, extraction rates have accelerated to 3.2 per cent per annum, mainly driven by significant investments in infrastructure and higher material living standards in developing and transitioning countries. Under a business-as-usual scenario, resource use will continue to grow to 190 billion tonnes by 2060, with industrial water withdrawals increasing by up to 100 per cent from 2010 levels.[36,37] This increase in global material extraction follows the same path as economic growth, with future global GDP in 2050 projected to be 2.4 times greater than at present in real terms.[38]

Ageing Water Infrastructure

Drinking water, wastewater, and stormwater services are provided through a network of treatment plants, pumps, pipes, storage facilities, and other assets operated by both public and private-owned utilities. These structures and facilities are referred to as 'water infrastructure'. In many countries, the water and wastewater systems were built over a century ago. As pipes, plants, and pumps reach the end of their expected lifespan, they need to be upgraded, replaced, or fortified. In addition, many water and wastewater systems are not equipped to meet the new demands of population growth, increased treatment requirements, and the impacts of climate change. Ageing infrastructure is resulting in significant leakage. For example, in the United States, drinking water systems currently lose around six billion gallons of treated water per day or 2.1 trillion gallons per annum.[39] Any contaminant on the exterior of a water distribution system can enter the potable water supplies during a leak. Chemical contaminants can include pesticides, petroleum products, fertilizers, solvents, detergents, pharmaceuticals, and other compounds. If chemical contaminants intrude in sufficient concentration or volume, it could result in acute toxicity. Microbial contaminants are also of concern because some microbes, such as viruses, can cause an infection with a single organism, even with dilution. Furthermore, treating and pumping this water only for it to be lost is economically costly, with the United States losing an estimated $7.6 billion of treated water in 2019 due to leaks.

Meanwhile, combined sewer systems were constructed based on models and population projections that are outdated now. Combined sewer overflows are likely to increase with climate change resulting in more frequent and intense storm events. Finally, even in high-income countries, water infrastructure is lacking, with portions of the population not having access to adequate drinking water quality. For example, in Europe, over 16 million people still lack access to basic drinking water and more than 31 million need basic sanitation.[40,41]

Water–Energy Nexus

Water and energy systems are interdependent, with water used in all energy production and electricity generation phases. Energy is required to extract, convey, and deliver water of appropriate quality for various human uses and treat wastewater before releasing it to the environment.[42] In 2014, around 4 per cent of global electricity consumption was used to extract, distribute, and treat water and wastewater, along with 50 million tonnes of oil equivalent of thermal energy, mostly diesel used for irrigation pumps and gas in desalination plants. Over the period from 2014 to 2040, it is estimated that the amount of energy used in the water sector will more than double. The most significant increase will come from desalination, followed by large-scale water transfer and increasing demand for wastewater treatment (and higher levels of treatment). As a result, electricity consumption in the water sector is projected to rise by 80 per cent.[43] At the same time, water is needed in the energy sector with water used in thermal power plants for cooling, for washing, dust suppression, and transportation of coal, in the output of hydropower plants which depend on inflows into the reservoir, and in the production of biofuels, which depends on water for energy crops.[44] The energy sector is responsible for 10 per cent of global water withdrawals. While water withdrawals for the energy sector between 2014 and 2040 are projected to rise by less than 2 per cent to reach over 400 billion cubic metres (bcm), the amount of water consumed (water withdrawn but not returned to a source) will increase by almost 60 per cent to over 75 bcm, mainly due to the power sector switching to advanced cooling technologies that withdraw less water but consume more as well as a rise in biofuel production and greater deployment of nuclear power.[45]

Water–Food Nexus

The challenge of feeding an increasing world population and meeting the demand for water is significant, with food demand by 2050 increasing by 60 per cent. Already, agriculture is the largest water user, accounting for more than 70 per cent of global freshwater withdrawals.[46] Worldwide, 1.2 billion people live in areas where severe water shortages and scarcity challenge agriculture. It is estimated that around 11 per cent of rainfed cropland and 14 per cent of pastureland experience severe recurring droughts, and over 60 per cent of irrigated cropland is highly water-stressed. Furthermore, demand for water will increase significantly due to changing dietary patterns, including a shift from unprocessed cereals towards highly processed foods, livestock products, and high-value crops, whose consumption is expected to increase, particularly in low-income and lower-middle-income countries continually. Changes in diets impact water demand as livestock products and oils require more water than cereals, starchy roots, fruits, and vegetables.[47] At the same time, agriculture causes water pollution through its discharge of pollutants and sediment to surface and/or groundwater, net loss of soil by poor agricultural practices, and salinization and waterlogging of irrigated land.[48] For example, in the European Union, 38 per cent of water bodies are under significant pressure from agricultural pollution. At the same time, in the United States, agriculture is the primary source of pollution in rivers and streams.[49]

Greenhouse Gas Emissions

Greenhouse gas emissions from the water sector are mainly associated with grid electricity use, which is consumed by a range of key processes: treating water to a potable standard, pumping water around the water supply network, pumping wastewater around the sewer network, and treating wastewater to a standard appropriate for discharge to receiving waters. With increased environmental regulation and higher water quality standards, treatment processes are becoming more high-tech and complex, often resulting in rising energy consumption and associated greenhouse gas emissions. Water utilities collectively influence up to 12 per cent of regional total primary energy consumption, with energy mainly used for water heating. Urban water utilities typically account for 1–2 per cent of aggregate global primary energy use and at times up to 6 per cent of regional electricity use. The result is that urban water management's regional greenhouse gas emissions are up to 17 per cent. It is estimated that 58 per cent of emissions from urban water utilities comes from energy use, while 40 per cent is attributed to treatment processes and 2 per cent from chemical use.[50,51]

Notes

1. Christina Cook and Karen Bakker, 'Water Security: Debating an Emerging Paradigm', *Global Environmental Change* 22, no. 1 (2012).
2. Robert G. Varady et al., 'Adaptive Management and Water Security in a Global Context: Definitions, Concepts, and Examples', *Current Opinion in Environmental Sustainability* 21 (2016).
3. Katherine Selena Taylor, 'Australian Water Security Framings across Administrative Levels', *Water Security* 12 (2021).
4. ADB, 'Asian Water Development Outlook 2016: Strengthening Water Security in Asia and the Pacific' (2016), https://www.adb.org/sites/default/files/publication/189411/awdo-2016.pdf.
5. Robert G. Varady et al., 'The Exigencies of Transboundary Water Security: Insights on Community Resilience', *Current Opinion in Environmental Sustainability* 44 (2020).
6. GWP, 'Water in the Green Economy' (2012), http://www.gwp.org/Global/ToolBox/Publications/Perspective%20Papers/03%20Water%20in%20the%20Green%20Economy%20(2012).pdf.
7. Ibid.

8. UN-Water, 'Water Security and the Global Water Agenda' (2013), https://www.unwater.org/publications/water-security-global-water-agenda/.

9. ADB, 'Asian Water Development Outlook 2016: Strengthening Water Security in Asia and the Pacific'.

10. GWP, 'Water in the Green Economy'.

11. Ibid.

12. UN-Water, 'Water Security & the Global Water Agenda' (2013), https://www.unwater.org/publications/water-security-global-water-agenda/#:~:text=The%20Brief%2C%20produced%20by%20UN,the%20umbrella%20of%20water%20security.

13. Charles J. Vörösmarty et al., 'Ecosystem-Based Water Security and the Sustainable Development Goals (Sdgs)', *Ecohydrology & Hydrobiology* 18, no. 4 (2018).

14. Ibid.

15. Mukand S. Babel et al., 'Measuring Water Security: A Vital Step for Climate Change Adaptation', *Environmental Research* 185 (2020).

16. IPCC, 'Summary for Policymakers' (2018), https://www.ipcc.ch/site/assets/uploads/sites/2/2019/05/SR15_SPM_version_report_LR.pdf

17. Peter Pfleiderer et al., 'Summer Weather Becomes More Persistent in a 2 °C World', *Nature Climate Change* 9, no. 9 (2019).

18. WHO, 'Heatwaves', https://www.who.int/health-topics/heatwaves#tab=tab_1.

19. I. Delpla et al., 'Impacts of Climate Change on Surface Water Quality in Relation to Drinking Water Production', *Environment International* 35, no. 8 (2009).

20. Nigel W. Arnell et al., 'The Implications of Climate Change for the Water Environment in England', *Progress in Physical Geography: Earth and Environment* 39, no. 1 (2015).

21. D. L. Swain et al., 'Increased Flood Exposure Due to Climate Change and Population Growth in the United States', *Earth's Future* 8, no. 11 (2020).

22. Nasrin Alamdari et al., 'Evaluating the Impact of Climate Change on Water Quality and Quantity in an Urban Watershed Using an Ensemble Approach', *Estuaries and Coasts* 43, no. 1 (2020).

23. UNESCO World Water Assessment Programme, 'UN World Water Development Report 2021: Water and Climate Change' (2021), https://www.unwater.org/publications/un-world-water-development-report-2021/.

24. Hossein Tabari, 'Climate Change Impact on Flood and Extreme Precipitation Increases with Water Availability', *Scientific Reports* 10, no. 1 (2020).

25. NASA, 'Carbon Emissions Could Dramatically Increase Risk of U.S. Megadroughts', https://climate.nasa.gov/news/2238/carbon-emissions-could-dramatically-increase-risk-of-us-megadroughts/.

26. Günter Blöschl et al., 'Changing Climate Both Increases and Decreases European River Floods', *Nature* 573, no. 7772 (2019).

27. United Nations Department of Economic and Social Affairs, 'World Population Prospects 2019: Highlights' (2019), https://population.un.org/wpp/Publications/Files/WPP2019_Highlights.pdf.

28. Alberto Boretti and Lorenzo Rosa, 'Reassessing the Projections of the World Water Development Report', *npj Clean Water* 2, no. 1 (2019).

29. Ibid.

30. Population Division UN Department of Economic and Social Affairs, '2018 Revision of World Urbanization Prospects' (2018), https://www.un.org/development/desa/publications/2018-revision-of-world-urbanization-prospects.html.

31. Boretti and Rosa, 'Reassessing the Projections of the World Water Development Report.'

32. Dustin Garrick et al., 'Rural Water for Thirsty Cities: A Systematic Review of Water Reallocation from Rural to Urban Regions', *Environmental Research Letters* 14, no. 4 (2019).

33. Martina Flörke, Christof Schneider, and Robert I. McDonald, 'Water Competition between Cities and Agriculture Driven by Climate Change and Urban Growth', *Nature Sustainability* 1, no. 1 (2018).

34. USGS, 'Urbanization and Water Quality', https://www.usgs.gov/special-topic/water-science-school/science/urbanization-and-water-quality?qt-science_center_objects=0#qt-science_center_objects.

35. Robert I. McDonald et al., 'Estimating Watershed Degradation over the Last Century and Its Impact on Water-Treatment Costs for the World's Large Cities', *Proceedings of the National Academy of Sciences* 113, no. 32 (2016).

36. International Resource Panel, 'Global Resources Outlook 2019: Natural Resources for the Future We Want' (2019), https://www.resourcepanel.org/reports/global-resources-outlook

37. System of Environmental Economic Accounting, 'Economy-Wide Material Flow Accounts and the Sustainable Use of Natural Resources in the Economy', https://seea.un.org/zh/news/economy-wide-material-flow-accounts-and-sustainable-use-natural-resources-economy.

38. FAO, 'More People, More Food, Worse Water? A Global Review of Water Pollution from Agriculture' (2018), http://www.fao.org/3/ca0146en/CA0146EN.pdf

39. American Society of Civil Engineers, 'The Economic Benefits of Investing in Water Infrastructure: How a Failure to Act Would Affect the Us Economic Recovery' (2020), http://www.uswateralliance.org/sites/uswateralliance.org/files/publications/The%20Economic%20Benefits%20of%20Investing%20in%20Water%20Infrastructure_final.pdf

40. Ibid.

41. WHO Europe, 'Water and Sanitation', https://www.euro.who.int/en/health-topics/environment-and-health/water-and-sanitation

42. R.C. Brears, *The Green Economy and the Water-Energy-Food Nexus* (London: Palgrave Macmillan UK, 2017).

43. IEA, 'Introduction to the Water-Energy Nexus', https://www.iea.org/articles/introduction-to-the-water-energy-nexus

44. European Commission, 'Water-Energy Nexus in Europe' (2019), https://publications.jrc.ec.europa.eu/repository/bitstream/JRC115853/online_ecj095x_policy_report_interactive_4.pdf.

45. IEA, 'Water-Energy Nexus: World Energy Outlook Special Report' (2017), https://www.iea.org/reports/water-energy-nexus.

46. Boretti and Rosa, 'Reassessing the Projections of the World Water Development Report.'

47. FAO, 'The State of Food and Agriculture 2020' (2020), http://www.fao.org/documents/card/en/c/cb1447en/.

48. 'Control of Water Pollution from Agriculture' (1996), http://www.fao.org/3/w2598e/w2598e00.htm#Contents.

49. 'More People, More Food, Worse Water? A Global Review of Water Pollution from Agriculture'.

50. WaCCLim, 'The Roadmap to a Low-Carbon Urban Water Utility' (2018), http://wacclim. org/wp-content/uploads/2018/12/2018_WaCCliM_Roadmap_EN_SCREEN.pdf.

51. Qian Zhang et al., 'Hidden Greenhouse Gas Emissions for Water Utilities in China's Cities', *Journal of Cleaner Production* 162 (2017).

3

Innovative Policies and Technologies to Achieve Water Security and Green Growth

Introduction

With challenges to the water sector increasing over the course of the century, there is an expectation that demand for innovative water management solutions will increase, in particular, solutions that enable the more efficient use of available water resources, enhance the quality of water for humans and nature, improve water resource planning to balance rising demand with limited, and often variable, supplies of water, enhance resilience to extreme weather events, and mitigate carbon emissions.[1,2] This chapter will first define the concept of innovative water management before discussing the various innovative policies and technologies available to achieve water security and green growth, including demand management, smart digital water management, alternative water supplies, nature-based solutions, renewable energy, and resource recovery.

Innovative Water Management

In the context of the water sector, innovation can be defined as 'the creation, development and implementation of a new product, technology, service, tariff design or process of production with the aim of improving efficiency, effectiveness or competitive advantage. It includes new ways of acquiring or deploying inputs, such as financial resources. The change may be incremental or fundamental.'[3] It should be noted that the definition includes the following:

- It deals with both products and processes.
- It refers to the creation, development, implementation of a new product/process developed either in-house or by other companies and sectors.

Financing Water Security and Green Growth. Robert C. Brears, Oxford University Press. © Robert C. Brears (2023).
DOI: 10.1093/oso/9780192847843.003.0003

- All products and processes to be new or novel.
- The aim must be to improve efficiency, effectiveness or increase competitive advantage.[4]

A vital aspect of the definition of innovation is that it must contain a degree of novelty, specifically one or more of the following:

- *New to the firm*: The innovation must be new to the firm. Other firms may have already implemented a product, process, marketing method, or organizational method, but if it is new to the firm (or in the context of products and processes, it is significantly improved), then it is an innovation for that firm.
- *New to the market*: Innovations are new to the market when the firm is the first to introduce the innovation to the market, where a market is defined as the firm and its competitors, and it can include a geographic region or product line.
- *New to the country*: An innovation is new to the country when the firm is the first to introduce the innovation for all domestic markets and industries.
- *New to the world*: An innovation is new to the world when the firm is the first to introduce the innovation for all markets and industries internationally.[5]

Innovative Water Management Technologies

In water resources management, the term 'technology' comprises hardware, software, and orgware. Hardware includes physical infrastructure and technical equipment, while software includes approaches, processes, and methodologies, for example, planning and decision support systems, models, knowledge transfer mechanisms, and capacity building. Finally, orgware includes organizational and institutional arrangements as well as ownership models.[6]

Demand Management

Demand management involves making better use of existing water supplies before increasing them further. Specifically, it promotes water conservation during normal and abnormal conditions through changes in practices, culture, and people's attitudes towards water resources. Demand management comprises a variety of interventions and organizational systems that intend to improve technical, social, economic, environmental, and institutional efficiencies in the various uses of water (Table 3.1) while providing a variety of benefits, including:

- Reducing loss and misuse in the various water sectors.
- Optimizing water use by ensuring reasonable allocation between various water users while considering the supply needs of streamflow processes, resource conservation, and quality, as well as the development of in situ uses of water, such as recreational use and energy.
- Adding more value per unit of resource mobilized.
- Facilitating significant financial and infrastructural savings for cities and countries, as well as companies.
- Helping reduce the pressure on resources by reducing or halting unsustainable exploitation of both renewable and non-renewable water sources.[7,8,9,10]

Table 3.1 Types of demand management tools

Type and description	Example of tools
Water allocation: This is the process whereby an available water resource is distributed (or redistributed) to legitimate claimants to ensure equity between users, protect the environment, achieve socioeconomic goals, and promote the efficient use of water	• *Pricing of water and water-related services*: Used to promote the efficient use of water and allocate water among competing uses • *Subsidies*: These are widely used by governments to encourage more environmentally beneficial behaviour • *Water trading*: This is the voluntary buying and selling of water in some quantifiable form, either now or in the future
Water augmentation: This aims to increase the available supply of water through active recharge or protection of water recharge areas	• *Conjunctive use and development of surface water and groundwater*: This is the combined use and development of surface water and groundwater as a strategy for sustainable use of water • *Managed aquifer recharge*: This consists of recharging an aquifer using either surface or underground recharge techniques, with the stored water available for use in dry years when surface water supplies may be low • *Source water protection*: This involves implementing programmes or activities targeted at reducing the likelihood of contaminants polluting surface water and groundwater supplies that provide drinking water to humans

Continued

Table 3.1 *Continued*

Type and description	Example of tools
Water efficiency: This involves actions to reduce water scarcity and maximize the benefits provided by existing water infrastructure. It also frees up water for other users, both human and natural	• *Water metering*: Smart meters capture high-resolution consumption data, which can be used to detect leaks in real-time, enhance conservation awareness, and provide performance indicators for large water users • *Reducing unaccounted-for water*: This is the difference between the volume of water treated and distributed and the volume the customer is invoiced. The difference can be due to poor operations and maintenance, lack of an active leak detection programme, or poor quality of underground assets • *Public education and awareness*: Education of the public is crucial in generating an understanding of water scarcity and creating acceptance of water conversation programmes

Smart Digital Water Management

Smart digital water management uses Information and Communication Technology (ICT) to provide real-time, automated data for use in resolving water challenges across a range of scales and differing contexts. There are many applications for smart digital water management, including water efficiency improvement, water quality monitoring, efficient irrigation, leak detection, pressure and flow management, and floods and drought monitoring. In addition, smart digital water management allows conventional water and wastewater systems to become:

- *Instrumented*: The ability to detect, sense, measure, and record data.
- *Interconnected*: The ability to communicate and interact with operators and people who manage the systems.
- *Intelligent*: The ability to analyse the situation, enable quick responses, and optimize troubleshooting solutions. Smart systems allow informed and systematic decision making for water utilities based on accurate and timely information.

Smart digital water management can be applied in various ways, including:

- *Smart water grids and smart water meters*: Smart grids integrate ICT into the management of the water distribution system. Sensors, meters, digital controls, and analytic tools are used to monitor and control water transmission and distribution automatically. Smart water grids aim to ensure water is efficiently delivered only when and where it is needed and that the water is of good quality.

- *Artificial intelligence (AI)*: AI is intelligence exhibited by machines or computers, allowing them to perform tasks such as understanding, learning, reasoning, planning, and more. In water resources management, AI can be used in a variety of contexts, including residential water use monitoring and management, optimization of industrial water use, predictive maintenance of water plants, and an early-warning system for water infrastructure.
- *Machine learning (ML)*: This subset of AI helps derive meaning from data generated by people, devices, and smart systems. Increasingly, the volume of data collected surpasses humans' ability to make sense of it and use it efficiently. ML uses this data to create predictions or answer questions. For example, water utilities could use AI to mine historical pump operational data to 'learn' the most efficient pump configuration for any time of the day or week.[11]

A few benefits can be realized by implementing smart digital water management, examples of which are summarized in Table 3.2.

Table 3.2 Benefits of smart digital water management

Benefit	Description
Environmental	• Lower water consumption through leak detection and reduced demand • Improved water quality through reduced pollution and contamination of waterways • Improved ecosystem health and protection through improved water quality and water quantity • Increased groundwater protection • Lower carbon emissions from reduced energy consumption and increased energy efficiency
Economic	• Increased efficiency in water and wastewater treatment systems • Reduced waste through lower leakage levels • Job creation through project research, design, development, and implementation • Reduction in future infrastructure costs by improving capacity and efficiency, resulting in less need for additional infrastructure

Continued

Table 3.2 *Continued*

Benefit	Description
Social	• Improved access to clean water and sanitation through water treatment and monitoring • Health improvements through access to clean, safe water • Improved livelihoods through job creation, higher productivity, and educational opportunities • Greater collaboration with community through increased engagement and knowledge-sharing • Increased gender equality through increased opportunities for capacity building and further education

Alternative Water Sources

Even with successful demand management measures, some locations will require alternative water sources, namely water reuse and water recycling initiatives. Regarding water conservation hierarchy terminology, reuse is the reuse of water within a single process or the use of harvested water for another purpose without treatment. At the same time, recycling is defined as using harvested water for another purpose after treatment. There are various water reuse and water recycling systems that can provide a reliable, climate-resilient, and economically sound water source for non-potable and potable uses while providing numerous benefits (Table 3.3):

- *Greywater*: Greywater is reusable wastewater from residential, commercial, and industrial bathroom sinks, bathtub shower drains, and clothes washing equipment drains. Greywater is reused onsite, usually for toilet flushing and irrigation. Greywater systems vary significantly in their complexity and size, ranging from small systems with simple treatment processes to large systems with more complex treatment processes. Nevertheless, most have standard features including a tank for storing the treated water, a pump, a distribution system for transporting the treated water to where it is needed, and some sort of (basic) treatment, such as filtering, settlement of solids, chemical, or UV disinfection.
- *Blackwater*: Blackwater, or sewage, is the wastewater from toilets. In blackwater recycling systems, all the blackwater is routed to an initial tank via gravity, from which it settles, and a primary colony of bacteria eats at the waste. The blackwater then goes through an aeration stage

Table 3.3 Water reuse and water recycling benefits

Benefit	Description
Water savings	Increase in the amount of potable water available for domestic uses by replacing it in irrigation of crops and amenity horticulture
Cleaner waterways	Reduction of the amount of stormwater and treated wastewater that is discharged into the environment
Reduced nutrient loads	Reduction of nutrient and contaminant loads in oceans and rivers
Reduced stress on ground and surface water	Reduction of stress on groundwater and rivers through the provision of alternative water sources
Liveable cities	Providing an opportunity to create a greener and more liveable landscape

and a sludge settling stage before it is chlorinated and used as irrigation water (watering lawns or non-food gardens).

- *Rainwater harvesting*: Rainwater harvesting systems collect and store rainfall for later use. When designed appropriately, they slow down and reduce runoff and provide a source of water. There are two main types of rainwater harvesting systems:
  - *Passive harvesting systems*: These are typically small volume systems designed to capture rooftop runoff. Rain barrels are usually used in residential applications where the flow from rain gutter downspouts is easily captured for outdoor use, for example, garden and landscape irrigation or car washing.
  - *Active harvesting systems*: These are larger volume systems that use cisterns to capture runoff from roofs or other suitable surfaces. Rainwater collected in active systems is typically used for irrigation or indoor non-potable water replacement, for example, toilet flushing, clothes washing, evaporative cooling.
- *Stormwater harvesting*: Stormwater harvesting systems involve collecting, storing, and treating stormwater from urban areas for reuse in various areas, including irrigation of public parks, gardens, and sports

fields. Stormwater harvesting systems can be large or small and typically consist of a collection area to capture stormwater, a network of pipes to transport stormwater from the collection site to the storage site, a treatment system to ensure the water is safe and suitable, and a network of pipes for distribution of the treated water.

- *Water recycling*: Recycled water can be used for a range of purposes, including in urban environments (households and recreational parks), industry (washing and cooling in power stations and mills), and agriculture (horticulture, forestry, pasture, flowers, viticulture), as well as in firefighting, groundwater recharge, irrigation of municipal landscapes, 'dualpipe' urban uses, and maintenance of environmental flows and wetlands.
- *Desalination*: Desalinated water can be produced for municipal/potable use and agricultural irrigation. It is also used in many other applications where high-quality water is required. For example, it is used in the manufacturing of pharmaceutics, semi-conductors, and hard disk drives.
- *Other alternative water sources*: Other alternative water sources include:
  - *Captured condensate*: Capturing water that condenses on cooling cells of mechanical equipment.
  - *Atmospheric water generation technology*: Producing potable water from surrounding air.
  - *Water purification systems*: Recovering and reusing discharge water for non-potable uses.
  - *Foundation water*: Collecting water around the foundations of buildings for non-potable uses.
  - *Blowdown water*: Collecting water that is drained from cooling equipment and boilers.
  - *Fog harvesting*: Collecting water from fog can be done with simple, low-cost collection systems knowns as fog collectors, particularly in coastal areas.[12,13,14]

Nature-based Solutions

Nature-based solutions involve the use of natural or semi-natural systems that utilize nature's ecosystem services in the management of water resources and associated risks. Nature-based solutions come in a variety of shapes and sizes and are implemented in a wide variety of contexts (Table 3.4) while providing multiple co-benefits, including:

Table 3.4 Types of nature-based solutions

Type and description	Examples
Green buildings and green streets: Green infrastructure at the building and street levels comprises a wide range of water features aimed at the management of both water quantity and water quality	• *Green roofs*: These are roofs with highly engineered contiguous systems of plantings, drainage layers, and watertight membranes. They provide runoff volume reduction and runoff peak rate attenuation • *Rain gardens*: These are depression gardens designed and located to receive water runoff from a roof, driveway, or lawn. They slow stormwater flow, help remove pollutants, recharge freshwater bodies, and look attractive • *Green parking lots*: These use green infrastructure that closely mimics the natural water cycle to manage stormwater through rainfall retention, pollutant removal, and water infiltration, examples of which include bioswales, infiltration systems, and vegetated filter strips
Green parks and urban forests: Parks can be designed to filter stormwater runoff from surrounding roadways and other impervious surfaces. Meanwhile, urban forests intercept and filter stormwater runoff, preventing flooding and improving water quality	• *Green parks*: Parks can use green infrastructure to remove contaminants from stormwater before diverting it away from the sewer system and returning it directly to the ground. Many green infrastructure solutions can be implemented to manage stormwater, including infiltration beds, stormwater planter boxes, and porous pavement • *Urban forests*: Designing urban forests involves creating sustainable living spaces that are beneficial to both humans and nature. Urban forest design can be applied to the creation of new forests and the redesign of existing ones, with the latter involving interventions that aim to improve existing green spaces to provide new services and facilities and enhance their sustainability

Continued

Table 3.4 *Continued*

Type and description	Examples
Water bodies: Land authorities protect, conserve, and enhance natural ecosystems, including water bodies. Incorporating green infrastructure that decreases flood risk or improves water quality into related plans and strategies can overcome the fragmentation of habitats and preserve or restore ecological connectivity, enhance ecosystem resilience, and ensure the continued delivery of ecosystem services	• *Retention ponds:* These are permanent pools of water with the capacity to capture and slowly release additional water over a period of time. They remove suspended solids, organic matter, and metals through sedimentation and soluble pollutants through biological processes • *Riparian buffers:* These are strips of vegetation established next to waterways in managed landscapes that are designed to capture runoff, nutrients, and sediment while restoring the natural aquatic environment • *Floodplain restoration:* This is the return of a floodplain's ecosystem to its natural conditions and functions before it underwent development. In addition to reducing flood levels and risk, this can improve water quality, provide a habitat for fish and wildlife, offer recreational opportunities, and provide erosion control
Agriculture: The utilization of land for agriculture is not traditionally acknowledged as a retention measure. Nonetheless, through various natural water retention measures (NWRM), retention of water within a catchment can be increased to reduce flooding risk while at the same time enhancing the natural functioning of the catchment and improving agricultural productivity	• *Buffer strips:* These are areas of natural vegetation cover at the margins of fields, arable land, and watercourses. Because of their permanent vegetation, they can slow runoff and absorb excess water. They also reduce the volume of suspended solids, nitrates, and phosphates originating from agricultural runoff • *Conservation tillage:* This practice excludes conventional tillage operations that invert the soil and bury crop residues. It slows water movement, which reduces the amount of soil erosion, potentially increasing infiltration • *Cover crops:* These are plants grown to provide soil cover and improve the physical, chemical, and biological characteristics of the soil. The benefits of their growth include increasing soil water storage and preventing erosion

Forestry: Forests regulate streamflow, support groundwater recharge, and, through evapotranspiration, contribute to cloud generation and precipitation. Forestry NWRM can store or recycle substantial amounts of water, thereby moderating floods. They can also improve water quality by filtering and cleaning water

- *Forest riparian buffers:* They include a mixture of trees, shrubs, and grasses, all of which provide flood control. Trees, with their deep roots, diffuse the energy of floodwaters, reducing damage downstream, and thus flood frequency and severity, as well as associated damage to life, property, and infrastructure
- *Floodplain Forests:* The essential natural function of a floodplain is to store water and sediment derived from the river basin, especially during floods. When floodplains are reforested, the forest contributes to this natural flood retention function by increasing the hydraulic roughness of the floodplain area, slowing the release of water stored on the surface even more

- Simultaneously restoring natural environmental features to urban environments that provide habitat for wildlife while mitigating flood risk.
- Managing stormwater runoff while filtering pollutants and degrading them biologically or chemically.
- Deferring or even replacing costly grey infrastructure projects, which take years to complete, making them vulnerable to rising costs of materials, labour, and financing.
- Creating jobs through the construction, maintenance, or management of various green infrastructure initiatives.
- Providing opportunities for people to exercise and relax, all of which increases physical and mental health.
- Offering enhanced public education opportunities to teach the community about mitigating the adverse environmental impacts of our built environment.[15,16,17]

Renewable Energy and Resource Recovery

Regarding climate change mitigation and circular economy thinking, water and wastewater treatment facilities and infrastructure provide opportunities to generate renewable energy and recover resources from wastewater. Table 3.5 summarizes the multiple benefits of implementing renewable energy schemes.

Renewable Energy from Wastewater

Energy derived from wastewater treatment is a renewable energy resource. It can include:

- *Biogas from anaerobic digestion*: Anaerobic digestion is a proven technology for sewage sludge treatment and allows renewable energy generation from the same process. During anaerobic digestion, microorganisms break down the organic matter contained in the sludge and convert it into biogas which can be used for electricity, heat, and biofuel production.
- *Biomethane*: Biomethane is produced via biogas upgrading, which is the removal of carbon dioxide before the biogas can be used as a vehicle fuel or injected into the natural gas grid, as the large volume of carbon dioxide reduces its heating value.
- *Combined heat and power (CHP)*: CHP is the most prevalent means of utilizing biogas. As the process of anaerobic digestion requires some

heat, it is suited to CHP. The ratio of heat to power varies depending on the scale and technology but typically 35–40 per cent is converted to electricity, 40–45 per cent to heat, and the balance lost as inefficiencies in the various stages of the process.

- *Anaerobic co-digestion*: In addition to sewage sludge, some wastewater treatment plants include other organic feedstock in the anaerobic reaction. Known as anaerobic co-digestion, it can lead to a significant increase in gas production as most co-substrates have higher methane production per tonne of fresh matter than sewage sludge.
- *Thermal conversion of biosolids*: Thermal oxidation (incineration), which is the complete oxidation of organics (biomass) to carbon dioxide and water in the presence of excess air, is a well-established technology.
- *Thermal energy recovery from wastewater*: Thermal energy can be recovered from raw wastewater or effluent by exploiting the significant temperature differential between wastewater and ambient conditions. This temperature difference can be recovered for use in heating and cooling systems.

Table 3.5 Benefits of renewable energy

Benefit	Description
Reducing air pollution	Increasing the use of renewable energy and improving energy efficiency can help reduce greenhouse gas emissions and air pollutants by decreasing consumption of fossil fuel-based energy
Reducing energy costs	Significant cost savings can be achieved by wastewater treatment plants generating their own electricity and increasing energy efficiency
Supporting economic growth	Investing in renewable energy systems and energy efficiency can support economic growth through job creation and market development of energy system services and energy efficiency markets
Demonstrating leadership	Investing in renewable energy systems demonstrates not only responsible government stewardship of tax revenue but also the environmental co-benefits that are obtained from reducing energy usage
Improving energy and water security	Renewable energy at wastewater treatment plants reduces electricity demand, avoiding the risk of brownouts or blackouts during high energy demand periods and helping avoid the need to build new power plants, which in turn lowers water-energy nexus pressures
Protecting public health	Improving the performance of treatment processes, reducing the risk of waterborne illness

Renewable Energy on Facility-owned Buildings

Water utilities can implement traditional renewable energy activities on facility-owned buildings and surrounding land, including:

- *Solar energy*: Wastewater treatment plants require many aeration tanks when treating sewage. These require a lot of space in the plant area, providing opportunities to utilize this space with solar photovoltaic (PV) systems to drive equipment or provide heat.
- *Floating PV installations*: Floating PV installations are similar to that of land-based PV systems, other than the fact that the PV arrays, and often their inverters, are mounted on a floating platform. They can be installed on reservoirs as well as ponds and lakes.
- *Wind power*: Wind energy, captured onsite using wind turbines, can be very cost-effective in areas with adequate wind resources. As opposed to large utility-scale wind farm turbines, which can have capacities as high as 3 MW, small wind turbines are often better suited for local facilities.
- *Hydropower energy recovery*: Recovering energy from the flow of wastewater entering or leaving a treatment plant using micro-hydropower turbines is a viable method of energy savings at plants with large flows rates. Hydropower energy recovery is cost-effective because it is constructed using existing infrastructure.

Resource Recovery

Numerous resources can be recovered from wastewater to generate new revenue streams for water utilities, including the following:

- *Nitrogen*: Nitrogenous materials present in the sewage can be removed from sewage effluent and converted into biomass through activated secondary treatment processes. Fertilizer grade ammonium sulphate can be produced from the high ammonia-nitrogen concentration sidestreams from sludge digestion processes by stripping and absorption.
- *Phosphorous*: Resource recovery technologies enable phosphorus recovery from the biosolids accumulated after the treatment of the main process stream or on sidestreams that have enriched phosphorus because of biological accumulation

- *Struvite*: This can be recovered to reduce phosphorus levels in effluents while simultaneously generating a valuable by-product such as a slow-release fertilizer or raw material for the chemical industry.
- *Cellulose*: Toilet paper often ends as fibrous particles in the wastewater treatment plant. By using fine-mesh sieves, the cellulose fibres can be successfully removed. The cellulose materials that are recovered can be used to dewater the wastewater treatment plant sewage sludge, in the production of asphalt, and as a raw material for insulation material.
- *Bioplastic*: One of the most non-traditional technologies under development is the production of biodegradable plastic using polymers isolated from biosolids. Polymers contain carbon, hydrogen, oxygen, and nitrogen, and therefore biological wastewater can be used to make polymers. The bioplastic can be used as a substitute for conventional petroleum-based plastics.
- *Bricks and tiles*: Sewage sludge ash is the by-product of the combustion of dewatered sewage sludge in an incinerator. The ash is primarily a silty material with some sand-sized particles and can be used in the brick and tile industry.
- *Mining wastewater for metals*: Metals can be potentially mined from wastewater. For instance, silver and cadmium is increasingly being found in wastewater and is expensive enough to potentially warrant recovery.[18,19,20]

Notes

1. Uta Wehn and Carlos Montalvo, 'Exploring the Dynamics of Water Innovation: Foundations for Water Innovation Studies', *Journal of Cleaner Production* 171 (2018).
2. R.C. Brears, *Climate Resilient Water Resources Management* (Cham, Switzerland: Palgrave Macmillan, 2018).
3. Vanessa L. Speight, 'Innovation in the Water Industry: Barriers and Opportunities for Us and Uk Utilities', *Wiley Interdisciplinary Reviews: Water* 2, no. 4 (2015).
4. Ibid.
5. Ibid.
6. R.C. Brears, *Water Resources Management: Innovative and Green Solutions* (De Gruyter, 2021).
7. *Urban Water Security* (Chichester, UK; Hoboken, NJ: John Wiley & Sons, 2016).
8. *Regional Water Security* (Wiley, 2021).
9. *Developing the Circular Water Economy* (Cham, Switzerland: Palgrave Macmillan, 2020).
10. GWP, 'Water Demand Management: The Mediterranean Experience' (2012), http://www.gwp.org/Global/ToolBox/Publications/Technical%20Focus%20Papers/01%20Water

%20Demand%20Management%20-%20The%20Mediterranean%20Experience%20
(2012)%20English.pdf.

11. Brears, *Water Resources Management: Innovative and Green Solutions*.

12. *Regional Water Security*.

13. *Water Resources Management: Innovative and Green Solutions*.

14. *Developing the Circular Water Economy*.

15. *Blue and Green Cities: The Role of Blue-Green Infrastructure in Managing Urban Water Resources* (Palgrave Macmillan UK, 2018).

16. *Nature-Based Solutions to 21st Century Challenges* (Oxfordshire, UK: Routledge, 2020).

17. *Regional Water Security*.

18. *Developing the Circular Water Economy*.

19. *Regional Water Security*.

20. *Water Resources Management: Innovative and Green Solutions*.

4

Financing Water Security and Green Growth

Introduction

Globally, yearly economic losses related to water security include $260 billion from inadequate water supply and sanitation, $120 billion from urban property flood damage, and $94 billion from water insecurity to existing irrigators. It is estimated that water-related losses in agriculture, health, income, and property could result in gross domestic product (GDP) declining by up to 6 per cent by 2050 and lead to sustained negative growth in parts of the world.[1,2] For example, inadequate sanitation causes India significant economic losses, equivalent to 6.4 per cent of the country's GDP, with premature mortality and other health-related impacts of inadequate sanitation the most costly at $38.5 billion, followed by productive time lost to access sanitation facilities at $10.7 billion, and drinking water-related impacts at $4.2 billion.[3] Drinking water distribution systems are vulnerable to interruption in service from extreme weather events and ageing infrastructure.[4] For instance, in the United States, the total capital spending on water infrastructure at the local, state, and federal levels in 2019 was around $48 billion, while investment needs totalled $129 billion, creating an $81 billion gap: this underinvestment will likely lead to a $2.9 trillion decline in GDP by 2039.[5] Regarding the Sustainable Development Goals (SDG), current annual investments to achieve the water supply, sanitation, and hygiene SDGs (targets 6.1 and 6.2) are not factoring in the impact of climate change.[6] Furthermore, despite the benefits of nature-based solutions, including green infrastructure, being more recognized in water resources management, with investment in green infrastructure growing by around 12 per cent per annum between 2013 and 2015, suggesting a rapid level of uptake, there is still underinvestment in nature-based solutions, with current direct investments appearing to be less than 1 per cent globally, and more likely to be closer to only 0.1 per cent of the total investment in water resources management.[7]

Financing Water Security and Green Growth. Robert C. Brears, Oxford University Press. © Robert C. Brears (2023).
DOI: 10.1093/oso/9780192847843.003.0004

It is estimated that an additional investment of $1.7 trillion is required to ensure universal and equitable access to safe and affordable drinking water for all, which is around three times the current investment levels. Meanwhile, the scale of investments in water infrastructure needs to increase significantly, with estimates ranging from $6.7 trillion by 2030 to $22.6 trillion by 2050. However, these figures do not cover water resources development for irrigation or energy.[8] Regarding nature-based solutions that enhance the resilience of ecosystems and address societal challenges, including water security, investments in nature-based solutions-relevant sectors will need to almost triple by 2030 and increase to over $536 billion/year by 2050, at least four times the total amount invested today.[9] Overall, it is globally recognized that innovative financing is required to close the gap between current investments in water resources management and the amount of investments required to achieve water security and green growth. This chapter will first define the concept of innovative financing to achieve water security and green growth. The chapter will then review the various sources of finance available. Finally, the chapter will provide a series of principles for fostering investment in water security and green growth projects.

Innovative Financing to Achieve Water Security and Green Growth

Closing the financing gap to achieve water security and green growth is a challenge as the water sector has relied historically on public funding to meet its investment needs. However, in many countries, the water sector's cash flow is insufficient to ensure the sustainable provision of services or sector development. Moreover, many parts of the sector are government departments where mobilizing private finance is non-existent. Even when they are established as corporate entities, such as water supply and service providers, it is rare for them to borrow from commercial lenders due to weak incentives and/or poor creditworthiness. Additionally, public and overseas development assistance funding combined does not adequately cover the needs related to water and sanitation. Nevertheless, countries have sought new sources of finance to meet water security challenges by expanding opportunities for private investment over the past couple of decades.

However, private investment in water and sanitation has constituted only a fraction of all private commitments to infrastructure to date. For example, in the Asia Pacific region, private finance in water and sanitation constituted only 5.4 per cent of all private commitments to infrastructure, including financing for energy, transport, and telecommunications. Moreover, while the private sector has recognized opportunities for investment in water infrastructure, it has not favoured the water sector due to uncertainties regarding revenues and the potential for political interference. Some of the specific barriers that create a gap between current financing and future needs are listed in Table 4.1.

As such, it is globally recognized that innovative finance is required to close the financing gap to achieve water security and green growth, where innovative finance is defined as 'a set of financial solutions and mechanisms that create scalable and effective ways of channelling both private money from the global financial markets and public resources towards solving pressing global problems'. Innovative financing helps generate additional funds by tapping new funding sources. For instance, looking beyond traditional mechanisms such as budget outlays from established donors and engaging new partners, such as private sector actors. Innovative financing also makes projects more

Table 4.1 Barriers to financing water security and green growth

Barrier	Description
Knowledge gaps	There are often knowledge gaps about financial products and viable investment opportunities for water projects. Additionally, financiers often lack knowledge of the water sector and view it as too political, with frequent opposition to charging for water services as well as tariff increases
Undervaluing of water	Water is an under-valued resource, not adequately accounted for by investors that depend on or affect its availability in other sectors such as urban development, agriculture, energy, etc.
Political pressure	There is often political interference in the tariff setting process, resulting in water services being under-priced, undermining water investments
Capital intensive infrastructure	Water infrastructure is capital intensive, with high sunk costs and long pay-back periods
Difficulty of monetizing benefits	Water management provides both public and private benefits, which cannot be easily monetized. This reduces potential revenue flows
Difficulty of scaling up projects	Water projects are often too small or too context-specific, raising transaction costs and making financing models difficult to scale-up
Fragmentation of water utilities	Often countries have small community water systems that serve small populations, all with various ownership models, making it difficult for a water system to fund or finance the infrastructure that is needed
Inadequate business models	Water utilities often fail to generate sufficient revenue to cover operational and maintenance costs due to low rates of cost recovery and persistent operational inefficiencies

Table 4.2   Collaboration to achieve water security and green growth

Stakeholder	Collaborative actions
Governments	They will need to:
	• Mobilize domestic finance by developing policies and incentives that improve efficiency and governance of service providers to make them more creditworthy
	• Improve the financial enabling environment, including price regulation and incentivizing, leveraging of public funds with commercial finance, and mobilizing additional blended finance into the sector and targeting those funds to the most productive uses
	• Encourage increased efficiency in the sector
Development partners	They need to:
	• Improve efficiency and creditworthiness and mobilize domestic finance
	• Increase the use of guarantees and other instruments to crowd commercial finance into the sector
Private sector	They need to:
	• Partner with the public sector towards improving capital and operating efficiency
	• Reach out to the public sector to explore potential financing relationships and transactions

effective and efficient by linking financing to results, redistributing risk, improving the availability of capital, engaging technology, and matching the length, or tenor, of investments with project needs. Overall, financing water security and green growth through innovative financing requires a collaborative approach where all stakeholders play a part, a summary of which is provided in Table 4.2.[10,11,12,13,14,15,16,17]

Principles for Innovative Finance

The High Level Panel on Water has defined a range of principles that innovative financing should follow to achieve water security and green growth:

- *Maximize the value of existing assets*: Investment should improve existing water infrastructure's operational efficiency and effectiveness. Improvements can result from good operation and maintenance of infrastructure and demand management.
- *Maximize water-related benefits over the long term*: The multiple benefits that water-related investments generate depend on how investments

are designed and sequenced to meet strategic goals, including climate change adaptation. This means projects should be designed to be scalable and adjustable to changing conditions.

- *Foster synergies and complementarities with investments in other sectors*: Policies outside of the water sector should be encouraged to factor in water risks, which in turn stimulates water-wise investments
- *Attract more financing by improving the risk-return profile of water investments*: Governments can employ a range of fiscal policy instruments to recover the costs of investments from beneficiaries, improve the financial viability of utilities, and provide a revenue stream to improve the risk-return profile of water-related investments.[18]

Governments Facilitating Financing of Water Security and Green Growth

Governments can support the principles mentioned above by:

- *Providing political support*: Governments can raise the importance of water on the political agenda at the level of climate protection.
- *Investing wisely*: Governments can invest in fit for purpose water resources management projects that quickly achieve water security objectives.
- *Planning and sequencing water-related investments strategically*: Investments in water security-related projects should follow a strategic direction to ensure the projects:
  - maximize benefits at the least cost to society;
  - benefit sectors that affect water demand or supply;
  - mitigate current and future water-related risks;
  - are assessed in a standardized way.
- *Developing an inventory for financial needs and options for the water sector*: The inventory should be at the basin and country-level and include a mechanism to track those needs and map financial flows that contribute to water-related investments at different scales (local, basin, national).
- *Stimulating demand for water-related investments and innovation*: This can be done by promoting the value of water and the polluter pays and the beneficiary pays principles.

- *Optimizing the operational efficiency and effectiveness of existing infrastructure*: This can be done jointly with service providers and water users by ensuring proper operation, maintenance, and financial sustainability of existing assets.
- *Identifying revenue sources to support projects*: This involves identifying ongoing revenue sources for operations and maintenance, preferably from water users, sufficient to ensure that infrastructure remains fully functional beyond the commissioning stages.[19]

Sources of Finance

There are various sources of finance available to achieve water security and green growth.

Public Finance

Public finance refers to the government's role in the economy, which is the minimization of market failure and the maximization of desirable effects. Public revenue is generated from taxation and tariffs and is used to finance public expenditures. Taxation is a levy by the government on an individual or legal entity using water or the environment, for example, a tax on fertilizers. The revenues generated can finance water projects, such as the restoration of waterways. Taxation is considered a stable form of revenue as non-payment usually leads to civil penalties. Tariffs are another source of public revenue and are payments made for access to water and the use of related services, for example, payment for water supply from a piped network and wastewater treatment. In addition to tariffs, additional fees may be charged, such as development impact fees, connection fees, drought surcharges, and other fixed fees. Tariffs and related fees are used to support operational and maintenance costs of providing these services and cross-subsidize services.

Nevertheless, tariffs and their related fees can be an unstable form of revenue due to uncertainty regarding the user base. For instance, if the user base diminishes, then the collected tariffs may be insufficient to cover the operational and maintenance costs of the service. Overall, taxes and tariffs are generally insufficient to generate the required revenue to match the lump investment needed for infrastructure development. So borrowing instruments are utilized to fund government services.[20,21]

International Public Finance

Public finance flows through multilateral development banks (MDBs) and bilateral development finance institutions (DFIs) at the international level. MDBs have been a significant component of development finance for decades. Examples of MDBs include the World Bank and Asian Development Bank. MDBs provide financial assistance to developing countries, usually through loans and grants for water infrastructure projects and water policy-based loans. The latter involves financing in exchange for an agreement by the borrowing country that policy reforms will be undertaken. DFIs are specialized development banks or subsidiaries that support private sector development in developing countries, including water projects. DFIs are usually owned by national governments and source their capital from national or international development funds. DFIs include Germany's KfW Bankengruppe, Japan Bank for International Cooperation, and the Netherlands Development Finance Company. DFIs provide a range of products and services, including lending and investment, guarantees, grants and technical assistance, advisory services, and research and policy expertise.[22]

Private Finance

Private finance is the raising, providing, or managing of private capital to conserve, restore, or sustainably use water resources or avoid a negative impact of water usage on biodiversity and ecosystem services. Specifically:

- Investors seek investment opportunities from the:
  - conservation and sustainable use of water resources;
  - conservation and restoration of ecosystems to protect water quantity and water quality.
- Investors direct financial flows away from projects with negative impacts on the environment and ecosystem services and towards projects that mitigate negative impacts or provide environmental co-benefits.

Funders and financiers providing finance for water security and green growth projects is broadening, increasing the pool of available capital. Foundations, as well as impact investors, are joining traditional sources of philanthropic funding. In addition, large asset owners, such as public pension funds and university endowments, are seeking to contribute capital into investments that combine financial returns with measurable environmental and social impact. Corporations are also a significant source of financing

Table 4.3 Costs from failing to implement environmental corporate social responsibility

Cost	Description
Planning permission refused or delayed	Not considering impacts on water quantity and/or water quality can lead to refused planning permissions, resulting in financial losses and potential losses of funders
Increased programme costs	In construction, there are increased costs associated with removing existing natural systems to be replaced with hard engineered systems
Increased flooding costs	Flooding can result in loss of revenue, devaluation of buildings, time spent out of productivity, and increased insurance requirements for the occupier
Higher maintenance costs	Hard engineered solutions often require more maintenance than nature-based solutions
Loss of client relationships/ investment	Funders and end-users place considerable value on a company's reputation. A loss of reputation could result in falling behind competitors
Declining staff well-being	Time is lost due to staff illness or loss of quality staff due to unappealing workplace

for investments in water projects, which may be part of corporate social responsibility strategies. Environmental corporate social responsibility aims to reduce any damaging effects on the environment from a business' processes. For example, environmental corporate social responsibility activities may focus on water efficiency measures to reduce water and energy use or nature-based solutions to adapt to climate change. A failure to implement environmental corporate social responsibility initiatives into planning, design, construction, and operation can increase business risks, lower reputation, and increase costs (Table 4.3). Finally, retail investors are another potential source of finance for water-related projects. Overall, private finance can come in various forms, including commercial bank loans, bonds, and equity.[23,24]

Blended Finance

Globally, there is a growing call for private financing to complement underfunded government budgets to finance natural resources management initiatives, including water-related investments.[25,26] The OECD defines blended finance as the 'strategic use of development finance for the mobilisation of additional finance towards the SDGs in developing countries'. Additional finance is commercial finance that does not have an explicit development purpose.[27]

Additionality

The concept of additionality is a critical aspect of blended finance and includes:

- *Financial additionality*: The investment would not have materialized without the private sector's contribution.
- *Development additionality*: Development results would not have materialized without the mobilization of commercial finance.
- *Operational (institutional) additionality*: There is an improved quality of the investment due to public finance and its technical, social, environmental, governance standards and practices.
- *Systemic additionality*: The potential that successful projects implemented with blended financial may help overcome investors' biased risk perceptions by sending a positive signal to the market.

Blended finance can involve various instruments (Table 4.4) and actors in blending operations, including aid agencies and public donors, multilateral and national development banks, private foundations, commercial banks, investors, think tanks, and non-governmental organizations

Table 4.4 Blended finance instruments

Instrument	Description
Investment grants	These cover the specific costs and activities to decrease overall project costs and increase chances of success. They are mainly used to purchase or upgrade existing fixed capital. Interest rate subsidies can help lower the costs of finance resulting from underdeveloped local financial markets
Grant-funded technical assistance	It is a versatile tool that can be used to mobilize additional sources of finance to meet sustainability objectives, including to support project preparation, project implementation, or the broader business environment
Loan guarantees	Protects investors against losses and/or improves the financing costs (government guarantees reduce borrowing costs)
Structured finance: first loss piece	Absorbs risks by making the public entity the first to take losses that may occur should the project incur losses
Equity investment	Equity investors take a percentage of the ownership of the company or project. The money provides funding for the project and demonstrates its viability

Table 4.5 Potential roles of blended finance

Role of blended finance	Example of instruments	Contribution to additionality
Identifying and enabling new finance structures	Grants, loans	• Researching to identify opportunities • Facilitating the design of new finance structures
Seeding new finance structures	Equity, debt	• Providing proof of concept funding and helping scale up financial instruments to engage additional private capital • Conducting due diligence that can be shared with potential investors • Acting as a reference lead to other investors
Risk mitigation	Guarantees, risk absorbing equity	• Changing the risk perception for private investors
Technical support	Grants	• Providing grant funding alongside an investment to help increase chances of success, e.g., technical assistance
Reward additional development impacts	Grants	• Assigning a financial value to a non-financial outcome
Market development	Grants	• Researching and publishing reports on the success of different interventions • Supporting the development of investor incentives (e.g., policy changes) • Supporting the development of consistent ways to monitor financial and developmental impact

(NGOs).[28,29,30,31] In addition, Table 4.5 summarizes the potential roles of blended finance and the contribution to additionality.[32,33,34]

Intermediaries

Intermediaries play a crucial role in blended finance by structuring the transaction, bringing the actors together, and facilitating the blending. Many donor countries rely on intermediaries as they already have a record of accomplishment and the skill set to engage with private sector actors that staff in governments and aid agencies lack. MDBs and DFIs usually take on this role as they are mandated and organized to work with the private sector. However, private fund managers, local financing institutions, and NGOs can also act as intermediaries in blended finance.[35,36]

Principles for Blended Finance

Overall, a set of principles to guide blended finance include:

1. *Additionality/rationale for using blended finance*: Support for the private sector should be beyond what is available or otherwise absent from the market and should not crowd out the private sector.
2. *Crowding-in*: Blended finance should contribute to catalysing market development and the mobilization of private sector resources.
3. *Commercial sustainability*: Support of the private sector and the impact achieved by the blended finance transaction should aim to be sustainable.
4. *Reinforcing markets*: Assistance to the private sector should be structured to address market failures effectively and efficiently and minimize the risk of disrupting or distorting markets or crowding out private finance, including new entrants.
5. *Promoting high standards*: Blended finance should promote the private sector's adherence to high standards of conduct, including in the areas of corporate governance, environmental impact, social inclusion, transparency, integrity, and disclosure.[37]

Financing Instruments

Actors who seek funding sources for water security and green growth projects should consider options and instruments that fit their needs and the specific context of their respective activities. There is an array of financing instruments available from public, international public, private, and blended financial sources to achieve water security and green growth, including:

- *Green bonds and green loans*: Such as green bonds issued for the construction of green-grey hybrid infrastructure.
- *Debt-for-nature swaps*: Such as countries restructuring their debt with Paris Club members to initiate water security projects.
- *Payments for watershed services (PWS)*: Such as PWS schemes that prevent agricultural pollution of waterways.
- *Market-based instruments*: Such as seasonal water pricing to encourage water conservation.
- *Public-private partnerships*: Such as local governments cooperating with local private sector actors on local water security projects.

- *Biodiversity offsets*: Such as biodiversity offset schemes that protect water resources and related biodiversity.
- *Tradable permits*: Such as water quality trading schemes that reduce or control water pollution.

Combination of Financing Instruments

A combination of different instruments, sources, and financial considerations must be applied to guarantee enough support throughout the entire water security and green growth project lifecycle, including the planning, implementation, and long-term operation and maintenance phases. Two general cost categories need addressing to ensure any project's success:

- *Investment costs*: These are the costs associated with investments in developing infrastructure, capacities, and technologies for water security and green growth. Examples of costs include research and development, human capacity development and coordination, construction material, and specialized equipment. Investment costs are usually the highest during the development phase of any project. To cover these costs, an external finance source that is either grant-based or expects a return on investment through the value generated by the measure is required.
- *Operating costs*: These are the ongoing expenses incurred to support the coordination and facilitation of the project throughout its lifetime. These include human resources, equipment, and communication costs, as well as administrative costs, such as financial oversight and the managing, monitoring, and evaluating of programmes, projects, and initiatives.[38,39]

Principles for Fostering Investment in Water Security and Green Growth Projects

Table 4.6 provides a series of principles for fostering investment in water security and green growth projects.[40]

Table 4.6 Principles for fostering investment in water security and green growth

Principle	Description
Maximize the value of existing water security investments	Increased efficiency in the operation and maintenance of existing water assets can be a cost-effective way of improving water security and services. Investments can be made in the areas of: • *Innovation*: For example, investments in water-efficient irrigation, adopting best practices that reduce nutrient flows into water bodies, or water-efficient and cleaner production methods • *Enhancing water allocation efficiency*: For example, investments in water allocation schemes that provide greater benefits from water use as compared to investing in new infrastructure to augment supply
Select investment pathways that reduce water risks at least cost over time	This requires performing a cost-benefit analysis on projects and considering how specific projects may foreclose future options. Beneficial investments in water security and green growth projects share three features: 1. *They have been proven to be cost-effective*: Cost-benefit analysis helps identify projects that generate more benefits 2. *They combine investments in infrastructures, information, and institutions*: Well-designed infrastructure only delivers expected outcomes when they are supported by appropriate institutions (for project design, financing, management, and accountability) and when they build on the best available knowledge and information 3. *They are consistent with water-wise, long-term development strategies*: The investments are dynamic and adaptive concerning changing circumstances
Ensure synergies and complementarities with investments in other sectors	Improving water security requires that investments in a range of sectors (urban development, food security, energy security, etc.) are water-wise and avoid increasing water-related risks. In addition, policies outside the water sector can stimulate water-wise investments when they factor in the costs of reducing water risks and deter investments and practices that inadvertently increase water-related risks
Scale-up financing through risk-return allocation schemes	Water infrastructure competes with other sectors for financial investments. The main criterion in that competition is the risk-return ratio (the return an investment can yield considering the level of risk exposure). The ratio can be improved by making the best use of economic and pricing instruments: • *Economic instruments*: They can play a key role in delivering water security at least cost for society and in providing a revenue stream for investments in water security and green growth • *Pricing instruments*. These, in combination with other instruments, for example, regulatory, voluntary, or other economic instruments, can contribute to water conservation, phase out negative externalities, for example, pollution, and improve the financial sustainability of water infrastructures and water services through cost recovery

Notes

1. OECD, 'Water, Growth and Finance' (2016), https://www.oecd.org/environment/resources/Water-Growth-and-Finance-policy-perspectives.pdf.
2. World Bank, 'High and Dry: Climate Change, Water, and the Economy' (2016), https://openknowledge.worldbank.org/handle/10986/23665?utm_source=Global+Waters+%2B+Water+Currents&utm_campaign=9905bbdc1e-Water_Currents_Water+Utiliti_12_dec_2018&utm_medium=email&utm_term=0_fae9f9ae2b-9905bbdc1e-25803553.
3. 'Economic Impacts of Inadequate Sanitation in India' (2011), https://documents.worldbank.org/en/publication/documents-reports/documentdetail/820131468041640929/economic-impacts-of-inadequate-sanitation-in-india.
4. US EPA, 'Water Security', https://www.epa.gov/emergency-response-research/water-security.
5. American Society of Civil Engineers, 'The Economic Benefits of Investing in Water Infrastructure: How a Failure to Act Would Affect the Us Economic Recovery' (2020), http://www.uswateralliance.org/sites/uswateralliance.org/files/publications/The%20Economic%20Benefits%20of%20Investing%20in%20Water%20Infrastructure_final.pdf
6. World Bank, 'The Costs of Meeting the 2030 Sustainable Development Goal Targets on Drinking Water, Sanitation, and Hygiene' (2016), https://openknowledge.worldbank.org/handle/10986/23681
7. UNESCO, '2018 Un World Water Development Report, Nature-Based Solutions for Water' (2018), http://www.unesco.org/new/en/natural-sciences/environment/water/wwap/wwdr/2018-nature-based-solutions/.
8. OECD, 'Financing Water: Investing in Sustainable Growth' https://www.oecd.org/water/Policy-Paper-Financing-Water-Investing-in-Sustainable-Growth.pdf.
9. UNEP, 'State of Finance for Nature' (2021), https://www.unep.org/resources/state-finance-nature.
10. International Labor Organization, 'Innovative Finance: Putting Your Money to (Decent) Work' (2018), https://www.ilo.org/wcmsp5/groups/public/—ed_emp/documents/publication/wcms_654680.pdf.
11. World Bank, 'Innovative Finance for Development Solutions' (2015), https://olc.worldbank.org/system/files/Innovative_Finance_for_Development_Solutions.pdf.
12. 'The Costs of Meeting the 2030 Sustainable Development Goal Targets on Drinking Water, Sanitation, and Hygiene'.
13. 'Financing Options for the 2030 Water Agenda' (2016), https://openknowledge.worldbank.org/handle/10986/25495.
14. ODI, 'Climate Change and Water Finance Needs to Flood Not Drip' (2018), https://odi.org/en/publications/climate-change-and-water-finance-needs-to-flood-not-drip/.
15. Hongjoo Hahm, 'Current Trends in Private Financing of Water and Sanitation in Asia and the Pacific', *Asia-Pacific Sustainable Development Journal* 26, no. 1 (2019).
16. Robert C. Brears, *Water Resources Management: Innovative and Green Solutions* (De Gruyter, 2021).

17. OECD, 'Making Blended Finance Work for Water and Sanitation: Unlocking Commercial Finance for Sdg 6' (2019), https://www.oecd.org/environment/resources/making-blended-finance-work-for-sdg-6-5efc8950-en.htm.

18. High Level Panel on Water, 'Making Every Drop Count: An Agenda for Water Action' (2018), https://sustainabledevelopment.un.org/content/documents/17825HLPW_Outcome.pdf.

19. 'Water Infrastructure and Investment' (2015), https://sustainabledevelopment.un.org/content/documents/hlpwater/08-WaterInfrastInvest.pdf.

20. Elena Humphreys, Andrea van der Kerk, and Catarina Fonseca, 'Public Finance for Water Infrastructure Development and Its Practical Challenges for Small Towns', *Water Policy* 20, no. S1 (2018).

21. Robert A. Greer, 'A Review of Public Water Infrastructure Financing in the United States', *WIREs Water* 7, no. 5 (2020).

22. OECD, 'Development Finance Institutions and Private Sector Development', https://www.oecd.org/development/development-finance-institutions-private-sector-development.htm.

23. R.C. Brears, *Nature-Based Solutions to 21st Century Challenges* (Oxfordshire, UK: Routledge, 2020).

24. World Bank, 'Mobilizing Private Finance for Nature' (2020), http://pubdocs.worldbank.org/en/916781601304630850/Finance-for-Nature-28-Sep-web-version.pdf.

25. Julian Rode et al., 'Why "Blended Finance" Could Help Transitions to Sustainable Landscapes: Lessons from the Unlocking Forest Finance Project', *Ecosystem Services* 37 (2019).

26. OECD, 'Making Blended Finance Work for Water and Sanitation: Unlocking Commercial Finance for Sdg 6'.

27. 'Blended Finance in the Least Developed Countries 2019' (2019), https://www.oecd.org/finance/blended-finance-in-the-least-developed-countries-2019-1c142aae-en.htm.

28. Karin Küblböck and Hannes Grohs, 'Blended Finance and Its Potential for Development Cooperation' (2019), https://www.econstor.eu/handle/10419/200507.

29. Ibid.

30. Oxfam, 'Blended Finance: What It Is, How It Works and How It Is Used' (2017), https://www-cdn.oxfam.org/s3fs-public/file_attachments/rr-blended-finance-130217-en.pdf.

31. Convergence, 'Blending with Technical Assistance' (2019), https://assets.ctfassets.net/4cgqlwde6qy0/3RZClckJliqSyQVy5zkxaT/d3154bf0a55836bd3ec26fb07258a913/Technical_Assistance_Brief_vFinal.pdf.

32. Küblböck and Grohs, 'Blended Finance and Its Potential for Development Cooperation'.

33. Tanja Havemann, Christine Negra, and Fred Werneck, 'Blended Finance for Agriculture: Exploring the Constraints and Possibilities of Combining Financial Instruments for Sustainable Transitions,' *Agriculture and Human Values* (2020).

34. OECD, 'Making Blended Finance Work for the Sustainable Development Goals' (2018), https://www.oecd.org/development/making-blended-finance-work-for-the-sustainable-development-goals-9789264288768-en.htm.

35. Küblböck and Grohs, 'Blended Finance and Its Potential for Development Cooperation'.

36. Gunnel Axelsson Nycander, 'Blended Finance: Finding Its Right Place' (2020), https://www.svenskakyrkan.se/filer/8333_SK19489_blended_finance_final.pdf.

37. IDFC, 'Idfc Blended Finance: A Brief Overview' (2019), https://www.idfc.org/wp-content/uploads/2019/10/blended-finance-a-brief-overview-october-2019_final.pdf.

38. Brears, *Water Resources Management: Innovative and Green Solutions*.

39. Brears, *Nature-Based Solutions to 21st Century Challenges*.

40. OECD, 'Water, Growth and Finance'.

5

Green Bonds, Environmental Impact Bonds, and Green Loans Financing Water Security and Green Growth

Introduction

Various debt instruments are available to implement and mainstream water security and green growth projects at various scales and in different contexts, including green bonds, environmental impact bonds (EIB), and green loans.[1,2,3] This chapter will first review the differences between green bonds and regular bonds. The chapter will then discuss how EIBs are a form of debt characterized by a pay for success component that determines the amount that investors are repaid based on environmental performance. Finally, the chapter will discuss how green loans support various green projects, including those focusing on achieving water security and green growth.

Green Bonds

Corporate and governmental organizations use bonds to borrow money from the market (Table 5.1). They are essentially a fixed-term IOU between the borrower (bond issuer) and their lenders (the bond investors): investors loan money to issuers by purchasing their bonds. In return, investors receive regular interest payments until the bond matures and the issuer repays the debt in full. Usually, bonds provide cheaper capital than bank loans, making them attractive for financing capital-intensive projects. Green bonds retain this loan structure. However, the main difference between conventional bonds, known as vanilla bonds, and green bonds is that the proceeds of green bonds are pledged to finance/refinance projects with environmental benefits. Therefore, green bonds have a broad appeal as they attract investors committed to environmental protection, enable companies to signal their commitment towards the environment by issuing green bonds, and enable investors to

Financing Water Security and Green Growth. Robert C. Brears, Oxford University Press. © Robert C. Brears (2023).
DOI: 10.1093/oso/9780192847843.003.0005

Table 5.1 Types of bond issuers

Issue type	Description
Government bonds	Bonds issued by a public entity, such as a city or state, are used to finance their activities
Corporate bonds	A bond issued by a company is referred to as a corporate bond. They can be designed for institutional investors (insurance companies, banks, hedge funds, etc.) or retail investors
Multilateral Development bank bonds	Bonds can be used by multilateral development banks or other supranational or international agencies

enhance their reputation and take a leadership position in the market. In 2017, the global green bond supply exceeded $155 billion, and by 2035, the global green bond market could be in the range of $4.7 trillion to $5.6 trillion, with annual issuances of between $620 billion and $720 billion.[4]

In the context of water security and green growth, green bonds can be issued to construct grey infrastructure, green infrastructure, and hybrid infrastructure. There are numerous types of green bonds, including:

- *General obligation bonds*: These are designed for green projects, with the full income base of the issuer used for collateral (the default credit rating is used).
- *Revenue obligation bonds*: These are designed for green projects, with the issuer's revenue streams, such as income from taxes and fees, used to pay for the issue costs.
- *Project bonds*: These are issued for specific green projects. The collateral security is only the assets created by the project and the revenue from the project.
- *Securitized bonds*: A securitization can be defined as green when the underlying cash flows relate to green assets or where the proceeds from the deal are earmarked to invest in green assets.[5,6,7,8,9]

Pricing of Green Bonds

Most green bonds are investment grade and are priced similarly to conventional debt at issuance. In addition, the bonds are usually asset-linked and often backed by the issuer's balance sheet. As a result, there is no price difference between green bonds and non-green bonds. While there are additional costs for issuers of green bonds, including the costs in external opinions and of annual reporting of the use of proceeds, the costs are minimal and do not disincentivize investors from shifting from traditional bonds to green bonds: it is estimated that globally, green bonds are more than three times oversubscribed.[10]

Benefits of Green Bonds

Green bonds provide a range of benefits in their use, including the following:

1. *Providing an additional source of green financing*: Traditional sources of debt financing are not sufficient in meeting green investment needs. Therefore, there is a need to introduce a new means of financing that can expand the investor base, including institutional investors, such as pension funds, insurance companies, and sovereign wealth funds
2. *Enabling more long-term green financing*: In many countries, the ability of banks to provide long-term green loans is constrained due to the short maturity of their liabilities and lack of instruments for hedging duration risks. Also, corporates that can only access short-term credit face refinancing risks for long-term green projects.
3. *Enhancing issuers' reputation*: Issuing a green bond enhances the issuer's credibility with investors and the public. It can also meet internal sustainable development policies.
4. *Facilitating the greening of brown sectors*: Green bonds can be a transition mechanism that encourages issuers in less environmentally friendly sectors to reduce their environmental footprint by engaging in green investment activities that can be funded via a green bond.
5. *Making new green financial products available to responsible investors*: Many institutional investors who have a preference for sustainable (responsible) investment are seeking new financial instruments to achieve their investment targets.[11]

Green Bond Issuing Process

The following steps are commonly taken when issuing a green bond:

1. *Select eligibility criteria*: Issuers can self-label and set their criteria and processes. Nonetheless, it is now rare for green bonds to not align with internationally recognized guidelines. Because most investors do not have the resources (technical expertise) and time to carry about extensive due diligence, they rely on international standards to assess

credibility. Investors are also often seeking products that contribute to more than one environmental goal and, at times, products that achieve both environmental and social goals.

2. *Establish project selection process*: The projects should undergo a rigorous review and approval process, including early screening, identifying, and managing potential environmental and/or social impacts, and obtaining approval from the organization's board. Environmental specialists then typically screen the approved projects to identify those that meet the green bond selection criteria.

3. *Earmark and allocate proceeds*: The issuer discloses how it will separate green bond proceeds and make periodic allocations to eligible investments. Usually, the proceeds are credited to a special account that invests the funds in eligible green bond projects, with funds periodically allocated in an amount equal to the disbursements of eligible projects.

4. *Monitor and report*: The issuer monitors the implementation of the green projects and provides reports on the use of proceeds and expected environmental impacts.[12,13]

Green Bond Principles

The International Capital Market Association (ICMA) has developed the Green Bond Principles (GBP), which are voluntary best practices that can be followed when issuing bonds that serve environmental purposes. The GBP provides issuers with guidance on launching a credible green bond, helps investors evaluate the environmental impacts of the green bonds they have invested in, and assists underwriters in facilitating transactions that preserve the integrity of the green bond market. There are four components for alignment with the GBP:

1. *Use of proceeds*: The foundation of a green bond is utilizing the proceeds for eligible green projects. All eligible green projects should provide clear environmental benefits, which are assessed, and, where feasible, quantified by the issuer. Eligible green project categories include:
   a. *Renewable energy*: including the production and transmission of renewable energy.
   b. *Energy efficiency*: for instance, in new and renovated buildings, energy storage, appliances, and products.

c. *Pollution prevention and control*: including greenhouse gas control, soil remediation, waste prevention/reduction/recycling, and waste to energy.

d. *Terrestrial and aquatic biodiversity*: including the protection of water-shed environments.

e. *Sustainable water and wastewater management*: including sustainable infrastructure for clean and/or drinking water, wastewater treatment, and green infrastructure.

f. *Climate change adaptation*: including initiatives that make infras-tructure more resilient to climatic extremes and the development of information support systems, such as early warning systems.

2. *Process for project evaluation and selection*: The green bond issuer should communicate clearly with investors:

a. The environmental sustainability objectives of the eligible green projects.

b. The process in which the issuer determines how the projects fit within eligible green project categories.

c. Additional information identifying and managing any environmen-tal or social risks of the project(s).

3. *Management of proceeds*: The proceeds of the green bond should be credited to a sub-account, moved to a sub-portfolio, or be tracked by the issuer and have it internally tracked. The GBP encourages trans-parency and recommends that the issuer's management of proceeds be verified by an external auditor or third party to verify the internal tracking method and allocation of funds from the green bond proceeds.

4. *Reporting*: Issuers should make available up-to-date information on the use of proceeds. The information should be renewed annually until full allocation and on a timely basis in case of material developments. The annual report should include:

a. A list of projects that the green bond proceeds have been allocated

b. A brief description of the projects

c. The amount allocated

d. Expected impact.[14]

Water Reporting Metrics

The GBP has developed a set of metrics for sustainable water and wastewater management projects (Table 5.2). The indicators aim to capture the environ-mental and sustainability benefits of these projects. In addition, the metrics are designed to facilitate quantitative reporting across geographies at the project and/or portfolio level.[15]

Table 5.2 Green bond principle's indicators for sustainable water and wastewater management projects

Project focus	Actions	Indicators
Sustainable water management	Annual water savings, for example, from: • Reduction in water losses in water transfer and/or distribution • Reduction in water consumption of economic activities (e.g., industrial processes, agricultural activities including irrigation, buildings, etc.) • Water reuse and/or water use avoided by waterless solutions and equipment (e.g., for sanitation, cooling systems for power plants, industrial processes, etc.)	• Annual absolute (gross) water use before and after the project in cubic metres/year • Reduction in water use in percentage
Wastewater treatment projects (including sewage sludge management)	Annual volume of wastewater treated or avoided: • Wastewater treated to appropriate standards or raw/untreated wastewater discharges avoided • Wastewater avoided, reused, or minimized at source	Annual absolute (gross) amount of wastewater treated, reused or avoided before and after the project in terms of: • Cubic metres/year • Per capita/year • Percentage
Treatment, disposal, and/or reuse of sewage sludge	Treatment, disposal, and/or reuse of sewage sludge (according to country legislation compatible with internationally recognized standards): • Sludge that is treated and disposed of (e.g., dewatering, sanitization, composting, digestion without biogas extraction)	• Annual absolute (gross) amount of raw/untreated sewage sludge that is treated and disposed of (in tonnes of dry solids/year and percentage) • Annual absolute (gross) amount of sludge that is reused (in tonnes of dry solids per annum and percentage)

	• Sludge that is reused (e.g., digestion with biogas recovery, phosphorous recovery, agriculture use, co-combustion)	
Improved water supply infrastructure and drinking water quality	Improved water supply infrastructure and facilities and/or improved quality of the supplied drinking water because of the project	Number of people with access to clean drinking water (or annual volume of clean drinking water in cubic metres/year supplied for human consumption) through infrastructure supporting sustainable and efficient water use
Improved sanitation facilities that have been constructed under the project	The increase in the share of the population connected to wastewater collection and treatment systems helps in domestic water pollution abatement and prevents long-lasting environmental damage to the aquifers	Number of people with access to improved sanitation facilities under the project
Improved measures to reduce the risk from adverse flooding impact	This can include, for example, improved hydrometeorological forecasting, improved early warning systems, infrastructure for flood mitigation (levees and reservoirs), flood zoning and improved basin planning	Number of people and/or enterprises (e.g., companies or farms) benefitting from measures to mitigate the consequences of floods
Sustainable land and water resources management (SLM) systems in place	SLM will be site-specific for preserving and restoring natural landscapes (such as floodplains, forests, watersheds, and wetlands) as different areas require different interventions. SLM includes: • Watershed plans and soil and water conservation zones • Agronomic and vegetative measures (e.g., afforestation) • Water-efficient irrigation	• Area covered by sustainable land and water resources management practices • Annual catchment of water (cubic metres/year) that complies with quantity (cubic metres/year) and quality (e.g., turbidity) requirements by utilities

Continued

Table 5.2 *Continued*

Project focus	Actions	Indicators
	• Structural measures (e.g., flood control and drainage measures or stormwater harvesting) • Active recharge by upstream activities to ensure adequate water supply	

Green Bond Certification

The Climate Bonds Initiative (CBI) is a non-profit organization that promotes large-scale investments that will deliver a low-carbon and climate-resilient global economy. A key component of CBI is the Climate Bonds Standard and Certification Scheme (Certification Scheme) that 'allows investors, governments, and other stakeholders to identify and prioritize low-carbon and climate resilient investments and avoid greenwash'. The Certification Scheme confirms that the bond is fully aligned with IMCA's GBP, uses best practices for tracking, reporting, and verification, and is consistent with achieving the goals of the Paris Climate Agreement. The Certification Scheme has two distinct phases:

1. *Pre-issuance requirements*: These need to be met by the issuers seeking certification ahead of the issuance.
2. *Post-issuance requirements*: These need to be met by issuers seeking ongoing certification following issuance.

Water Infrastructure Criteria
A crucial part of the Certification Scheme is that it contains a range of sector-specific eligibility criteria. Each criterion sets climate change benchmarks for that sector, which are used to screen assets and capital projects to ensure only those with climate integrity (either climate change mitigation and/or adaptation and resilient to climate change) are certified. The Water Infrastructure Criteria specifies the requirements that water infrastructure assets and/or projects must meet to be eligible for inclusion in a Certified Climate Bond. The bond must also meet the reporting and transparency requirements of the Climate Bonds Standard to receive certification. Water infrastructure

assets that can be certified are generalized into two main categories. Both the assets and projects must meet both the requirements of the mitigation and the adaptation and resilience components to be eligible for inclusion as a certified bond:

1. *Engineered water infrastructure or water-use systems that collect, treat, and distribute water or protect against floods or drought. Built assets include:*
   - *Water monitoring*: Built assets include smart networks, early warning systems, water quality monitoring processes, for example:
     - Stormwater warning systems
     - Floodwater warning systems
     - Drought warning systems.
   - *Water storage*: Built assets include rainwater harvesting systems, stormwater management systems, infiltration ponds, aquifer storage, groundwater recharge systems, sewer systems, pumps, etc. Examples of projects include:
     - Improving water management and efficiency by reducing leaks and reducing urban runoff.
     - Installing or upgrading water capture and storage infrastructure.
     - Improving energy efficiency or using low-carbon fuel sources.
   - *Water treatment*: Built assets include water recycling systems, wastewater treatment facilities, slurry treatment facilities, etc. Examples of projects include:
     - Separating solids from wastewater management systems
     - Generating renewable energy from methane or biogas production
     - Waste energy recovery
     - Improving energy efficiency or using low-carbon fuel sources
     - Installing or upgrading water treatment infrastructure.
   - *Desalination*: Built assets include the construction and/or operation of seawater desalination plants or brackish water desalination plants. Examples of projects include:
     - Reverse osmosis/forward osmosis desalination with onsite low-carbon energy
     - Integrated water and power plants
     - Desalination plants supplying water for fossil/nuclear power stations.

- *Water distribution*: Built assets include rainwater harvesting systems, terracing systems, etc. Examples of projects include:
  - Installing or upgrading water irrigation systems, such as high-efficiency drip.
- *Flood defence*: Built assets include surge barriers, pumping stations, levees, etc. Examples of projects include:
  - Installing or upgrading of flood monitoring and warning systems.
2. *Nature-based solutions that collect, store, treat, or distribute water or to buffer floods or drought*: The nature-based solutions and hybrid infrastructure covered by the Water Infrastructure Criteria include:
- *Water storage*: Nature-based assets include rainwater harvesting systems, aquatic ecosystems, aquifer storage, groundwater recharge systems, riparian wetlands, stormwater management, etc. Examples of projects include:
  - Using natural areas for stormwater management
  - Creating groundwater recharge areas for aquifer storage.
- *Flood defences*: Nature-based assets include ecological retention and relocation of assets from floodplains, etc. Examples of projects include:
  - Restoration of riparian wetlands for flood storage
  - Creation of safe delta flood zones for rivers to naturally expand into
  - Altering flows to reduce the force of flood stage flows.
- *Drought defence*: Nature-based assets include aquifer/groundwater storage, wetland storage, recharge zone management, etc. Examples of projects include:
  - Using pumps to transfer waters to/from the natural aquifers
  - Metering/monitoring systems to detect and warn against low flow
  - Planting/removing vegetation to reduce demand for irrigation.
- *Water treatment*: Nature-based assets include natural filtration/recycling systems, such as wetlands and forests, engineered natural filtration systems, and forest and fire management for water quality management, etc. Examples of projects include:
  - Wetlands for water filtration and nutrient management
  - Integration of existing natural features with water treatment.
- *Stormwater management*: Nature-based assets include permeable surfaces, groundwater recharge, rainwater harvesting, constructed wetland ponds, forests for water quality management, etc. Examples of projects include:

- Removal of pavements to increase groundwater absorption and reduce runoff
- Creation of wetland restoration ponds.

- *Ecological restoration*: Nature-based assets include erosion control systems, hydrological restoration, etc. Examples of projects include:
  - Development of environmental flow regimes
  - Restoration of hydrological function and aquatic species
  - Restoring downstream deposition of sediment.[16]

Case 5.1 Government Bond: New Jersey's Green Bonds Financing Water Infrastructure Upgrades

In 2021, in partnership with the New Jersey Department of Environmental Protection (DEP), the New Jersey Infrastructure Bank sold $122.5 million of AAA/Aaa rated environmental infrastructure bonds. The bonds, issued as green bonds, with maturities through 2050 and an effective interest rate of 1.875 per cent, leveraged DEP's zero-interest loans to provide a total of $386 million in projects, creating over 4,500 direct construction jobs across the state. The types of projects funded include green infrastructure, sewer system collection and treatment improvements, drinking water treatment and distribution enhancements, and projects to reduce or eliminate combined sewer overflows. Examples of projects funded include:

- *Passaic Valley Sewerage Commission*: $6.5 million has been invested in increasing wet weather treatment capacity, reducing the frequency and duration of combined sewer overflows.
- *Plumsted Township*: The construction of a $22.8 million advanced wastewater treatment facility has been initiated to eliminate failing septic systems.
- *Little Egg Harbor Municipal Utilities Authority*: $6.1 million will be invested in replacing ageing potable water mains and constructing a new potable water treatment plant to increase the system capacity and resilience.
- *Camden County Municipal Utilities Authority*: $72 million has been invested in sludge digester improvements at the wastewater treatment facility to reduce the amount of sludge generated and to generate enough biogas to meet 50 per cent of the treatment facility's power needs.[17]

Case 5.2 Corporate Bond: Anglian Water Funding Capital Investments

Anglian Water, owned by its parent company, Anglian Water Services Limited, is the largest water and recycling company in England and Wales by geographic region. Since

Anglian Water announced its first green bond in 2017, it has funded 850 capital investment projects through green bonds totalling £876 million. All capital expenditure is subject to British Standards Institute verification, a standard launched by the Green Construction Board. The water company now has six green bonds in operation, funding various schemes including water abstraction projects, drought and flood resilience work, and water recycling and water resource management projects. The proceeds from the green bonds must contribute to one or more environmental objectives of:

- Climate change mitigation
- Climate change adaptation
- Natural resource conservation
- Biodiversity conservation
- Pollution prevention and control.[18]

Case 5.3 Multilateral Development Bank Bond: Asian Development Bank's Green Bonds Supporting Water Projects

The Asian Development Bank (ADB) has raised around $7.6 billion since its green bond programme was launched in 2015, with the green bond issuances being diverse, with transactions across multiple currencies. In 2019, the ADB followed up its inaugural 2018 euro-denominated green bond with another issuance of €750 million, with maturity in 2029. The green bonds help promote ADB's priorities of climate change mitigation, climate and disaster resilience, and environmental sustainability, with climate change adaptation projects including those in the areas of water and other urban infrastructure and services. In 2020, the ADB announced an investment of up to $20 million in green bonds to be issued by Georgia Global Utilities JSC (GGU), with the proceeds used to upgrade water supply and sanitation in Tbilisi and nearby municipalities and refinance the debt of renewable energy and water operations. The investments are part of a $250 million issue by GGU of five-year green bonds listed on the Irish Stock Exchange.[19,20]

Environmental Impact Bond

EIBs are a form of debt characterized by a pay for success component that determines the amount that investors are repaid based on environmental performance. Investors take on a portion of the risk of project performance and are rewarded in the case of over-performance. Investors in EIBs receive principal and interest as with traditional bonds. In addition, an EIB has performance tiers based on key performance thresholds of a designated outcome metric. Performance payments are tied to achieving these pre-determined environmental outcomes, which a third-party evaluator verifies. EIBs can be issued for projects that generate avoided costs in the future, such as reduced costs of green infrastructure compared to grey infrastructure solutions, avoided regulatory enforcement or punishment for non-compliance, or reduced costs from extreme weather events. For example, EIBs are typically used for green infrastructure projects such as stream and floodplain restoration, stormwater planters in right-of-ways, and constructed wetlands. There are various metrics available to determine the success of the projects, including:

- *Water quality*: Improving water quality by capturing and treating combined sewer overflows.
- *Climate resilience*: Promoting climate resilience through flood relief and mitigation.
- *Quality of life*: Enhancing the quality of life associated with the restoration of rivers, waterways, and waterfronts by removing harmful contaminants and pollutants.
- *Responsible management*: Various environmental, social, and governance criteria can be achieved at the project level, such as environmental impacts and community involvement.[21,22,23]

Benefits of Environmental Impact Bonds

EIBs can help deliver private capital to make more efficient use of existing resources and potentially bring new funds to meet a range of objectives, including:

- *Starting projects sooner*: EIBs provide capital now rather than waiting for revenue to come through in the future. Accelerating the timetable for water project financing, initiating, and completing will help bring down the cost of these projects and speed the rate at which these projects are implemented.
- *Attracting additional payers*: EIBs create a multi-stakeholder transaction in which project beneficiaries share some aspect of EIB costs.
- *Piloting new projects*: EIBs allow the piloting of new projects that may be viewed as risky and share these risks with investors if the projects are not successful.

- *Providing an incentive for good project construction and performance*: EIB's have an 'over-performance payment' structure if the project continues to achieve desired outcomes over time.[24]

Case 5.4 City of Atlanta's Environmental Impact Bond

In 2019, the City of Atlanta's Department of Watershed Management, in partnership with Quantified Ventures and Neighborly, announced the closing of the first publicly issued EIB, which will finance green infrastructure in an area of the city frequently impacted by polluted stormwater runoff and flooding. The $14 million EIB provides funding for a range of urban ecosystem restoration and green stormwater management practices in both combined and separate sewer systems of the Upper Proctor Creek watershed. The projects, which began construction in 2021 and will be completed by 2024, aim to mitigate localized flooding by reducing stormwater runoff by 55 million gallons annually. In addition, the projects will provide a range of multiple co-benefits, including improving stream health, providing access to green space, improving air quality, providing public environmental education, restoring native habitat, and creating green jobs. The EIB has a two-tiered performance structure with the high-performance threshold set at 6.52 million gallons of capacity for stormwater captured or detained by green infrastructure, as measured by hydrological surveys. Volume was chosen as it is:

- A straightforward metric that can be applied to and aggregated across all projects (types and geography).
- Reflects both flood reduction and water quality improvement.
- Easy for investors to understand and is related to their environmental interests.
- Allows consistent prediction and measurement of results.[25,26,27]

Green Loans

Green loans are any type of loan instrument made available to exclusively finance or refinance, in whole or part, new and/or existing eligible green projects, including projects that focus on achieving water security and green growth.[28,29] There are multiple benefits for borrowers of green loans, including:

- *Enhancing sustainability management*: Green loans can be used to develop governance, strategy, and management structures related to sustainability within organizations. It can also improve the medium- and long-term environmental, social, and governance (ESG) assessment of the borrower, which can help it raise its corporate value.

- *Gaining public acceptance*: Borrowers can demonstrate that they are actively promoting green projects by procuring green loans, which could increase their public acceptance.
- *Reinforcing the funding base and building relationships with new lenders*: Diversifying financing instruments enables borrowers to reinforce their funding bases. Procuring green loans and disclosing relevant information enables borrowers to consolidate their funding base by building new relationships with financial institutions which value ESG loans.
- *Raising funds on relatively favourable terms*: If organizations take out green loans, they may be able to raise funds on relatively favourable terms from financial institutions who are well versed in evaluating the feasibility of such businesses.[30]

Green Loan Principles

The Loan Market Association has developed the Green Loan Principles (GLP) to facilitate and support environmentally sustainable economic activities. The GLP build on the GBP to promote consistency across financial markets. The GLP comprise voluntarily recommended guidelines that can be applied on a deal-by-deal basis to categorize the loan as 'green'. The eligibility categories for green loans, including those that focus on achieving water security and green growth, are summarized in Table 5.3. The GLP provides a framework that enables market participants to understand the characteristics of a green loan, which is comprised of four components:

1. *Use of proceeds*: Green loans require the proceeds to be used for green projects, including research and development. The use of loan proceeds for green projects should be described in the finance documents and any marketing materials. The green projects should have clear environmental benefits, measured and reported by the borrower. If the funds are used for refinancing, the borrowers should estimate the share of financing versus refinancing. The GLP recognizes a broad range of categories of eligibility for green projects to address crucial areas of environmental concern, including climate change, natural resource depletion, loss of biodiversity, and air, water, and soil pollution.
2. *Process of project evaluation and selection*: The borrower of a green loan should communicate to its lenders their environmental objectives, the process of how its projects fit within the GLP eligibility categories, and

Table 5.3 Categories of eligibility for green projects

Category	Examples of activities
Sustainable water and wastewater management	• Sustainable infrastructure for drinking water and/or wastewater treatment • Sustainable urban drainage systems • River training and other forms of flooding mitigation
Environmentally sustainable management of living natural resources and land use	• Environmentally sustainable agriculture • Climate-smart farming, such as drip-irrigation • Preservation or restoration of natural landscapes
Terrestrial and aquatic biodiversity conservation	• Protection of coastal, marine and watershed environments
Climate change adaptation	• Information support systems, such as climate observation and early warning systems
Eco-efficient and/or circular economy adapted products, production technologies, and processes	• Development and introduction of environmentally sustainable products, with an eco-label or environmental certification
Renewable energy and energy efficiency	• Production of renewable energy • Energy storage, smart grids, and efficient appliances and products

any related eligibility criteria, such as the process of identifying and managing potential material environmental risks associated with the proposed projects. Borrowers should also disclose any green standards or certifications they are seeking to conform with.

3. *Management of proceeds*: The proceeds of the loan should be credited to a dedicated account or tracked by the borrower to maintain transparency and promote the integrity of the financial product. Borrowers should establish an internal governance process to track the allocation of funds towards green projects.

4. *Reporting*: Borrowers should make available information on the use of proceeds, renewed annually until fully drawn. The information should include a list of green projects for which the green loan proceeds are used, a brief description of those projects, and the amounts allocated and their expected impact. The GLP recommends the use of qualitative performance indicators and, where possible, quantitative performance measures and discloses the methodology and/or assumptions used in the quantitative determination.[31]

Case 5.5 Border Bank's Green Loans

Border Bank, a mutual financial institution servicing the Department of Home Affairs and the Australian Border Force community, is launching its Green Loan programme. It rewards customers with a special low rate when they borrow for a green initiative. The green loan has a fixed rate of 5.79 per cent per annum compared to the standard 5.92 per cent per annum. The loan can be up to seven years and qualifies for the bank's Reduced Fees Program. Green loans are available for a range of environmentally friendly activities, including installing rainwater tanks, water pumps, greywater treatment systems, and solar hot water systems and purchasing water-efficient white goods and appliances (minimum 4.5-star rating out of 6).[32]

Case 5.6 Water and Waste Disposal Loan Guarantee

The United States Department of Agriculture's Water and Waste Disposal Loan Guarantee programme helps private lenders provide affordable financing to qualified borrowers to improve access to clean, reliable water and waste disposal systems for households and businesses in rural areas. The funds can be used to construct or improve facilities for drinking water, sanitary sewers, solid waste disposal, and stormwater disposal. Lenders can be federal or state-chartered banks, savings and loans agencies, farm credit banks, or credit unions, while eligible borrowers are public bodies, Tribes, and non-profit businesses. The loan guarantee percentage is published annually in a Federal Register notice, with loans disbursed receiving an 80 per cent guarantee. The lender will establish and justify the guaranteed loan term based on the use of the loan funds, the economic life of the assets and those used as collateral, including revenue taken as security, and the borrower's repayment ability. The loan's interest rates are negotiated between the lender and borrower, and rates can be fixed or variable.[33]

Case 5.7 Malaysia's Green Technology Financing Scheme

The Malaysian Government's Green Technology Financing Scheme (GTFS) is a special financing scheme introduced to support the development of green technologies in Malaysia. The GTFS is a soft loan supported by the government with participating financial institutions offering green loans to finance the production of green products and to finance investment for the utilization of green technology (Table 5.4). GTFS has defined that any product, equipment, or system that satisfies the following criteria is categorized as green technology:

- Minimizes environmental degradation
- Reduces greenhouse gas emissions
- Safe for use and promotes a healthy and improved environment for all forms of life
- Conserves energy and natural resources
- Promotes the use of renewable resources

Various sectors can be funded, including water (Table 5.5), with participating financial institutions receiving from the government a two per cent per annum interest/profit rate subsidy for the first seven years and a 60 per cent government guarantee of green component cost.[34]

Table 5.4 Malaysia's green technology financing scheme

Financing offer	Details
For producers (RM 100 million per applicant)	*Purpose*: To finance investment for the production of green products *Finance tenure*: Up to 15 years *Eligibility Criteria*: Legally registered Malaysian companies that have at least 51 per cent Malaysian shareholding
For users (RM 25 million per applicant)	*Purpose*: To finance investment for the utilization of green technology *Financing tenure*: Up to 10 years *Eligibility criteria*: Legally registered Malaysian companies that have at least 51 per cent Malaysian shareholding

Table 5.5 Criteria for water sector

Criteria for water	Examples of projects
Scope: Adoption of green technology in the management and utilization of water resources: - Better quality of water supply to users - Efficient use of water resource - Rainwater harvesting - Recycling and reuse - Reduction use of chemicals - Use of green materials and/or equipment	- Better water treatment technology - Leakage monitoring and minimization - Lower-grade water for industrial process - Recycling and reuse of water - High efficient treatment plant

Notes

1. R.C. Brears, *Water Resources Management: Innovative and Green Solutions* (De Gruyter, 2021).
2. Amanda Medori Hallauer et al., 'Environmental Impact Bond: An Innovative Financing Mechanism for Enhancing Resilience in the City of Atlanta through Green Infrastructure' (paper presented at the World Environmental and Water Resources Congress 2019, Pittsburgh, Pennsylvania, 2019 2019).
3. Zhenghui Li et al., 'Green Loan and Subsidy for Promoting Clean Production Innovation', *Journal of Cleaner Production* 187 (2018).
4. IDB, 'Transforming Green Bond Markets: Using Financial Innovation and Technology to Expand Green Bond Issuance in Latin America and the Caribbean' (2019), https://publications.iadb.org/en/transforming-green-bond-markets-using-financial-innovation-and-technology-expand-green-bond
5. Ryan Jones et al., 'Treating Ecological Deficit with Debt: The Practical and Political Concerns with Green Bonds', *Geoforum* 114 (2020).
6. Caroline Flammer, 'Corporate Green Bonds', *Journal of Financial Economics* (2021).
7. World Bank, 'What Are Green Bonds?' (2015), https://documents.worldbank.org/en/publication/documents-reports/documentdetail/400251468187810398/what-are-green-bonds.
8. Pauline Deschryver and Frederic de Mariz, 'What Future for the Green Bond Market? How Can Policymakers, Companies, and Investors Unlock the Potential of the Green Bond Market?', *Journal of Risk and Financial Management* 13, no. 3 (2020).
9. Candace Partridge and Francesca Romana Medda, 'The Evolution of Pricing Performance of Green Municipal Bonds', *Journal of Sustainable Finance & Investment* 10, no. 1 (2020).
10. Lloyd Freeburn and Ian Ramsay, 'Green Bonds: Legal and Policy Issues', *Capital Markets Law Journal* 15, no. 4 (2020).
11. OECD, 'Mobilising Bond Markets for a Low-Carbon Transition, Green Finance and Investment' (2017), https://www.oecd.org/env/mobilising-bond-markets-for-a-low-carbon-transition-9789264272323-en.htm.
12. World Bank, 'What Are Green Bonds?'.
13. Climate Bonds Initiative, 'Summary of Faqs: Guide for Issuers on Green Bonds for Climate Resilience' (2020), https://www.climatebonds.net/files/files/Summary%20of%20FAQs_Green%20Bonds%20for%20Climate%20Resilience.pdf.
14. IMCA, 'Green Bond Principles' (2021), https://www.icmagroup.org/assets/documents/Sustainable-finance/2021-updates/Green-Bond-Principles-June-2021-140621.pdf.
15. 'Suggested Impact Reporting Metrics for Sustainable Water and Wastewater Management Projects' (2017), https://www.icmagroup.org/assets/documents/Regulatory/Green-Bonds/Water-Wastewater-Impact-Reporting-Final-8-June-2017-130617.pdf
16. Climate Bonds Initiative, 'Water Infrastructure Criteria under the Climate Bonds Standard' (2021), https://www.climatebonds.net/files/files/Water%20Criteria%20Document%20Final_17Jan21.pdf
17. New Jersey Environmental Digital Library, 'Murphy Administration Invests $386m in Water Infrastructure, Creating 4,600+ Construction Jobs', https://njedl.rutgers.edu/news/murphy-administration-invests-386m-water-infrastructure-creating-4600-construction-jobs.

18. Anglian Water, 'Anglian Water Funds 850 Capital Investment Projects through Green Bonds since 2017', https://www.anglianwater.co.uk/news/anglian-water-green-bond-investment/#:~:text=Since%20it%20announced%20its%20first, Bonds%20totalling%20£876%20million.&text=Since%20then%2C%20the%20projects% 20delivered,company's%202010%20capital%20carbon%20baseline.

19. ADB, 'Adb Green Bond Newsletter and Impact Report 2021' (2021), https://www.adb. org/publications/adb-green-bonds.

20. 'Adb to Invest up to $40 Million in Ggu Green Bonds to Upgrade Water, Sanitation in Georgia,' https://www.adb.org/news/adb-invest-40-million-ggu-green-bonds-upgrade -water-sanitation-georgia#:~:text=TBILISI%2C%20GEORGIA%20(27%20July%202020, debt%20of%20renewable%20energy%20and.

21. Hallauer et al., 'Environmental Impact Bond: An Innovative Financing Mechanism for Enhancing Resilience in the City of Atlanta through Green Infrastructure'.

22. CPIC, 'Conservation Investment Blueprint: Environmental Impact Bond for Green Infrastructure' (2019), http://cpicfinance.com/wp-content/uploads/2019/01/CPIC-Blueprint-Environmental-Impact-Bond-for-Green-Infrastructure.pdf.

23. Ibid.

24. Diego Herrera et al., 'Designing an Environmental Impact Bond for Wetland Restoration in Louisiana', *Ecosystem Services* 35 (2019).

25. City of Atlanta Department of Watershed Management, 'Environmental Impact Bond (Eib) for Green Infrastructure in Proctor Creek Watershed', https://www. atlantawatershed.org/environmental-impact-bond/.

26. P.E. Glen R. Behrend, Amanda Hallauer, and David Bell, PWS, 'Atlanta's Environmental Impact Bond for Green Infrastructure', in *National Watershed and Stormwater Conference* (Charleston, South Carolina 2019).

27. Quantified Ventures, 'Atlanta: First Publicly Offered Environmental Impact Bond', https:// www.quantifiedventures.com/atlanta-eib.

28. Li et al., 'Green Loan and Subsidy for Promoting Clean Production Innovation'.

29. Brears, *Water Resources Management: Innovative and Green Solutions*.

30. Ministry of the Environment, 'Green Bond Guidelines: Green Loan and Sustainability Linked Loan Guidelines' (2020), https://www.env.go.jp/policy/guidelines_set_version_ with%20cover.pdf

31. Loan Market Association, 'Green Loan Principles. Supporting Environmentally Sustainable Economic Activity' (2018), https://www.lma.eu.com/application/files/9115/4452/ 5458/741_LM_Green_Loan_Principles_Booklet_V8.pdf.

32. Border Bank, 'Green Loan', https://www.borderbank.com.au/loans/green-loan/.

33. USDA, 'Water & Waste Disposal Loan Guarantees', https://www.rd.usda.gov/programs-services/water-environmental-programs/water-waste-disposal-loan-guarantees.

34. Malaysian Green Technology Corporation, 'What Sector Can Be Funded?', https://www. gtfs.my.

6

Debt-for-Nature Swaps Financing Water Security and Green Growth

Introduction

Many developing countries have large international (public sector) debts, and debt servicing absorbs a significant proportion of total budget expenditure. In 2019, debt for developing countries had reached more than $8 trillion. Due to the COVID-19 pandemic, debt servicing alone is estimated to be more than $3 trillion in developing counties in 2020 and 2021. The large scale of the debt contributes significantly to environmental degradation and the deterioration of the natural resource base. Furthermore, post-COVID-19 economic recovery costs could deplete the financial resources needed to address environmental degradation. As such, there are growing calls for the scaling-up of debt-for-nature (DFN) swaps to ensure the economic recovery benefits the environment and its ecosystems, including implementing water security and green growth initiatives.[1,2,3] This chapter will first discuss the concept of DFN swaps before discussing how they can be operationalized and administered. The chapter will then provide an overview of best practices for DFN swaps. Finally, the chapter will provide case studies of DFN swaps implemented to achieve water security and green growth.

Debt-for-Nature Swaps

There are three main types of debt swaps. Debt-debt swaps are a transaction between creditors who interchange foreign loans. Debt-equity swaps involve converting external debt into some form of equity with a foreign organization continuing to hold a claim on debtor country resources. Debt-rescue swaps, or 'buy backs', consist of the repurchasing of a country's debt in the secondary markets. DFN swaps are similar to debt-equity swaps. They involve the purchase (at discounted value) of a developing country's debt in exchange for environmental-related action on the part of the debtor nation.[4] Specifically,

Financing Water Security and Green Growth. Robert C. Brears, Oxford University Press. © Robert C. Brears (2023).
DOI: 10.1093/oso/9780192847843.003.0006

DFN swaps are typically a voluntary transaction in which an amount of hard-currency debt owed by a developing country government (the debtor) is cancelled or reduced (i.e., discounted) by a creditor in exchange for financial commitments to conservation—in local currency—by the debtor. These transactions usually involve countries that are financially distressed and experiencing difficulties in servicing debts.

The DFN swap mechanism provides relief and generates local currency funding for priority environmental programmes and projects. DFN swaps can be used to finance 'brown' (pollution abatement, development of environmentally friendly infrastructure, etc.) or 'green' (nature conservation, preservation of biological diversity, etc.) environmental programmes and projects. They can also be designed to alleviate poverty and foster economic development. As such, DFN swaps can be viewed as a mechanism that blends local and foreign financing to implement environmental programmes and projects that also support economic development and poverty reduction, but that would otherwise have not been financed because of their public goods character.[5,6,7]

The first DFN swap was signed in 1987 when Bolivia and Conservation International negotiated the exchange of $650,000 of Bolivarian commercial debt for a commitment to conserve 1.5 million hectares of forest. The Nature Conservancy, World Wildlife Fund, and Conservation International then brokered DFN swaps around this time, mainly in Latin America. In 1991, the Paris Club, a forum for negotiating debt restructurings between indebted countries and official bilateral creditors, introduced a clause allowing members to convert all official public debt through debt swaps with social or environmental objectives. After which, there was an increase in DFN swaps with Canada, Finland, France, Sweden, and Switzerland among the first countries to use the new clause for environmental purposes.

Nearly 30 countries have utilized DFN swaps since the 1980s to provide more than $1 billion to protect the environment. For example, in the early 1990s, the United States initiated the Enterprise for the America's Initiative that involved DFN swaps. As a result, the United States restructured and, in one case, sold debt equivalent to a face value of over $1 billion owed by Latin American countries. The transactions generated nearly $177 million for environmental and social projects within debtor countries.[8]

However, during the mid-1990s, the overall number of DFN swaps declined due to various factors, including the improved overall debt position of many developing countries because of previous debt-relief efforts.

Nonetheless, there has been a re-emergence of debt swaps in numerous sectors, including debt-for-education, debt-for-health, and debt-for-climate swaps. Debt swaps will more likely increase in demand with total debt before the COVID-19 pandemic reaching $253 trillion in 2019, with more than 60 countries spending more on debt servicing than on public health.[9,10,11,12]

Debt-for-Nature Swap Actors and Motivations

All DFN swaps involve a creditor and debtor. Some may also involve conservation investors or donors. These key actors and their motivations are as follows:

- *Creditor*: Creditors have loaned money and are holders of the debt. They can be commercial banks, commercial suppliers, government export credit agencies, and government aid agencies. Creditors are willing to donate or sell debt because they believe the benefits of reducing debt through debt swaps outweigh the benefits of waiting for uncertain future payment and/or have a desire to improve liquidity and/or have a desire to reduce credit exposure.
- *Debtor*: Debtors have borrowed money and are obligated to repay these debts. For a DFN swap transaction to work, the debtor needs to be interested in and able to provide local currency or another asset of value to environmental programmes or projects in exchange for the cancellation of the debt. The debtor is primarily interested in retiring its hard currency debt (in local currency) at the highest possible discount from face value (i.e., at the lowest possible price). A debtor government will also be interested in the potential for increased investment in conservation.
- *Donor*: Donors provide the funding that makes DFN swaps possible. The donors are typically developed country governments or private foundations, international conservation organizations, or commercial banks. Donors are interested in leveraging their funds to have the most significant impact on their environmental objectives. For government donors, promoting the developing country's economic growth through debt reduction is another motivation. Usually, donors are involved in approving the financial terms of debt swaps and continue to monitor project performance. Donors also recognise that DFN swaps can increase accountability and transparency of the debtor government's operations.[13]

Benefits of Debt-for-Nature Swaps

Numerous benefits can be attained by DFN swaps, as summarized in Table 6.1.[14]

Types of Debt-for-Nature Swaps

There are two main types of DFN swaps:

- *Commercial debt swaps*: These swaps involve selling commercial bank debt on secondary markets at discounted rates. Specifically, commercial debt swap transactions involve a commercial company creditor and government debtor and are typically brokered by third-party non-governmental organizations (NGOs). Such debt is either donated by the bank for tax advantages or sold on the secondary market at a discounted price, having been written off as unlikely to be repaid. The discount rate is related to the creditworthiness of the debtor government.
- *Bilateral debt swaps*: These swaps involve government debt and typically requires that the Paris Club creditors agree to a debt restructuring plan for the debtor country and include a debt swap clause in the plan. Bilateral debt swaps involve a government creditor and a government debtor and can be assisted by a third-party conservation NGO.

Table 6.1 Benefits of debt-for-nature swaps

	Benefits
Debtor	• Help reduce the level of external debt • Encourage international aid by broadening investment opportunities, including in conservation and sustainable development activities • Improving the balance of payment situation by replacing foreign currency liability with local currency liability • Facilitate the domestic flow of funds to a sector that is generally neglected (environment) • Strengthen government institutions and private organizations involved in environmental conservation • Facilitate the funding of medium- and long-term projects, with the issuing of deferred maturity bonds
Creditor/donor	• Achieve biodiversity conservation • Enhance bargaining power if the debt is negotiated on the secondary market at a significant discount • Multiply the value of the donated amount in local currency • Enhance international agency/debtor country coordination without affecting national sovereignty • Generate spin-off benefits and social well-being by helping to reduce debt-servicing pressures and uncertainty

These transactions are usually negotiated directly between the creditor and debtor and involve two types of transactions: debt buy-backs and debt-forgiveness. In exchange, the debtor agrees to invest a specified amount in local environmental programmes or projects. The amount of local currency generated usually reflects a discount rate relative to the face value of the original debt. Nevertheless, only a handful of creditor governments have participated in bilateral DFN swaps. Due to the significant technical expertise required to execute a DFN swap, most involve third-party NGOs with experience brokering such deals.[15,16]

General Elements of a Debt-for-Nature Swap

The general elements of a DFN swap are detailed in Table 6.2.[17,18]

Table 6.2 General elements of a debt-for-nature swap

Element	Description
Amount and type of debt converted or cancelled	The main debt categories include commercial and non-commercial, and non-overseas development aid and Paris Club and non-Paris Club, for example, a debt owned by the German public-owned development bank KfW
Redemption price and/or discount rate	This is the reduction of debt principal or face value if sold or the amount of debt service if maintained. This determines the cost-effectiveness of the operation and the value of the proceeds to be invested in environmental programmes or projects. It varies from debt forgiveness (cancellation of the debt obligation) to marginal discounts on the interest burden. For example, the $32 million bilateral debt owned by the United States to the Philippines was converted at a 50 per cent redemption rate in exchange for the Philippines agreeing to transfer $16 million in Peso to an environmental foundation
Exchange rate and currency	Foreign debt may be held in the debtor's currency, of the creditor (a most likely scenario), or a third country. Currency markets in developing countries are a main source of vulnerability. With DFN swap payments made within the country in the debtor currency, the identification of the exchange rate can be crucial in setting the repayment scheme, particularly where negotiations can last several years
Schedule of payment of the conservation commitments	Based on the savings accrued in the debt service, this is the obligation of the debtor country to make periodic investments in conservation. The schedule can involve regular payments to a financial institution or foundation
Terms of the utilization of the proceeds, including evidence of compliance	This may include creating special funds with board members, including the creditor/donor representatives. The creditor is interested in obtaining evidence of the impact of DFN swap proceeds

Operationalizing Debt-for-Nature Swaps

The typical steps to operationalize DFN swaps are as follows:

1. A national (government or NGO) conservation organization wishing to enact a DFN swap contacts one or several international organizations or representatives of supportive governments interested in funding environmental programmes or projects of mutual interest. The international organization(s) obtains or allocates funds to acquire part of the secondary market debt at below face value. The process can also be initiated externally by international NGOs wishing to fund and implement projects in a specific country. The DFN swap will proceed if the government's natural resource authority and the country's central bank agree to allocate local funds to conclude the swap process.

2. If the swap process is approved, the central bank will communicate its decision to the conservation organization stating the details under which the process may proceed:
   a. Face value sum authorized for the swap and its end-use.
   b. Donor characteristics, indicating that donors must be international organizations involved in the conservation of natural resources.
   c. Type of debt instruments to be purchased on the secondary market.
   d. Type of local currency bonds to be issued in the swap, which details the exchange rate, bond maturity, and annual rate of interest.

3. The central bank determines that the funds from the swap should be deposited in and administered by an intermediary national bank.

4. Once the domestic regulations are defined, the national conservation organization informs the international organizations that their funds can be used for the debt swap approved by the central bank.

5. The international organizations acquire the discounted debt instruments on the secondary market through an international broker.

6. The international organizations then pass the instruments on to the national conservation organization for transmittal for the selected intermediary bank, which will initiate the swap transaction with the central bank.

7. The central bank or the appointed intermediary bank exchanges the debt instruments for local currency bonds based on the terms specified in the second step, which it then deposits in a trust fund made out to the national conservation organization.

8. The national conservation organization prepares the budgets and allocates funds to the various conservation projects.[19,20]

Scheduling Revenue Flows

There are two main options for scheduling revenue flows from DFN swaps: a 'one-time swap' of an agreed amount of the present value of debt and a 'swap-as-you-repay annually' over an agreed period. Nevertheless, DFN swaps can have an inflationary impact if the size of the swaps is large compared to the debtor's economy and the funds are disbursed too quickly in a short period. In the traditional DFN swap model, a flow of annual debt repayments in foreign currency is converted into an annual expenditure in local currency equal to a sum of discounted present values of future repayments. In response, DFN swaps can mitigate the risk of inflation by:

- Ensuring the swaps are small in comparison to the money supply in the national economy.
- Issuing long-term bonds to spread the period of disbursement.
- Designing the transaction as a flow of annual debt service swaps instead of a one-time swap of debt stock.[21]

Administering Debt-for-Nature Swap Funds

DFN swaps can be disbursed locally, either directly for specific projects agreed with a creditor, or transferred to an established domestic financial facility that selects projects under the supervision of relevant stakeholders, including creditors. There are two main ways the DFN swaps can be made as follows.

Debt-for-Nature Swaps on a Project-by-Project Basis

DFN swaps on a project-by-project basis involve transactions that link individual swaps to specific projects from the start. International experience has shown that project-specific DFN swaps are attractive to some creditors for a variety of reasons, including:

- It gives creditors strong assurance on how exactly their money will be spent.

- It enables the creditors to determine how procurement will occur with the debtor country purchasing goods and services from creditors' suppliers.
- As an ad-hoc arrangement, it usually requires lower transaction and administrative costs as it does not involve setting up and operating a specialized institution to manage the project cycle. The overseeing of projects can be incorporated into existing operations of government and/or non-governmental institutions at a lower cost, while project cycle management can be contracted out to short-term consultants.

Debt-for-Nature Swaps through a Domestic Financial Facility

DFN swaps through a domestic financial facility are transactions that transfer money to a domestic financial facility that manages the programme's expenditures and project pipelines (including project appraisal and selection) according to agreed procedures and criteria. Specifically, the DFN swap is conducted through a specially established, local financial facility that manages the whole project cycle (project identification, development, appraisal, financing, and monitoring) under the rules and controls agreed between the parties to the transaction. Some of the benefits of conducting DFN swaps this way include the following:

- Projects are selected on a competitive basis, encouraging more efficient use of resources and increased environmental benefits of the swap.
- The establishment of a locally managed facility to administer DFN swap funds contributes to the better management of local and global common goods.
- Having in place a transparent and credible institution, which efficiently and effectively selects and finances environmental programmes and projects, can attract additional financing from donor countries, international institutions, NGOs, or other financing sources (grants, loans, etc.).

Lifecycle of Domestic Financial Facilities

Once a decision has been made on establishing a domestic financial facility, the next step is determining the institution's life cycle. The options include the following:

- *Perpetual funds*: These are created by a one-off injection of capital from creditors, donors, or other investors. It is not intended that this initial capital be replenished. The capital is kept in a bank account as an endowment or is invested in other revenue-generating assets. The domestic financial facility disburses only the net income earned on these assets.

- *Sinking funds*: These are created by a one-off injection of capital from creditors, donors, or other investors. It is not intended that this initial capital be replenished. The domestic financial facility disburses the income from these assets and the entire principal over a fixed period.
- *Revolving funds*: These are designed to be replenishable. They frequently receive new resources, which are added to the domestic financial facility's assets to replace the funds that have been spent, therefore replenishing or augmenting the original principal. The new funds may come from external transfers in instalments or as revenues from fiscal instruments, such as taxes or fees.[22]

Domestic Financial Facility Disbursement Instruments

Due to the numerous external benefits provided by projects supported by DFN swaps, domestic financing facilities should provide financing to environmental programmes and projects on more favourable terms than those available on the market. This 'soft' financing can be disbursed in numerous forms, including direct grants, low-interest loans, low premium, high-risk loan guarantees, or equity with a low expected return and higher accepted risk. Direct loans are viewed as the most attractive option for disbursing its resources as loans can provide some return on assets to replenish the domestic finance facility. Loans for projects that could generate financial revenue can incentivize project owners to implement projects quickly and more efficiently. Direct grants are considered the most transparent form of financing, the least risky, and the easiest to manage. It is also considered the most market-friendly form of financing as it does not compete with financial products provided by the private sector.

Furthermore, domestic financial facilities can use their limited resources to mobilize additional finance for environmental programmes and projects, maximizing their environmental effectiveness. However, the domestic financial facilities should never finance 100 per cent of project costs. Instead, co-financing is required to achieve financial leverage and additionality and can be done by providing matching grants that cover only a limited portion of the programme's or project's financial needs. The amount provided to cover eligible project costs (the rate of assistance) can be different for different projects, depending on the priority area, type of project (for example, the capacity to generate revenues), and type of beneficiary. Criteria for determining the maximum grant rate should be transparent and straightforward.[23,24]

Table 6.3 Guidelines for domestic financial facilities

Guideline	Description
Clear legal status	Clearly defined, stable, and internationally understood legal status
Clear objectives	It should have clearly defined environmental objectives and narrowly targeted spending priorities
Political independence	The domestic financial facility should be operationally independent of ad hoc politics
Accountable management	It should have an effective and accountable management structure with provisions for conflicts of interests, checks and balances, transparent decision-making, and operational procedures
Predictive revenues	The domestic financial facility should have predictable, long-term revenues
Effective and efficient management	It should be effective and efficient in achieving its objectives, with appropriate incentives, strong leadership, highly qualified staff, and cost-effective projects in the pipeline
Reporting standards	Accounting, financial management, and reporting procedures should be compatible with international standards and national laws
Capacity	It should have the capacity and incentive to leverage funding from other sources
Reasonable costs	It should have reasonable transaction and administrative costs

Guidelines for Domestic Financial Facilities

The OECD has listed a set of guidelines that are considered essential for the successful operation of domestic financial facilities, a summary of which is provided in Table 6.3.[25]

Best Practices for Debt-for-Nature Swaps

Overall, reaching a DFN swap agreement is complex, with each bargaining process unique. Nevertheless, a range of general best practices can be followed in DFN swaps as follows.

Debtor

The debtor could:

- *Establish DFN swap programmes*: DFN swap programmes signal to investors that the debtor country is interested in debt exchanges and that regulatory obstacles to debt exchange programmes have been dealt with.

The outputs of DFN swaps should be broad, such as conservation, sustainable development programmes, training, education, etc. to attract more investors and donors.

- *Keep track of who owns the country's debts*: Information should be gathered on the transactions being made of the country's debt in the secondary debt market.
- *Support and, where necessary, strengthen local management authorities*: These institutions are crucial partners who are often responsible for the swap proceeds. They function as a guarantee for donors and conservation investors that the exchange proceeds will be managed efficiently and according to the agreement. Reaching a DFN swap deal would take longer without these institutions and their absence may keep interested investors away from the exchange discussions. Good relations with existing national management bodies are also crucial as these organizations often receive large foreign support through the exchange, therefore becoming more influential.
- *Inform the central bank on the DFN swap concept*: The central bank's support is crucial as it plays an active role in the preparation of the DFN swap programmes. However, benefits acquired from DFN swaps are usually non-monetary, for example, improved environmental quality, etc. The central bank may not appreciate the value of the swap as its focus is on traditional economic indicators. As such, central banks must be involved at the early stages about the value of such programmes to overcome this barrier, which could result in the central bank opposing an exchange.
- *Include representatives of local residents and interest groups in the DFN swaps planning process*: DFN swaps can quickly become top-down exercises that exclude local people from decision-making. Also, local needs can be perceived as being less important when large debt reductions are at stake. However, the active participation of local people in the planning process is the best guarantee that agreements are reached that meet the approval and have the support of local groups.
- *Inform the public and media of the functioning of DFN swaps*: DFN swaps can be misunderstood due to the complicated and not always transparent transactions. The public can perceive transactions as transferring land or other national resources to foreign interests. Therefore, governments, with NGOs, have an essential educational task to fulfil by informing the media and public on DFN swap exchanges, including the question of sovereignty.

Conservation Investor

The conservation investor could:

- *Create a good working relationship with other financial institutions to find the 'right debt, at the right quantity, and at the right price'*: Economic advisers can also be essential partners in debt negotiations with the debtor country.
- *Initiate DFN swap discussions as a part of regular management consultations with governments*: Because the process to reach any DFN swap agreement is time-consuming, both actors should provide information on possible areas of agreement before any serious negotiations occur. Such information could also be an important factor in taking advantage of temporary 'bargains' in the secondary debt market.
- *Consider potential resource use conflicts carefully and safeguard the rights and needs of local people*: There is a great risk that DFN swap agreements that are reached without sufficient consultation with local people and examination of local resource use patterns and conflicts will be unsuccessful. Instead, the experiences of local groups should be considered at an early stage of the planning process. They should also be given a chance to express their opinion regarding how the DFN swap proceeds should be used and administered.
- *Develop working relationships with local partners*: Local NGOs are not only essential discussion partners for the involvement of local communities, but they may also help explain the benefits of DFN swaps to suspicious debtor governments and the media. NGOs also play a significant and responsible role in carrying out DFN swaps too.
- *Try to coordinate DFN swaps with other DFN swap investors*: Cooperation with other investors could reduce the transaction costs involved in reaching an agreement. The possibility for achieving more significant debt reductions due to investor cooperation could also increase the interest of debtor countries to participate in DFN swaps.

Creditor Bank

The creditor bank could:

- *Initiate discussions with potentially interested DFN swap investors*: This can generate new business opportunities, including the chance of selling non-performing debt.

- *Inform shareholders on the benefits of DFN swaps*: From the shareholder's perspective, it is not logical that the bank sells its loans at a loss to a conservation investor who then makes a debt exchange investment profit. The bank should, therefore, inform shareholders on the potential benefits the bank can get from selling non-performing debts, at a loss, for environmental programmes and projects, including the scope for improved relations with the debtor country and with the increasingly important environmental sector.
- *Consider adopting a green policy based on an assessment of the environmental impacts of bank policy*: One consequence of the growing public concern for the environment is that an increasing number of people are interested in how their savings are invested. Green funds, which make available savings to work for, not against, the environment, are becoming increasingly popular, and a green policy could also see that non-performing debts are donated to conservation investors for DFN swaps.[26]

Case 6.1 United States-Costa Rica Debt-for-Nature Swap

In 2007, the first debt swap between the United States and Costa Rica was established through the signing of four agreements:

1. *Debt Exchange Agreement*: Between the Government of the United States and the Central Bank of Costa Rica (BCCR).
2. *Debt Exchange Program Agreement*: Between the Government of the United States and the Government of the Republic of Costa Rica (GOCR).
3. *Contractual Exchange Commission Agreement*: Between the Government of the United States, The Nature Conservancy, and Conservation International (the NGOs).
4. *Forest Conservation Agreement*: Between the GOCR, the BCCR, and the NGOs.

The agreement resulted from negotiations between the governments of the United States and Costa Rica and the NGOs, The Nature Conservancy and Conservation International, to restructure the debt that the BCCR maintains with the United States Agency for International Development. Under terms laid out in the US Tropical Forests Conservation Act, Costa Rica was forgiven over US$20 million in debt in return for directing payments into a new conservation fund. As a result, by 2018, 42 executing entities of 52 projects have received donations from the debt swap. The projects that have benefited include:

- 50 rural tourism ventures being promoted.
- Ten forest fire brigades were created.

- Around 60,000 trees are being planted to improve forest connectivity.
- Over $2 million in land acquired in perpetuity for conservation.
- Over ten biological corridors benefiting from the development of at least five strategic plans.
- 150 producers having been trained in sustainable development, agroforestry, silvopastoral systems, and environmental awareness.

Some of the specific achievements of the debt swap include:

- *Strengthening producer organizations through the implementation of rotational grazing to improve productive capacity and promote the conservation of biodiversity and forest connectivity in protected wild areas as a mitigation measure for COVID-19 effects*: The Centro Agrícola Cantonal para el Progreso de Sarapiquí has held five workshops on regenerative livestock farming where nearly 40 farmers and their families have committed to transforming their farms by making better use of their pasture area, conserving their patches of forest, planting more trees and protecting water sources in and around the two largest Mixed National Wildlife Refuges in the country: Maquenque and Barra del Colorado. Participating farms will increase the effectiveness of their production while implementing conservation practices for soil, water, wildlife and wetlands in common and fragile ecosystems in the region.
- *Guardians of Nature Movement*: La Voz de Guanacaste seeks to create an identity of 'guardians of nature' by raising awareness, sharing knowledge, changing attitudes, and enhancing skills in teachers and school children on environmental issues with a particular focus on watersheds, biological corridors, protection of forest ecosystems, and the conservation of hunted species. La Voz de Guanacaste' activities include working with 19 schools on environmental education workshops, book donations, planting native trees in the schools, cleaning rivers and communities, developing nature commitments, conducting eco-tours, and developing interactive learning videos. The initiative also promotes outstanding students. In addition, La Voz de Guanacaste trained 61 teachers in the area. The initiative also succeeded in launching a free digital educational platform with the creation of more than 100 lessons and interactive environmental education tools linked to basic subjects.

A second DFN swap was signed between the United States and Costa Rica to finance the consolidation of the National System of Conservation Areas protected wildlife areas within the framework of the commitments assumed by the Government of Costa Rica before the United Nations Convention on Biological Diversity. Some of the achievements of the swap to date include:

- *Development of indicators and monitoring protocols for terrestrial and freshwater ecological integrity*: Throughout 2020, a conceptual framework and detailed ecological integrity indicators were developed for 32 prioritized protected areas. After a series of face-to-face and virtual workshops, interviews, working sessions and field trips, it will be possible to measure and analyse the 'state of health' of ecosystems and natural terrestrial and freshwater populations at the level of the system of protected wild areas, and on that basis, to make management decisions.
- *Design and construction of the wastewater treatment plant in Chirripó National Park*: The official handover and inauguration of the wastewater treatment plant and its energy supply system using photovoltaic panels for the 'Base Crestones' Refuge took place. As part of the works, two septic tanks, drains, and grease traps were installed. In addition, the energy needed to keep the system oxygenated is provided by a photovoltaic system, consisting of 19 solar panels, 12 batteries, and two inverters. The project will provide the sanitary conditions required for the operation and management of the lodge, which recently reopened its doors to park rangers, researchers, tourists, and concessionaires.[27,28,29,30]

Notes

1. Romy Greiner and Allyson Lankester, 'Supporting on-Farm Biodiversity Conservation through Debt-for-Conservation Swaps: Concept and Critique', *Land Use Policy* 24, no. 2 (2007).
2. Stein Hansen, 'Debt for Nature Swaps—Overview and Discussion of Key Issues', *Ecological Economics* 1, no. 1 (1989).
3. Paul Steele and Sejal Patel, 'Tackling the Triple Crisis: Using Debt Swaps to Address Debt, Climate and Nature Loss Post-Covid-19' (2020), https://pubs.iied.org/sites/default/files/pdfs/migrate/16674IIED.pdf
4. Stein Hansen, 'Debt for Nature Swaps: Overview and Discussion of Key Issues' (1988), http://documents1.worldbank.org/curated/en/823691493257754828/pdf/Debt-for-nature-swaps-overview-and-discussion-of-key-issues.pdf.
5. Ibid.
6. OECD, 'Debt-for-Environment Swap in Georgia: Pre-Feasibility Study and Institutional Options' (2006), https://www.oecd.org/env/outreach/35178696.pdf.
7. CBD, 'Debt-for-Nature Swaps' (2001), https://www.cbd.int/doc/nbsap/finance/Guide_Debt_Nov2001.pdf
8. Pervaze A. Sheikh, 'Debt-for-Nature Initiatives and the Tropical Forest Conservation Act (Tfca): Status and Implementation' (2018), https://fas.org/sgp/crs/misc/RL31286.pdf.

9. Danny Cassimon, Martin Prowse, and Dennis Essers, 'The Pitfalls and Potential of Debt-for-Nature Swaps: A Us-Indonesian Case Study', *Global Environmental Change* 21, no. 1 (2011).

10. Institute for Governance & Sustainable Development, 'Debt-for-Climate Swaps' (2020), http://www.igsd.org/wp-content/uploads/2020/08/Background-Note-on-Debt-Swaps-11Aug20.pdf

11. Jennifer McGowan et al., 'Prioritizing Debt Conversion Opportunities for Marine Conservation', *Conservation Biology* 34, no. 5 (2020).

12. Timothy B. Hamlin, 'Debt-for-Nature Swaps: A New Strategy for Protecting Environmental Interests in Developing Nations', *Ecology Law Quarterly* 16, no. 4 (1989).

13. CBD, 'Debt-for-Nature Swaps'.

14. Greiner and Lankester, 'Supporting on-Farm Biodiversity Conservation through Debt-for-Conservation Swaps: Concept and Critique'.

15. Ibid.

16. John M. Shandra et al., 'Do Commercial Debt-for-Nature Swaps Matter for Forests? A Cross-National Test of World Polity Theory1', *Sociological Forum* 26, no. 2 (2011).

17. Greiner and Lankester, 'Supporting on-Farm Biodiversity Conservation through Debt-for-Conservation Swaps: Concept and Critique'.

18. UNDP, 'Debt for Nature Swaps' (2017), https://www.sdfinance.undp.org/content/sdfinance/en/home/solutions/debt-for-nature-swaps.html.

19. FAO, 'Debt for Nature Swaps to Promote Natural Resource Conservation' (1993), http://www.fao.org/3/T0670E/T0670E00.htm#cont.

20. Greiner and Lankester, 'Supporting on-Farm Biodiversity Conservation through Debt-for-Conservation Swaps: Concept and Critique'.

21. OECD, 'Debt-for-Environment Swap in Georgia: Pre-Feasibility Study and Institutional Options'.

22. Ibid.

23. Ibid.

24. OECD, 'Lessons Learnt from Experience with Debt-for-Environment Swaps in Economies in Transition' (2007), https://www.oecd.org/env/outreach/39352290.pdf.

25. 'Debt-for-Environment Swap in Georgia: Pre-Feasibility Study and Institutional Options'.

26. P. Dogsé and B. von Droste, *Debt-for-Nature Exchanges and Biosphere Reserves: Experiences and Potential* (Unesco, 1990).

27. CBD, 'Investing in Nature for Sustainable Development' (2010), https://www.cbd.int/financial/debtnature/costarica-naturalsolutions.pdf.

28. Primer Canje de Deuda por Naturaleza, 'What Is the 1st Us Debt Swap—Cr?', https://primercanjedeuda.org/que-es-el-i-canje-de-deuda/.

29. Forever Costa Rica Association, 'I Debt-for-Nature Swap', https://costaricaporsiempre.org/en/programas/i-canje-de-deuda-por-naturaleza/.

30. Forever Costa Rica, 'Ii Debt-for-Nature Swap U.S.—C.R.', https://costaricaporsiempre.org/en/programas/ii-canje-de-deuda-por-naturaleza-ee-uu-c-r/.

7

Payments for Watershed Services Financing Water Security and Green Growth

Introduction

Payments for Ecosystem Services (PES) schemes are a transparent system for the provision of ecosystem services through conditional payments to voluntary providers. Globally, they are viewed as an important tool in resource and environmental management, land conservation, and reducing water conflicts in upstream and downstream regions of watersheds.[1,2] In the context of water resources management, Payments for Watershed Services (PWS) schemes are an instrument for watershed protection and management and have been implemented in both developing and developed countries at different scales around the world to achieve water security and green growth.[3,4] This chapter will first discuss the concept of PES, the benefits they provide, and the various design considerations that should be addressed. The chapter will then discuss the concept of PWS, the various benefits these schemes provide, and a guideline to ensure a scheme's success.

Payments for Ecosystem Services

Natural ecosystems provide a range of ecosystem services, such as clean water, biodiversity, carbon sequestration, and recreational opportunities. Sustainable land use can maintain these services; however, land users receive no direct compensation for those services as they are rarely sold and bought in the environmental market. The failure of markets to provide incentives to producers of ecosystem services creates environmental externalities, where productive or consumptive activities can inflict involuntary costs on others. In response, PES schemes have gained popularity over time to

Financing Water Security and Green Growth. Robert C. Brears, Oxford University Press. © Robert C. Brears (2023).
DOI: 10.1093/oso/9780192847843.003.0007

internalize externalities associated with the use of ecosystem services. PES schemes provide direct incentives to improve the ecological impacts of private land-use decisions in both developed and developing nations. Specific PES incentive tools include direct public payments, direct private payments, tax incentives, cap and trade markets, voluntary markets, and certification programmes.[5,6]

PES is defined by five criteria: (1) they are a voluntary transaction, (2) they involve a well-defined ecosystem service, (3) the service is 'bought' by at least one buyer, (4) the service is 'provided' by at least one provider, and (5) the transaction is conditional on provision of that service. There are four main types of PES schemes:

- Carbon sequestration and storage, for example, electricity companies paying farmers to plant and maintain additional trees.
- Biodiversity protection, for example, paying local people to set aside or naturally restore areas to create a biological corridor.
- Watershed protection, for example, downstream water users paying upstream farmers to adopt land uses that limit deforestation, soil erosion, flooding risk, etc.
- Landscape beauty, for example, a tourism operator paying a local community to not hunt in a forest where tourists visit to view wildlife.[7]

Additionality and Conditionality

PES scheme payments are made for actions over and above those that land or resources managers would generally be expected to undertake. While 'additionality' will vary from case to case, the actions paid for must at least go beyond regulatory compliance. At the same time, payments are dependent on the delivery of ecosystem service benefits (conditionality). In practice, payments are usually based on implementing management practices that the contracting parties agree are likely to give rise to the benefits.[8]

Benefits of Payments for Ecosystem Services Schemes

PES schemes can provide numerous benefits compared to other conservation interventions, including the following listed in Table 7.1.[9,10]

Table 7.1 Benefits of payments for ecosystem services schemes

Benefit	Description
Proactive response to future regulations	PES schemes can anticipate certain developments and try to motivate relevant actors to become active to be better prepared when foreseen developments actually take place. Examples of developments could be changes in environmental regulation or increasing environmental standards
Enhancing innovation of environmental technologies and processes	PES schemes can spur innovation to reduce environmental degradation and solve environmental problems. For instance, competitiveness between ecosystem service providers can increase environmental effectiveness and cost-efficiency
Directly incentivizing conservation	PES schemes use direct incentives to reach biodiversity targets, which is considered more cost-effective than traditional and indirect conservation policy tools, such as protected areas or integrated conservation and development projects, because it is not as complex to implement and is targeted specifically at project outcomes
New financing sources	In a time when biodiversity conservation financing is scarce, PES schemes can attract new funding sources
Poverty alleviation	While PES schemes are not designed to be a poverty alleviation scheme, they can result in more sustainable livelihoods through the provision of in-kind benefits to participants, especially when targeted at rural or indigenous populations

Auctions or Performance Payments

Poor targeting of ecosystem services can lead to low economic efficiency and environmental effectiveness of PES schemes. Targeting payments to areas where they are most needed increases the PES scheme's environmental effectiveness. Site selection tools for spatial targeting usually consider the ecosystem service provided, degradation risk, and participation cost. Spatial targeting can be combined with either auctions or performance payments to enhance economic efficiency and environmental outcomes further:

- *Auctions*: Auctions (also reverse auctions or procurement auctions) are a contractual design feature that invites potential ecosystem service suppliers to submit price offers at which they are willing to sign a PES contract. Bids need to be competitive as only reasonable offers will be contracted. Auctions help reveal private willingness to accept and private opportunity costs. They are a mechanism to enhance the economic efficiency and environmental effectiveness of PES contracts.

- *Performance-based payments*: Performance-based payments, also known as payments by results or outcome-based payments, relate payments to actual ecosystem service provision, in contrast to payments prescribing specific actions or inputs. Performance payments can result in the use of local knowledge and promote innovative land-use practices. Service providers usually know more about needed inputs and land-use practices, enabling ecosystem service supply at lower costs. Performance payments need to be tied to observable indicators; therefore, reliable indicators need to be developed to ensure the scheme's success.[11]

Market Type

Payments for PES schemes are implemented through various mechanisms, including exchanges, clearinghouses, mitigation or conservation banks, and bilateral agreements. The most appropriate mechanism depends on factors such as the number of interested buyers and sellers, the homogeneity of the ecosystem service, and transaction costs:

- *Exchanges*: These are market institutions where numerous buyers and sellers trade a homogeneous, fungible (interchangeable) commodity in a single market. With large numbers of buyers and sellers, each buyer and seller are small relative to the size of the market and therefore cannot impact market price. Theoretically, such a market leads to efficient outcomes where the commodity (ecosystem service) is traded to those who value it the most. Furthermore, the high number of trading partners and a standardized commodity results in minimal transaction costs.
- *Clearinghouses*: Clearinghouses acquire ecosystem service credits and act as intermediaries between buyers and sellers. Clearinghouses normalize credits by establishing appropriate trade ratios so that each unit can be sold as a homogenous unit. Because clearinghouses own the credits, it is their responsibility to find buyers, allowing ecosystem service producers to reduce the risks associated with demand uncertainty.
- *Mitigation or conservation banks*: Mitigation or conservation banks are similar to clearinghouses, except that the banks acquire property that perpetually provides services, such as habitat restoration, rather than credits for fixed amounts of ecosystem services.
- *Bilateral agreements*: These involve customized trading transactions between a buyer and a seller and can allow PES in cases where

heterogeneity is high. It typically involves bilateral agreements between a regulatory authority and private landowners.[12]

Intermediaries

At a minimum, PES schemes require two actors: buyers (beneficiaries) of ecosystems and sellers (providers) who affect ecosystem services supply. At times, a third group called intermediaries is needed. PES intermediaries are actors who take on roles that connect and facilitate transactions between buyers and sellers. Intermediaries also connect with each other to strengthen connections between buyers and sellers. Intermediaries can range from individuals to organizations to collaborative groups connected to different PES stakeholders. These intermediaries can span scales, including local, regional, national, and international, and include public, private, civil, and academic organizations. Intermediaries perform various tasks, depending on their strengths/abilities, the local context they operate in, and regulatory measures. Table 7.2 provides examples of roles intermediaries can play.[13]

Table 7.2 Role of intermediaries in payments for ecosystem services schemes

Role	Description
Information exchange	Providing accessible information about the concept of PES to stakeholders and the public Providing information to potential participants about how the scheme works Assisting with information between buyers, sellers, and other groups involved in the PES scheme
Scheme design	Convening stakeholders to obtain input into scheme design (for example, target ecosystem services, landowner eligibility, payment structure, geographic boundaries) Ensuring region-specific and stakeholder-specific concerns are incorporated into PES scheme design considerations Developing PES scheme standards and guidelines, including protocols for monitoring and evaluation
Networking, representation, and mediation	Representing interests and concerns related to buyers, sellers, and other participants At times acting as a neutral third party Representing buyers and/or sellers in the negotiation process
Administration and project coordination	Promoting and publicizing information about the PES scheme Project administration (managing contracts, administering project funds) Monitoring and evaluation Assisting with scheme eligibility requirements

Bundling and Layering of Services

While PES schemes can make payments exclusively for the provision of a particular ecosystem service, such as enhancing biodiversity, there are two other approaches available:

- *Bundling*: This is defined as the grouping of multiple ecosystem services together in a single package to be purchased by an individual or multiple buyers, for example, climate mitigation, water quality, biodiversity, and visitor benefits could be bundled together in a single scheme designed to pay for peatland restoration.
- *Layering*: Layering, also called stacking, refers to schemes where payments are made for different ecosystem services separately from the same system, for example, a peatland restoration project running a carbon offset scheme in parallel with a scheme targeting water companies to pay for water quality benefits, while taking in money from a visitor scheme linked to cultural and aesthetic values.[14,15]

Payments for Watershed Services

PWS is a sub-category of PES and involves a relationship between multiple users of the same watershed. Initially, PWS was conceptualized as downstream users incentivizing sustainable land-use practices upstream to secure their water quality and water quantity access. In reality, PWS schemes are very diverse, involving multiple private and public stakeholders and using various financial and non-financial incentives.[16] PWS schemes have been developed at various scales to provide various watershed services, including protecting water supplies, preventing floods, and maintaining aquatic habitats for commercial and recreational fish species.[17,18,19,20,21,22]

Buyers and Sellers

PWS buyers include a wide range of public and private actors, motivated by their desire to protect water resources for various public and private purposes:

- *Public sector buyers*: PWS schemes are attractive when the cost of watershed protection payments is less than the cost of filtration that would be required if surface water quality were diminished.

- *Private sector buyers*: Private sector buyers are helping secure or maintain their business interests in clean, abundant water. In addition, private sector buyers are also addressing the future possibility of regulation.
- *Philanthropic buyers*: PWS schemes can be funded by the voluntary contributions of water users to support watershed enhancement projects.
- *Eco-certification*: Voluntary eco-certification offers farm and forest producers an opportunity to differentiate their products and demonstrate a commitment to environmental protection. In the context of PWS, eco-certified products help protect water quality and aquatic habitat through various measures the producer implements, such as water conservation.

Meanwhile, landowners have multiple reasons for participating in PWS schemes. These reasons include:

- Cash payments.
- Various non-cash financial benefits, for example, new infrastructure or physical improvements to land.
- Increased agricultural yield or reduced costs associated with the adoption of new practices.
- Access to information and technical assistance.
- Personal interest in environmental stewardship.[23]

Payments for Watershed Services and Source Water Protection

PWS schemes often focus on source water protection, which is to maintain or protect the quality of drinking water sources. These schemes can be divided into filtration avoidance programmes and watershed protection programmes, with the former driven by regulations and the latter voluntary:

- *Filtration avoidance programmes*: Municipalities may be required to filter water supplies but can receive a filtration avoidance notice from an environmental regulator, waiving the requirements to filter drinking water supplies if the municipality can demonstrate to the environmental agency that their source watersheds are adequately protected, therefore the risk of contamination to water supplies is low. As filtration plants incur significant capital, operational and maintenance costs, these waivers can result in significant savings for water providers without filtration infrastructure. Actions that are taken in these schemes include:

- ○ Compensating farmers and private forest landowners for adopting best management practices (BMPs) that reduce or prevent downstream pollution.
- ○ Purchasing conservation easements.
- ○ Sharing costs with government agencies, such as a forestry department, for management actions that benefit water quality.

- *Watershed protection programmes*: These programmes are designed to maintain water quality and/or water quantity. They are not driven by regulations as the utilities involved usually have filtration facilities or use groundwater supplies that do not require filtration. Instead, these programmes are developed to reduce risks to water supplies related to increasing development in the watershed and avoid costs associated with treating pollution and sediment in water supplies from non-point sources, such as agriculture. The actions taken in these schemes are generally the same as filtration avoidance programmes.[24]

Payments for Watershed Services and Utilities

There is a growing use of PWS schemes by drinking water, wastewater, and electric utilities to meet various objectives. Utilities are uniquely positioned to pursue PWS initiatives as they have a direct relationship with many potential buyers: their customers. As utilities already have established financial relationships with customers, the infrastructure for payment is already in place, and there is a process for establishing funding mechanisms, such as through rate increases or voluntary contributions on utility bills. Furthermore, utilities are usually connected to their surrounding watersheds and are aware of their ecological and social conditions. In recent years, utilities in the United States have developed PWS schemes to offset impacts and maintain the provision of beneficial ecosystem services. Some of these schemes compensate farmers and forest owners for changing management practices to reduce downstream pollution and sedimentation. These schemes avoid the need to construct costly filtration plants and reduce utility operational and maintenance costs among others.[25]

Payment Mechanisms

In PWS schemes, there are four main types of payment mechanisms:

- *Private payment schemes*: In these schemes, private entities agree amongst themselves to provide payments in return for maintenance or restoration of a watershed service. The transaction mechanism can take many forms, including:
  - *Transfer payments*: Direct payment schemes, where a service seller receives a payment from a service buyer in return for the protection or restoration of a watershed service.
  - *Land purchases*: A private party may purchase land from another private party to safeguard the watershed service originating from that land.
  - *Cost-sharing*: Beneficiaries of watershed services can agree among themselves to share the costs that must be met by service sellers upstream to maintain or restore watershed services.
  - *Purchase of development rights*: In this mechanism, property rights are separated from development rights. For example, a forest owner may retain the property rights for their land but can sell the development rights. The buyer and seller then agree in the purchase contract on restrictions on land use and BMPs that protect watershed services.
- *Cap-and-trade schemes*: Under a cap-and-trade scheme, a cap is established for the release of pollutants or the abstraction of groundwater. Trading increases the economic efficiency of water and environmental management by enabling companies or landholders to buy permits from those able to generate them in a cheaper way.
- *Certification schemes for environmental goods*: Certification schemes, or eco-labelling schemes, are another payment mechanism for PWS schemes. Transactions occur between private partners, but payment is embedded in the price paid for a traded product, such as organic produce. The buyers in these schemes are consumers who prefer products from suppliers who comply with verifiable environmental standards. Intermediaries play a role either as a certification agency or as traders in certified products.
- *Public payment schemes*: These are the most common form of payment scheme for ecosystem services. Service buyers are public authorities, such as municipalities or national governments, motivated by the need

to provide safe drinking water or regulation of river flows. Mechanisms for payment in these schemes include user fees and purchasing
of development rights.[26]

Guideline Framework for Effective Targeting

The following guideline framework for targeting in PWS schemes (where targeting is the process of selecting participating parcels among those eligible for
a PES scheme) is recommended to ensure a scheme's success:

1. *Definition of scheme goals, ecosystem services, and targeting criteria:*
   a. *Consider using valuation services to identify ecosystem services:* Stated
      preferences and benefit transfer can be employed to identify the
      ecosystem services most valued by users. Ecosystem services con-
      sensually prioritized by providers and users should be identified and
      targeted for PWS schemes.
   b. *Consider scheme goals when selecting targeting criteria:* Single or mul-
      tiple scheme goals need considering when selecting criteria and
      indicators for targeting PWS areas. The lack of a precise definition
      of PWS goals can lead to selecting areas that do not provide targeted
      services.
   c. *Consider service users' spatial demand and distribution:* The
      definition and measurement of ecosystem services and identifica-
      tion of priority areas should consider users' distribution regarding
      the spatial-temporal flow of ecosystem services. This is mandatory
      for watershed services, which has a local, not global, demand.
   d. *Consider the impacts of spatial synergy:* Spatial synergy occurs when
      the conservation of two or more parcels provides more benefits
      when proximate or contiguous than spatially isolated in the land-
      scape. In areas of potential spatial synergy, PWS applications should
      be selected according to the land use pattern of the surrounding
      parcels. For example, parcels not attractive to the PWS scheme
      should be enrolled if they are likely to affect ecosystem service
      provision in a neighbouring priority parcel. The enrolment of con-
      tiguous rural properties enables coordination between landowners,
      facilitates collaborative resource management, and optimizes the
      achievement of conservation goals. Besides targeting criteria for
      contiguity, PWS scheme managers can also employ agglomeration

bonuses to encourage the enrolment of adjacent areas by making an extra payment of areas enrolled contiguously in other PWS parcels.

e. *Other considerations include*:

    i. *Consider setting a single or priority goal*: PES schemes that aim to achieve multiple goals, such as watershed conservation, carbon stock, biodiversity, and poverty alleviation, may not find sufficient target areas that contribute simultaneously to achieving these goals. The spatial targeting of PWS schemes should consider all such goals, but it may be more appropriate and effective to have a single or priority objective to pursue.

    ii. *Consider the planning data produced for the area*: The goals and priorities of a PWS scheme can be defined based on planning data available for the area. Landscape plans provide a detailed spatial information database on ecological and social functions, local pressures, and impacts, indicating the goals and priorities of the PWS scheme.

    iii. *Consider a combined definition of targeting criteria by scheme managers and landowners*: Typically, landowners make better decisions on recruiting areas within their property, while scheme managers make better selections on the properties to be enrolled at the landscape level. Therefore, in areas with several small properties and high administrative costs, targeting criteria can be defined by combining the scheme manager's and landowners' preferences.

    iv. *Consider the existence of service provision thresholds*: The selection priority areas for PWS schemes should focus on enrolling parcels that contribute to achieving thresholds, not on parcels that do not contribute. The threshold is the point where watershed service provision is significantly improved in a certain number of enrolled areas.

    v. *Contemplate the effect of social diffusion on targeting areas with additionality*: The selection of areas with little or no additionality may not compromise the scheme's effectiveness. A behavioural change in a small share of the population can affect it entirely through spillover effects, such as conservation in a non-enrolled area. If this effect is likely, it is more effective to enrol areas with low additionality but whose landowners are willing to fulfil PWS contract obligations without high payments than areas with high additionality and higher enforcement costs.

2. *Measurement of indicators*:
   a. *The scale of indicators*: Using landscape-scale indicators to select PWS priority areas is satisfactory, and the production of fine-scale indicators is unnecessary.
   b. *Measurement of ecosystem services*: Modelling can identify areas where specific management practices can provide ecosystem services. If projects face budgetary constraints, a group of experts can evaluate the ecosystem services provided.
3. *Criteria aggregation and targeting methods*:
   a. *Employ cost-effective targeting methods*: Additionality/cost targeting is considered the most effective method.
   b. *Define criteria weights*: The relevance of each criterion in achieving scheme goals should be considered in the targeting procedure. The selection of priority parcels to achieve PWS goals may be hindered if greater weights are not assigned to meet the most important criteria.
   c. *Validate the targeting method*: The method is deemed effective by comparing its selected areas with those obtained through another targeting method or those enrolled in a PWS scheme.
4. *Planning, implementation, and operation*:
   a. *Undertake collaborative design of the PWS scheme*: Landowners' participation in the design and implementation processes strengthens collaboration between providers, contributes to the community's legitimization of the targeting approach, and favours landscape-scale management of the scheme.
   b. *Strengthen partnerships with local intermediaries*: Intermediaries are crucial in providing assistance and information to providers. They select relevant areas to achieve scheme goals, elaborate competitive applications regarding environmental benefits and increase providers' interest. Intermediaries can facilitate cooperation among landowners at the landscape scale and the accessibility of small landowners by assisting them in the eligibility and documentation phases.
   c. *Promote the PWS scheme in the most relevant areas to achieve scheme goals*: Adverse self-selection and inefficient targeting can strongly affect the effectiveness of PWS as they favour targeting unthreatened or low-benefit areas. Adverse selection is more likely when willingness to participate is low. Promoting the PWS scheme in the most relevant areas where providers have low willingness to participate can help avoid self-selection bias.

d. *Adaptive management of the scheme*: Adaptive management enables learning from practice, as the measurement, monitoring, valuation, and management of ecosystem services contain uncertainties. It can improve PWS targeting over time as systematic monitoring and impact assessment can inform policy and generate feedback and facilitate the reshaping of policy in response to feedback. Adaptive management can be facilitated by:

  i. A policy environment that supports experimentation, critical thinking, and long-term funding.
  ii. Availability of high-quality data and technical capacity.
  iii. Participation of stakeholders and external evaluators in implementing and redesigning the scheme.[27]

Case 7.1 Wessex Water's Somerset Catchment Market

Wessex Water in the United Kingdom has created and operates online markets for nature-based solutions, solving environmental challenges through nutrient neutrality, biodiversity net gain, net-zero carbon, and flood risk management. Specifically, its EnTrade trading platform optimizes investments and delivers environmental improvement measures through carbon offsetting, Catchment Nutrient Balancing, nutrient/nitrogen neutrality, source protection, net biodiversity gain, rewilding, and increasing landscape connectivity and permeability. Markets can be created on EnTrade through the following process:

1. *Identify the problem*: Any organization, public or private, can create a marketplace on EnTrade's platform to enable environmental improvement measures, for example, planting trees or cover crops to offset nutrient runoff.
2. *Define the solution*: EnTrade works with the applicant to come up with a defined set of outcomes, a workable plan to achieve them, and measurement methodologies required to verify them.
3. *Ensuring the science is right*: EnTrade retains an agronomy and environmental science team to provide advice and support on how best to achieve the environmental objectives, utilizing local expertise when required.
4. *Establish supply*: EnTrade maintains a database of registered EnTrade farmers and provides on-the-ground support if required to recruit more in the applicant's area.
5. *Launch the marketplace*: Over a 2–4 week period, registered farmers submit prices for delivering some or all of the measures. The total delivery costs are determined when the market closes, and winning bids are notified. EnTrade takes payment for the project, holding it in escrow until all the work is completed.

6. *Manage and measure*: EnTrade uses various technologies, including the EnTrade smartphone app and remote sensing via satellite, to verify that work has been carried out. The growing portfolio of technology solutions enables EnTrade to reduce overheads, reduce paperwork for farmers, and minimize the need for site visits for verification. EnTrade releases electronic payment to each farmer on completion of agreed work, ensuring accountability and improved cash flow for the farmer.

EnTrade operates the Somerset Catchment Market in parts of the River Tone and Parrett catchments (including the Yeo) to improve water quality and biodiversity. Wessex Water offers payments to farmers to create projects on farms that improve the environment. These projects generate a known quantity of environmental benefits, known as a credit, which can be bought by other industries required to offset nutrient and biodiversity losses. The buyers include private companies, such as water companies and building developers, public bodies, government, local councils, and private investors. Water companies have a regulatory requirement to reduce phosphorous entering watercourses from their wastewater treatment processes. In addition to upgrading wastewater treatment plants, some water companies are also investing in schemes that help reduce phosphorous runoff from farmland. Industry can also deliver environmental benefits on behalf of another industry, known as offsetting. Furthermore, housing developers will have a mandatory requirement to soon deliver biodiversity net gain from their developments. Through the EnTrade Catchment Market, farmers can create nature-based projects on farmland that delivers nutrient and biodiversity credits. Through the EnTrade platform, farmers can sell these credits to organizations needing to offset their impact on the environment, providing an opportunity for farmers to earn a financial return while improving the local environment. Farmers can potentially generate multiple environmental credits from the same nature-based project, attracting investment from various buyers. Regarding the pricing of credits, once the Catchment Market confirms the farmer's project(s) meet the basic criteria, the farmer is invited to bid for funding on the EnTrade platform. Farmers can set their minimum price to guarantee their required return. The eligible nature-based projects include:

- Growing cover crops
- Livestock watercourse exclusion fencing
- Hedgerow planting
- Woodland creation
- Wetland/pond creation
- Edge-of-field/in-field buffer strips
- Arable reversion to species-rich grassland.[28,29]

Notes

1. Katherine Brownson and Laurie Fowler, 'Evaluating How We Evaluate Success: Monitoring, Evaluation and Adaptive Management in Payments for Watershed Services Programs', *Land Use Policy* 94 (2020).
2. Jian Sun, Zhiliang Dang, and Shaokui Zheng, 'Development of Payment Standards for Ecosystem Services in the Largest Interbasin Water Transfer Projects in the World', *Agricultural Water Management* 182 (2017).
3. Marcela Muñoz Escobar, Robert Hollaender, and Camilo Pineda Weffer, 'Institutional Durability of Payments for Watershed Ecosystem Services: Lessons from Two Case Studies from Colombia and Germany', *Ecosystem Services* 6 (2013).
4. R.C. Brears, *Water Resources Management: Innovative and Green Solutions* (De Gruyter, 2021).
5. Bhim Adhikari and Gemma Boag, 'Designing Payments for Ecosystem Services Schemes: Some Considerations', *Current Opinion in Environmental Sustainability* 5, no. 1 (2013).
6. Kelly J. Wendland et al., 'Targeting and Implementing Payments for Ecosystem Services: Opportunities for Bundling Biodiversity Conservation with Carbon and Water Services in Madagascar', *Ecological Economics* 69, no. 11 (2010).
7. S. Wunder, 'Are Direct Payments for Environmental Services Spelling Doom for Sustainable Forest Management in the Tropics?', *Ecology and Society* 11 (2006).
8. Center for International Forestry Research, 'Payments for Ecosystem Services (Pes): A Practical Guide to Assessing the Feasibility of Pes Projects' (2014), https://www.cifor.org/publications/pdf_files/Books/BFripp1401.pdf.
9. Claudia Sattler and Bettina Matzdorf, 'Pes in a Nutshell: From Definitions and Origins to Pes in Practice—Approaches, Design Process and Innovative Aspects', *Ecosystem Services* 6 (2013).
10. Wendland et al., 'Targeting and Implementing Payments for Ecosystem Services: Opportunities for Bundling Biodiversity Conservation with Carbon and Water Services in Madagascar'.
11. Sarah Schomers and Bettina Matzdorf, 'Payments for Ecosystem Services: A Review and Comparison of Developing and Industrialized Countries', *Ecosystem Services* 6 (2013).
12. Simanti Banerjee et al., 'How to Sell Ecosystem Services: A Guide for Designing New Markets', *Frontiers in Ecology and the Environment* 11, no. 6 (2013).
13. Heidi R. Huber-Stearns, Joshua H. Goldstein, and Esther A. Duke, 'Intermediary Roles and Payments for Ecosystem Services: A Typology and Program Feasibility Application in Panama', *Ecosystem Services* 6 (2013).
14. M. S. Reed et al., 'A Place-Based Approach to Payments for Ecosystem Services', *Global Environmental Change* 43 (2017).
15. Wendland et al., 'Targeting and Implementing Payments for Ecosystem Services: Opportunities for Bundling Biodiversity Conservation with Carbon and Water Services in Madagascar'.
16. Patrick Bottazzi et al., 'Payment for Environmental "Self-Service": Exploring the Links between Farmers' Motivation and Additionality in a Conservation Incentive Programme in the Bolivian Andes', *Ecological Economics* 150 (2018).

17. Matthias Bösch, Peter Elsasser, and Sven Wunder, 'Why Do Payments for Watershed Services Emerge? A Cross-Country Analysis of Adoption Contexts', *World Development* 119 (2019).

18. Yan Lu and Tian He, 'Assessing the Effects of Regional Payment for Watershed Services Program on Water Quality Using an Intervention Analysis Model', *Science of The Total Environment* 493 (2014).

19. Brownson and Fowler, 'Evaluating How We Evaluate Success: Monitoring, Evaluation and Adaptive Management in Payments for Watershed Services Programs'.

20. Lu and He, 'Assessing the Effects of Regional Payment for Watershed Services Program on Water Quality Using an Intervention Analysis Model'.

21. Muñoz Escobar, Hollaender, and Pineda Weffer, 'Institutional Durability of Payments for Watershed Ecosystem Services: Lessons from Two Case Studies from Colombia and Germany'.

22. Brears, *Water Resources Management: Innovative and Green Solutions*.

23. EcoAgriculture Partners, 'Innovations in Market-Based Watershed Conservation in the United States: Payments for Watershed Services for Agricultural and Forest Landowners' (2011), https://ecoagriculture.org/publication/innovations-in-market-based-watershed-conservation-in-the-united-states/.

24. Drew E. Bennett et al., 'Utility Engagement with Payments for Watershed Services in the United States', *Ecosystem Services* 8 (2014).

25. Ibid.

26. IUCN, 'Pay: Establishing Payments for Watershed Services' (2006), https://www.iucn.org/content/pay-establishing-payments-watershed-services.

27. Ligia Maria Barrios Campanhão and Victor Eduardo Lima Ranieri, 'Guideline Framework for Effective Targeting of Payments for Watershed Services', *Forest Policy and Economics* 104 (2019).

28. EnTrade, 'A New Deal for the Natural Environment', https://www.entrade.co.uk.

29. Somerset Catchment Market, 'About the Somerset Catchment Market', https://www.somersetcatchmentmarket.org.uk/about.

8

Market-based Instruments Financing Water Security and Green Growth

Introduction

Environmental policy in the 1970s and early 1980s was driven mainly by regulations of emissions, environmental quality, processes, and technologies. Such regulations were referred to as 'command and control'. However, over the past several decades, market-based instruments (MBIs), also known as economic incentives, have become the preferred environmental policy tool for influencing environmental outcomes for a range of reasons, including a new orientation towards markets and deregulation in public policy, increasing recognition of the limitations of government in general, and of traditional command and control systems of environmental regulation in particular, an increasing concern that regulations may not adequately cope with emerging environmental problems, and a desire to further implement the polluter pays principle and to internalize environmental costs into the prices of goods and services.[1,2] This chapter will discuss the various MBIs available for locations to finance water security and green growth, particularly water pollution taxes, various water pricing structures, subsidies, and incentives.

Environmental Taxes and Environmental Charges

Environmental taxes and environmental charges can be defined as a 'price' to be paid on the use of the environment. While they operate similarly, there is a difference between the two. Environmental taxes are designed to internalize environmental or social costs in private consumption and production decisions. Environmental taxes aim to reduce pollution to a level that equates the environmental and social cost of the pollution with the economic cost of further reductions. Therefore, there is a cost of pollution to the polluter, giving

Financing Water Security and Green Growth. Robert C. Brears, Oxford University Press. © Robert C. Brears (2023).
DOI: 10.1093/oso/9780192847843.003.0008

them an incentive to reduce pollution to the level where environmental and social effects can be compensated, and the economic benefits of further production exceed the environmental costs associated with it. Environmental taxes can be levied on emissions, effluents, solid waste released into the environment, inputs or materials known to be a source of environmental pressure, and final products linked to environmental degradation. There are two types of environmental taxes:

- *Incentive taxes*: An environmental tax can be levied purely to change environmental damaging behaviour without any intention of raising revenue. The level of an incentive tax can be set according to estimates of the cost of the environmental damage and what price signal is required to achieve this environmental objective. Often revenue from incentive taxes is used to further encourage behaviour change via grants or tax incentives.
- *Fiscal environmental taxes*: A tax may change environmental behaviour and yield substantial revenues over and above those required for related environmental regulation. The revenues can be used to finance budget deficits or shift taxes from income taxes towards taxes on the consumption of resources and environmental pollution. This is commonly known as green tax reform.[3,4]

Meanwhile, per the polluter pays principle, the cost of regulation should be paid by those being regulated. Environmental charges contribute to or cover the cost of monitoring or controlling that use. Cost-covering charges can be of two types:

- *User charges*: This is where a charge is paid for a specific environmental service, for example, treating wastewater.
- *Earmarked charges*: This is where the revenue from the charge is spent on related environmental purposes, but not in the form of a specific service to the charge-payer.[5]

In the context of water resources management, environmental taxes and environmental charges are an effective incentive for pollution prevention and reduction and to recover the costs of providing water and related services and incentivize the conservation of scarce water resources, all the while generating various benefits (Table 8.1).[6,7]

Table 8.1 Benefits of environmental taxes and environmental charges

Benefit	Description
Internalize external environmental costs	This is the main reason for using environmental taxes instead of regulations. They incorporate the costs of environmental services and damages directly into the prices of goods and services or activities that give rise to them
Create incentives	They create incentives for producers and consumers to shift away from environmentally damaging behaviour, particularly if they are reinforcing controls/permits
Cost-effectiveness	They can achieve more cost-effective pollution control than regulations
Spur innovation	For producers, environmental taxes and environmental charges can spur innovation. When water becomes taxed, taxpayers will develop new modes of production and general consumption to reduce their tax liability, helping to achieve more eco-efficiency, implement the precautionary principle, and improve both sustainability and international competitiveness
Raise revenues	They raise revenues that can be used directly to improve the environment or give others the incentive to do so

Water Pollution Taxes

Water pollution degrades water ecosystems and negatively impacts economic activities and human health. Many countries have been applying different MBIs to reduce the amount of pollutants discharged into bodies of water, improve the quality of wastewater, and help protect the environment. Government actions to control pollution can be implemented by establishing environmental taxes, which aim to correct market failures by influencing the actions of the polluting actors, who must pay for environmental costs.[8] Environmental taxes are often applied to pesticide and chemical fertilizers to reduce the environmental impacts associated with their application and promote sustainable agricultural practices.

Pesticides and chemical fertilizers play a crucial role in maintaining and increasing agricultural productivity. Nevertheless, certain products containing toxic contents can adversely impact the environment and human health and generate negative externalities, including water contamination.

Therefore, taxes on pesticides and chemical fertilizers are frequently used to incorporate in the price of pesticide/fertilizer its social and environmental costs and reduce increases in the use of the most harmful pesticides and fertilizers. Furthermore, the tax can generate a revenue stream earmarked to mitigate the environmental impacts of pesticides and fertilizers or encourage farmers to adopt more sustainable agricultural practices. Therefore, the design of taxes on pesticides and fertilizer usage needs to determine the following:

- Tax base (the tax can be based on the sales value, dosage, weight of active ingredient or the environmental impact of a product)
- Tax rate (fixed or differentiated among product classes or toxic content; it can be set as either a fixed amount or as a percentage)
- Point of application
- Revenue allocation.[9]

Case 8.1 Denmark's Pesticide Tax

Over the past several decades, one of the largest challenges to Denmark's water supply has been the pollution of well fields with pesticides from urban areas and farmland. In 2013, Denmark's current pesticide tax came into force. The tax on pesticides changed from a value-based tax to a quantity-based tax differentiated according to health and environmental criteria. The new tax includes information about the individual pesticide's human health risks, their toxicity towards non-target organisms, and risk to groundwater. Therefore, the higher the toxicity, the higher the tax on the individual products. Moreover, in 2015, a new regulation banned many pesticides for non-professionals without a spraying certificate. Also, from 2015 onwards, only ready-to-use pesticides can be kept on the shelf for self-service at the retailers, while the concentrated products that need dilution must be kept behind the counter or in locked cabinets. The rationale is that customers should contact qualified sales personnel and receive advice on correct dilution, use, disposal, etc. and guidance on alternative methods to control pests.[10]

Water Pricing

Water pricing is used to recover the costs of providing water and related services to users. It establishes a direct link between what the users gain and the costs of providing the service. Full-cost pricing is where customers are charged for the actual cost of water and related services, including operation costs, treatment, storage, and distribution, and provides funds for future investments. Furthermore, full-cost pricing signals scarcity and encourages water conservation. When designing a water pricing structure to cover the costs of providing water and related services and encouraging conservation, a range of factors should be considered, including:

- *Water price stability*: Customers are more likely to pay for water price increases to cover increasing costs if their rates are generally stable. For example, it is likely to be more acceptable for water prices to increase by 2 per cent per annum for five years than 10 per cent once every five years.
- *Water price predictability*: Water utilities need to know how much revenue they expect to generate each year. However, predicting revenue can be difficult, as water use can vary from year to year. For instance, water use can increase significantly in dry years and decrease during a wet year. Water utilities that promote conservation are likely to see a reduction in water use, requiring a water price increase. As such, the water price should be set to generate and keep sufficient reserves so that the system can survive a sudden decrease in water use.
- *Number of customers*: Water utilities with a small customer base may take the revenue that is required and divide it among its customers. Water utilities with a large customer base may choose an alternative pricing structure, such as increasing block rates.
- *Customer classes*: Some water systems only serve residential customers while others serve industrial, commercial, or agricultural customers. Each customer class has different patterns of water use, and the cost of servicing these customers may be different too. Therefore, water utilities with several customer classes often use different water prices and pricing structures to meet their specific needs.
- *Water use*: If customers use significantly different volumes of water, water utilities can consider charging for the amount of water used. As water is a scarce commodity, water pricing structures can send a price signal to customers and encourage conservation. Customers that recognize the value of the service being provided will more likely use the product in a way that reflects its true value.
- *Customer needs*: There may be differences among customers within a class that affect their ability to pay for that service. For example, some residential customers may have lower incomes and difficulty paying

their water bills. As such, pricing structures could allow for different rates for customers with different needs within a single customer class.[11,12]

Water utilities typically price water using the following rate structures:

- *Flat rate/fixed rate*: Customers pay the same amount regardless of how much water they use. However, when water use is higher than average, the system will not generate the additional revenue needed to meet higher demand, for example, additional treatment costs. Furthermore, the structure has no incentive for customers to conserve water.
- *Volumetric rate*: A volumetric rate is a charge for the volume or amount of water consumed. It requires metering to be implemented. The main types of volumetric rate charges are:
  - *Uniform rate*: Customers are charged a uniform rate per unit of water (for example, kilolitre), regardless of the amount of water used. The structure can also include a fixed service charge. The structure can guarantee a stable revenue stream and helps encourage conservation.
  - *Block rate*: Under a block rate structure, the customer is charged a unit price for water that changes according to the amount of water used. Water use is divided into two or more blocks, and different unit prices are established for each block. The number and size of each block vary by utility, depending on the characteristics of the water demand and the customers:
    - *Decreasing block rate*: Customers are charged lower rates per unit of water for successive blocks (fixed quantities). Systems can charge a fixed fee in addition to decreasing block rates. The structure is beneficial for industrial or commercial customers who use large amounts of water. However, it offers little incentive for customers to conserve water.
    - *Increasing block rate*: Customers are charged higher rates per unit of water for successive blocks (fixed quantities). Systems can charge a fixed fee in addition to the increasing block rates. The structure sends a strong signal to customers about the value of water. The reduction in water use from conservation can postpone or eliminate the need for expensive upgrades or new equipment.
- *Two-part rate*: A two-part rate combines both a fixed charge and volumetric pricing:

- ○ *Fixed charge*: The purpose of the fixed charge is to cover fixed costs, provide revenue stability, and cover customer-related costs, such as billing, meter reading, etc. Types of fixed charges include:
  - ▪ *Service charge*: Covers the costs of servicing the account, such as meter reading and billing cost.
  - ▪ *Meter charge*: Varies with meter size. It recovers costs such as repair and replacement.
  - ▪ *Minimum charge*: This entitles customers to a specific water use level.
  - ○ *Variable charge*: The variable charge, also called a volumetric or consumption charge, is for the volume of water used or the amount of water consumed.
- *Seasonal rate*: Changes in water consumption patterns from season to season occur in most water systems. Water utilities can either set one rate for the off-peak season and one for the peak season (these rates can be uniform or block rates) or set one rate (uniform or block rate) and apply excess usage charges (the charge for water used in excess of that used on average off-peak times) during peak season. Seasonal rates can encourage conservation, reducing peak use and therefore reducing the need to expand the system capacity.[13,14,15]

Case 8.2 Greater Western Water's Charges

In 2021, Greater Western Water became a new water corporation for Melbourne's Central Business District and western region following a merger of City West Water and Western Water. As a state-owned water distributor and retailer, the prices charged are regulated by Victoria's Essential Services Commission (ESC). As part of the integration, Greater Western Water successfully applied to the ESC to adjust the prices over the next two financial years (2021–2023) to ensure all customers experience the same level of service at a fair price. The new water charges for residential customers are detailed in Table 8.2. The water charge contributes to:

- The supply, treatment, and transfer of water
- The collection, treatment, reuse, and disposal of wastewater
- The delivery and maintenance of local water and sewer pipes
- Information technology systems
- Customer service and community programmes
- Income tax
- Environmental contributions.[16]

Table 8.2 Residential charges for customers in the Greater Western Water area

Residential charges	Old price (1 July 2020–30 June 2021)	New price (1 July 2021–30 June 2022)	Price change compared to last year
Water network charge	$52.70 per quarter	$51.89 per quarter	-$0.81 per quarter
Water usage charge			
Block 1: First 440 litres of water used per day	$2.7748 per kilolitre	$2.7562 per kilolitre	-$0.0186 per kilolitre
Block 2: Water usage above 440 litres of water used per day	$3.2313 per kilolitre	$3.2112 per kilolitre	-$0.0201 per kilolitre
Recycled network charge	$7.09 per quarter	$7.98 per quarter	+$0.008 per quarter
Recycled water usage charge	$2.5787 per kilolitre	$2.6074 per kilolitre	+$0.00287 per kilolitre
Sewerage network charge	$63.15 per quarter	$55.64 per quarter	-$7.51 per quarter
Sewage disposal charge	$0.8644 per kilolitre	$0.7647 per kilolitre	-$0.0997 per kilolitre

Irrigation Water Pricing

In irrigation systems, once the magnitude of total charges has been established for an irrigation project, there is a range of ways to design individual billing structures. Irrigation project expenses include fixed expenses (repayment of loans, basic salaries, basic maintenance, long-term improvements, etc.) and variable fees that depend on the volume of water delivered in a year (pumping charges, water purchases, etc.). Irrigation water prices can be divided into various categories:

- *Base fees*: Base fees provide a stable annual income to pay for a certain percentage of the fixed fees that the project will have in all years. These fees are usually based on the irrigated area. The fee is fixed, with no aspect of volumetric charging in it.
- *In-kind fees*: In some projects, in-kind fees are accepted as part, or all, of the payment for water delivery service. For example, the only fee may be to clean a canal.
- *Charges based on crop type*: Projects with inflexible water deliveries and inexpensive water often use this as a basis for fees, with the assumption

being that crop 'x' will be irrigated more times than crop 'y' and therefore should have a higher charge.

- *Charges based on the number of irrigations per hectare*: Often, projects have a standard size and flow rate and have a certain number of hours for irrigating a specific field size.
- *Volumetric water charges*: These water fees depend on the volume of water diverted or delivered in a season or year. The delivered volume may fluctuate, depending on the water supply and the variable costs associated with receiving, conveying, and delivering the water. There are many variations of allocating volumetric water fees among farmers, including:
  - Charges for the volume of water used in a season or year, with a flat rate per volume.
  - Charges for the volume of water used in a season or year, with a tiered rate, with the use of 'x' cubic metres of water per hectare having one price, and any water used beyond that threshold having a higher charge rate.[17]

Case 8.3 South San Joaquin Irrigation District's Volumetric Charges

South San Joaquin Irrigation District's volumetric charges are based on acre-feet of water delivered as recorded for each irrigation event by division managers, who record quantities of water used by each parcel of land. Water usage is determined by the flow rate multiplied by the duration of the water run. Flow rate is determined based on the predetermined capacities of gates, laterals, and turnouts throughout the distribution system. As a result, there are two pricing tiers:

- *Tier 1*: $3 per acre-foot of water for the first 48 inches
- *Tier 2*: $10 per acre-foot for water used in excess of 48 inches.[18]

Stormwater Fees

Stormwater programmes have transitioned from single-purpose drainage systems to multipurpose programmes that provide a range of services, including storm drainage, water quality, mitigation of land-use impacts, floodplain management, and green space amenities. The main drivers of this transition are increasingly more stringent and costly environmental regulations, ageing infrastructure, degraded waterways, and flood protection. As such, cities have traditionally found it difficult to develop and finance comprehensive stormwater programmes that support multiple sustainable development and public health and safety goals. In response, there has been a shift in financing from taxes to user fees: Traditionally, the cost of stormwater management was paid for through various taxes, such as property tax, or included in monthly water bills. However, the trend is to direct the cost of stormwater management towards properties that generate the most runoff.

Stormwater fees generate a revenue stream to address the increased investment required to control stormwater runoff and combined sewer overflows. Stormwater fees are considered a fair, equitable method for charging people who benefit from the stormwater infrastructure. Often stormwater fees are based on impervious surface areas of customers, as runoff from the impervious surface is the main contributor to the storm sewer system, with Table 8.3 listing the various ways stormwater fees can be calculated.

Stormwater fees can be used to support the direct costs of stormwater management, including improvement of stormwater quality and waterway health, flood control measures, development of drainage plans, river restoration, adding or improving green space, installation of stormwater management systems, including green infrastructure, provision of aesthetic values within the urban landscape, and water for reuse. Overall, stormwater fees can positively affect customers' behaviour, especially when based on impervious

Table 8.3 Various stormwater fee methods

Method	Description
Equivalent residential unit (ERU)	The stormwater fee is determined by usage based on the impervious area. One ERU is equivalent to the average impervious area on residential/commercial properties. Typically, the stormwater fee is assessed per ERU used
Tier	The stormwater fee is tiered, with different fees charged for different customer types
Meter	The stormwater fee is based on the size of a parcel's water meter
Parcel area	The stormwater fee is based on a rate per parcel area of imperviousness
Square foot	The stormwater fee is based on the rate per parcel square feet of imperviousness
Usage	The stormwater fee is based on the parcel's water usage (volume of runoff and rate at which runoff is produced). Runoff volume and rates are usually based on the impervious area

surfaces or if a stormwater fee credit is included in the system. At the minimum, the stormwater fee directly connects human development activities with polluted runoff.[19,20,21,22,23]

Case 8.4 Baltimore City's Stormwater Fees

Since 2013, Baltimore City has operated a stormwater utility that property owners in the city fund. The purpose of the fee is to provide a sustainable, dedicated revenue source for maintaining, operating, and improving the stormwater management system, including installing practices to improve stormwater quality. The stormwater fee is based on the impervious area on a property. The fee appears as a line item on the monthly water bill. Single-family properties are charged one of three rates:

- Tier 1 properties have no more than 820 square feet of impervious surface area and pay $40 per annum ($3.33 each month).
- Tier 2 properties have more than 820 square feet but no more than 1,500 square feet of impervious surface area and pay $60 per annum ($5 per month).
- Tier 3 properties have more than 1,500 square feet of impervious surface area and pay $120 per annum ($10 per month).

Non-single family properties are billed based on an ERU, which is the size of the impervious surface area (1,050 square feet) of the median-sized house in the city: the larger the impervious surface area parcel, the higher the stormwater fee for the property. Non-single family properties pay $60 per ERU per annum.[24]

Subsidies

Subsidies are a form of direct financial government support for businesses to offset their operating costs over a lengthy period, such as offsetting the costs of implementing environmentally friendly practices and technologies. Subsidies are used to:

- Encourage the use of eco-friendly substitute products and discourage the use of products that cause environmental damage.
- Accelerate environmental performance that could not otherwise be afforded, and then reduce or eliminate the subsidy once the necessary changes have been accomplished.
- Reduce and share the investment risk in innovative and environmentally desirable technology, which often does not have adequate access to traditional sources of venture capital.

Subsidies include direct payments, loan guarantees, and special tax breaks. The following principles should be followed to ensure subsidies promote environmentally friendly conduct or technologies:

- *Subsidies should achieve the intended policy outcome*: Subsidies require a smart design and clarity about what the policy objectives and short- and long-term objectives are.
- *Subsidies should reach the intended target groups*: They require clarity on the intended target group and how they can best be reached. It also requires rigorous monitoring to track how subsidies are reaching the intended groups.
- *Subsidies should be financially sustainable*: A thorough understanding of the programme's potential costs is required. Costs include both upfront capital costs and long-term operational and maintenance costs.
- *Subsidies should integrate local peoples' needs*: To guarantee the sustainability of the subsidized environmental technology, it is of prime importance to facilitate the integration and participation of the local beneficiaries and to develop a sense of ownership towards the new infrastructure.
- *Subsidies should be implemented clearly and transparently*: As subsidies involve public funds, subsidy programmes need to be clear and transparent, enabling eligible households or communities to access them and providing precise recourse mechanisms in cases where there is a suggestion of impropriety.[25,26,27]

In the context of water security and green growth, if subsidies are well-designed, they 'can be powerful and progressive tools, ensuring that all people benefit from water supply and sanitation services'. Currently, most subsidies go to water, urban, and networked services, including low-interest loans to small farmers to implement nature-based solutions or tax credits for businesses to invest in water-efficient technologies in industrial processes. However, subsidies can also be targeted at specific communities to ensure water supply and sanitation are affordable, and those in need are not left behind.[28]

Case 8.5 Netherlands Environmental Investment Allowance

The Netherlands' Environmental Investment Allowance (MIA) enables Dutch companies to deduct 36 per cent of their capital outlay from taxable profit, in addition to regular depreciation. The deduction concerns purchase costs, production costs, modification costs, and the cost of environmental consultancy (only for small and medium-sized enterprises). Companies can claim for the MIA if they invest in a business asset on the Environmental List, with a minimum investment of €2,500 per annum up to a maximum investment of €25 million per annum. The Environment List includes the following:

- *Rainwater installation*: Intended for the use of rainwater as flushing, cooling, or process water.
- *Water-saving facility*: Intended for reducing the intake of groundwater, surface water, or tap water for use as cooling, flushing, or process water through more efficient use of water or closing the cycle.
- *Facility for utilizing waste or process water from neighbouring companies*: Intended for the use of wastewater or process water from a nearby company for a company's process.
- *Recovery installation for raw materials from wastewater or water treatment sludge*: Intended for the recovery of one or more substances from wastewater or water treatment sludge.
- *Installation for breaking down micropollutants in water*: Intended for demonstrably reducing the emission of substances to a sewage treatment plant or surface water by completely breaking them down into harmless components.
- *Removal plant for micropollutants in water*: Intended for demonstrably reducing the emission of substances to a sewage treatment plant or surface water by removing them from wastewater.
- *Underground water storage*: Intended for the individual or collective storage of water in underground soil layers for use as irrigation or irrigation water in livestock farming, arable farming, flower bulb, tree cultivation, fruit, open field, or covered cultivation.
- *Water storage under the greenhouse*: Intended for individually or collectively storing rainwater or recirculation water under a horticultural glasshouse in a closed facility for use in glasshouse horticulture.
- *Installation for desalination of the drain(age) water in greenhouse horticulture*: Intended for demonstrably more frequent recirculation of drain(age) water within the cultivation process compared to the existing situation, by improving the removal of (sodium) salts so that the discharge of drain(age) water is reduced or avoided and where the investment at company level does not lead to the discharge of more brine.
- *Equipment for reduced use of groundwater as irrigation water in glasshouse horticulture*: Intended for reducing the amount of groundwater pumped up to produce irrigation water for use in glasshouse horticulture by at least 45 per cent compared to the existing situation.

- *Horse riding arena or sports field with rainwater collection and infiltration*: Intended for collecting rainwater from at least one's own company buildings in a watertight riding arena or watertight sports field with an overflow to an infiltration area that is not a drainage ditch.
- *Rainwater buffering facility*: Intended for buffering rainwater from industrial sites and industrial buildings in the built environment during heavy rainfall, other than sites or buildings associated with agriculture and (greenhouse) horticulture.[29,30]

Case 8.6 Saskatchewan's Farm Stewardship Program

Saskatchewan's Farm Stewardship Program (FSP) provides producers funding to implement best management practices (BMPs) in three priority areas—water quality, climate change, and biodiversity. The FSP focuses on four outcomes:

- Demonstrated improvements in water quality
- Demonstrated reductions in greenhouse gas emissions
- Enhanced resilience of the agricultural sector
- Biodiversity maintained.

Each BMP has its funding limits and eligibility criteria, with the programme payments subject to a minimum claim of $500:

- *Native rangeland grazing management*: The subsidy is 50 per cent of costs, with a funding cap of $10,000.
- *Riparian grazing management*: The subsidy is 50 per cent of costs, with a funding cap of $10,000
- *Permanent native forage*: The subsidy is 90 per cent of costs, with a funding cap of $10,000
- *Drainage stewardship*: The subsidy is 50 per cent of costs, with a funding cap of $20,000
- *Livestock stewardship*: The subsidy is 30–50 per cent of costs, with a funding cap of $100,000[31]

Incentives

Grants, rebates, and performance-based incentives directly support the development and deployment of practices and technologies to achieve water security and green growth:

- *Grants*: They are usually provided by local governments, utilities, and/or non-profit organizations to fund research and development, feasibility studies, system demonstrations, or installation of new technologies. Grants are sums that do not have to be repaid but are to be used for defined purposes. They can be provided before a technology is installed or after a system is fully operational.

- *Rebates*: They are often provided by utilities and funded through utility customer payments. Rebates are usually applied to discrete purchases, such as water-efficient appliances and are often provided after purchase and/or installation. They are commonly used for water efficiency home improvements and construction, water-efficient appliances, and on-site water reuse systems.
- *Fee discounts*: These are often provided by water utilities to encourage retrofits of existing properties and implementation of green infrastructure in new developments for stormwater quantity reductions and pollution reductions for improved water quality. They are the most common incentive programme to reduce runoff from private properties and decrease burdens on the city stormwater system.
- *Performance-based incentives*: They commonly support water efficiency upgrades in new developments or retrofits based on overall water saved and are usually funded through utility customer payments.[32,33,34]

Incentive Design and Good Practices

Various elements and good practices should be considered when designing financial incentives to achieve water security and green growth, including:

- *Designing incentives to align with overall policy goals*: While water conservation and water efficiency financial incentives usually focus on supporting the increased deployment of targeted technologies and practices, they can also be used to support other high-level goals, such as improving livelihoods in low-income communities, reducing energy consumption and greenhouse gas emissions, or improving environmental flows of water bodies. Goals can be defined through engagement with stakeholders and communities, the private sector, utilities, local government institutions, and others.
- *Basing incentive design on robust economic, financial, and market analysis*: How an incentive is designed is dependent on local markets and consumer preferences, availability of public sector resources, and broader financial infrastructure. Robust analysis should be conducted to determine target markets and technologies or actions to be incentivized and

any potential impacts associated with the incentive. Also, by analysing the local financial environment, the incentive can complement existing private sector finance initiatives rather than duplicate or replace these efforts. For example, incentives may target lower-income households that have limited access to finance.

- *Engaging the private sector and finance community*: Incentives should be designed to avoid any impacts that could lead to market distortion. Policymakers can engage the private sector to help understand market gaps and identify opportunities to support private investment and market development. Public–private partnerships can support a multiplier effect for public funds invested in water security and green growth initiatives. For example, loan guarantees can attract large amounts of private capital while reducing public sector funding requirements.
- *Establishing a stable policy environment and appropriate incentive time-frame to support sustained investment*: Providing market certainty through long-term policy signals can enhance the success of financial incentive programmes. Financial incentives can be implemented over long time horizons, with incentive levels reducing over time as the market matures and the uptake of the technology or action increases.
- *Establishing a robust policy foundation for financial incentives*: Strong water conservation and water efficiency policies and regulations can provide a crucial foundation for the success of financial incentives. Furthermore, robust standards for various water efficiency technologies, supporting flexible business models, and training in water conservation and water efficiency is integral in supporting the development of a robust market.
- *Coordinating incentive programmes and/or bundle incentives to support policy efficiency*: Many countries and jurisdictions provide a diverse portfolio of grants, rebates, and loans targeted at various markets and technologies. Implementing an incentive programme can be coordinated or bundled to improve overall programme and policy efficiency.
- *Expanding outreach and building capacity to support market development and long-term finance*: Often, there is a need to educate and build market awareness of the benefits of water conservation, water efficiency, smart water technologies, and nature-based solutions and on the specific financial incentives offered. Well-defined public education and outreach programmes can support financial incentive outcomes.

Also, ensuring that participation procedures in financial incentive programmes are easy to understand can improve participation levels. Furthermore, there is often the need to build the capacity of various water-related service providers to ensure sustainable outcomes, such as building the capacity of organizations to inspect and certify water-efficient technologies.

- *Monitoring and evaluating*: Financial incentive programmes should plan to monitor water conservation and water efficiency or water quality outcomes. This information can inform potential changes to the level of incentive and improvements to the incentive programme overall.[35]

Case 8.7 Grants: State of Illinois' Green Infrastructure Grant Opportunities Program

The State of Illinois' Green Infrastructure Grant Opportunities (GIGO) Program funds projects to construct green infrastructure BMPs that prevent, eliminate, or reduce water quality impairments by decreasing stormwater runoff into the state's waterways. The GIGO Program encourages applications for multiple BMPs in a series and/or multiple BMPs within the same watershed to increase their effectiveness and efficiency. The Illinois Environmental Protection Agency (EPA) will award $5 million annually beginning FY2021–FY2025 and anticipates distributing this amount across two to 10 awards per year, with a maximum total grant award of $2.5 million and a minimum of $75,000. The GIGO Program is a reimbursement model with the grantee performing the work, paying approved project costs, and submitting an invoice with supporting documentation before Illinois EPA will reimburse the grantee for approved project costs. The GIGO Program's grant will be up to 75 per cent of the approved project costs, except for those applicants within disadvantaged areas who may be eligible for up to 85 per cent GIGO Program assistance. The remaining 25 per cent (15 per cent for disadvantaged areas) is the grantee's responsibility and constitutes the match. The match can include money spent or in-kind services utilized to complete the project. Eligible projects will improve water quality through the construction of BMPs and include:

- Reconnecting streams with their floodplains.
- Treatment and flow control of stormwater runoff at sites directly upstream or downstream of an impervious area that currently impacts a waterway.
- Treatment and flow control of water generated from impervious surfaces associated with urban development (roads, buildings, etc.).

Examples of BMPs that can be funded through the GIGO Program include:

- Bioinfiltration
- Retention/infiltration
- Detention ponds
- Wetland creation/modification
- Floodplain reconnection
- Watershed-wide projects that involve multiple smaller BMPs
- Rainwater harvesting.[36]

Case 8.8 Rebates: Tucson Water's Gray Water Rebate

Tucson Water's Gray Water Rebate programme encourages the uptake of greywater systems to collect wastewater from hand washing sinks, showers, bathtubs, and clothes washing machines for reuse as greywater for irrigation of landscape plants, fruit trees, and lawns. When a permanent greywater irrigation system is installed, Tucson Water customers can seek a rebate of 50 per cent of qualifying costs, up to $1,000. The rebate is available for retrofitting existing homes and connecting new homes to greywater irrigation systems. The rebates cover the eligible rebate design costs (up to $200), materials, storage tanks, filters, pumps, backflow prevention assembly, and installation. Tucson Water customers must also attend a free, two-hour Gray Water Rebate Workshop, which covers appropriate methods to design, operate, and maintain a greywater system.[37]

Case 8.9 Fee Discounts: City of Guelph's Stormwater Credits

Industrial, commercial, institutional, and multi-residential properties of six or more units in the City of Guelph, Canada, may qualify for a credit on their stormwater bill if they implement a range of BMPs, including installing infiltration galleries, permeable pavement, rainwater cisterns, constructed wetlands, rain gardens, and green roofs, among others. Reducing runoff provides multiple benefits, including preventing floods, protecting Guelph's water supply and wildlife habitat, and reducing costs for property owners and the City of Guelph. Stormwater credits are available in four categories, as listed in Table 8.4. Many of the practices could be eligible for more than one type of credit. For example, a BMP may provide peak flow reduction and reduce volume runoff reduction. In such cases, credits may be awarded for both categories. The cumulative maximum credit available to any property is 50 per cent. Each applicant must provide documentation on the design details, function, and proof of regulatory/permitting compliance.[38]

Table 8.4 Stormwater credit categories

Credit category	Description and basis for charge reduction	Maximum credit (%)
Peak flow reduction	Facilities that control the peak flow of stormwater discharge from the property, based on the outlet rate in comparison to natural hydrologic conditions	15
Runoff volume reduction	Facilities that control the amount of stormwater retained on the property, based on retention volume resulting from increased infiltration, evapotranspiration, or reuse	40
Water quality treatment	Facilities that control the quality of stormwater discharged from the property, based on treatment type, pollutant load reduction, or Ontario Ministry of the Environment and Climate Change level of protection	15
Operations and activities	Non-structural measures, including education programmes and pollution prevention/risk management practices	15
Maximum credit available (capped)		**50**

Case 8.10 Performance-based Incentives: Toronto Water's Water Efficiency for Business Programmes

Toronto Water offers a number of programmes and services to help businesses better manage their water use, including the Industrial Water Rate Program and the Capacity Buyback Program. The Industrial Water Rate Program offers a discounted water rate to manufacturers in Toronto to help encourage water conservation and support economic growth. The programme is open to manufacturers that use more than 5,000 cubic metres of water per annum, fall within the industrial property tax class, are in full compliance with Toronto's Sewers By-Law, and submit a comprehensive water conservation plan to the satisfaction of Toronto Water. Successful applicants are charged the general water rate on the first 5,000 cubic metres of water use (Block 1 Rate). Water use over that amount is eligible for a rate reduction of 30 per cent (Block 2 Rate). The difference in water rate is:

- General Water Rate (Block 1 Rate): $4.0735 per cubic metre
- Industrial Water Rate (Block 2 Rate): $2.8514 per cubic metre.

The Capacity Buyback Program encourages and rewards commercial and institutional organizations by offering a free water audit to help identify ways of reducing water use, rewarding participants that implement permanent water-saving measures with a one-time case rebate of up to 30 cents per litre of water saved per average day and helping participants reduce their water bills over the long-term. The audit report will include a list of eligible processes or equipment changes the organizations can make and the estimated savings expected. Water efficiency upgrades eligible under the programme are:

- Cooling towers
- Boilers
- Refrigeration equipment
- Foodservice equipment
- Process equipment and other site-specific water-saving measures, for instance, greywater reuse, rainwater harvesting systems, etc.[39,40]

Notes

1. Valérie Boisvert, Philippe Méral, and Géraldine Froger, 'Market-Based Instruments for Ecosystem Services: Institutional Innovation or Renovation?', *Society & Natural Resources* 26, no. 10 (2013).
2. US EPA, 'Economic Incentives', https://www.epa.gov/environmental-economics/economic-incentives#subsidies
3. EEA, 'Environmental Taxes: Implementation and Environmental Effectiveness', (1996), https://www.eea.europa.eu/publications/92-9167-000-6/download.
4. Ministry for the Environment, 'Market-Based Approaches to Marine Environmental Regulation: Stage 2: Instrument Assessment Framework and Case Study' (2006), https://environment.govt.nz/publications/market-based-approaches-to-marine-environmental-regulation-stage-2-instrument-assessment-framework-and-case-study/.
5. EEA, 'Environmental Taxes: Implementation and Environmental Effectiveness'.
6. 'Assessment of Cost Recovery through Water Pricing' (2013), https://www.eea.europa.eu/publications/assessment-of-full-cost-recovery.
7. 'Environmental Taxes: Implementation and Environmental Effectiveness'.
8. Leticia Gallego Valero, Encarnación Moral Pajares, and Isabel M. Román Sánchez, 'The Tax Burden on Wastewater and the Protection of Water Ecosystems in Eu Countries', *Sustainability* 10, no. 1 (2018).
9. UNDP, 'Taxes on Pesticides and Chemical Fertilizers' (2017), https://www.undp.org/content/dam/sdfinance/doc/Taxes%20on%20pesticides%20and%20chemical%20fertilizers%20_%20UNDP.pdf.
10. Ministry of Environment and Food of Denmark, 'Pesticides and Gene Technology' (2017), https://www.ohchr.org/Documents/Issues/ToxicWaste/PesticidesRtoFood/Denmark.pdf.
11. Global Water Partnership, 'Water as a Social and Economic Good: How to Put the Principle into Practice' (1998), https://www.ircwash.org/resources/water-social-and-economic-good-how-put-principle-practice.
12. US EPA, 'Water and Wastewater Pricing: An Informational Overview' (2003), https://nepis.epa.gov/Exe/ZyNET.exe/901U1200.txt?ZyActionD=ZyDocument&Client=EPA&

Index=2000%20Thru%202005&Docs=&Query=&Time=&EndTime=&SearchMethod=
1&TocRestrict=n&Toc=&TocEntry=&QField=&QFieldYear=&QFieldMonth=&QField
Day=&UseQField=&IntQFieldOp=0&ExtQFieldOp=0&XmlQuery=&File=D%3A%
5CZYFILES%5CINDEX%20DATA%5C00THRU05%5CTXT%5C00000011%5C901U1
200.txt&User=ANONYMOUS&Password=anonymous&SortMethod=h%7C-
&MaximumDocuments=1&FuzzyDegree=0&ImageQuality=r75g8/r75g8/
x150y150g16/i425&Display=hpfr&DefSeekPage=x&SearchBack=ZyActionL&Back=
ZyActionS&BackDesc=Results%20page&MaximumPages=1&ZyEntry=2#.

13. 'Setting Small Drinking Water System Rates for a Sustainable Future: One of the Simple
Tools for Effective Performance (Step) Guide Series' (2006), https://www.ircwash.org/
resources/setting-small-drinking-water-system-rates-sustainable-future-one-simple-
tools-effective.

14. Christopher N. Boyer et al., 'Factors Driving Water Utility Rate Structure Choice: Evidence from Four Southern U.S. States', *Water Resources Management* 26, no. 10 (2012).

15. Chicago Metropolitan Agency for Planning, 'Full-Cost Water Pricing Guidebook for
Sustainable Community Water Systems' (2012).

16. Greater Western Water, 'Charges Explained', https://www.citywestwater.com.au/billing/
charges_explained.

17. Charles M. Burt, 'Volumetric Irrigation Water Pricing Considerations', *Irrigation and
Drainage Systems* 21, no. 2 (2007).

18. South San Joaquin Irrigation District, 'Billing and Customer Service', https://www.ssjid.
com/district-services/billing-and-customer-service/.

19. Conservation Ontario, 'Market-Based Instruments within the Green Economy'
(2013), https://conservationontario.ca/fileadmin/pdf/policy-priorities_section/Green
Economy_Literature_Review.pdf.

20. US EPA, 'Green Infrastructure Municipal Handbook' (2008), https://www.epa.gov/green-
infrastructure/green-infrastructure-municipal-handbook.

21. Neil S. Grigg, 'Stormwater Programs: Organization, Finance, and Prospects', *Public Works
Management & Policy* 18, no. 1 (2012).

22. F. A. Tasca, L. B. Assunção, and A. R. Finotti, 'International Experiences in Stormwater
Fee', *Water Science and Technology* 2017, no. 1 (2018).

23. Fabiane Andressa Tasca, Alexandra Rodrigues Finotti, and Roberto Fabris Goerl, 'A
Stormwater User Fee Model for Operations and Maintenance in Small Cities', *Water
Science and Technology* 79, no. 2 (2019).

24. Baltimore City Department of Public Works, 'Stormwater Fee', https://publicworks.
baltimorecity.gov/stormwater-fee.

25. OECD, 'Policy Instruments for the Environment' (2017), https://www.oecd.org/env/
indicators-modelling-outlooks/policy-instrument-database/.

26. Government of Alberta, 'Environmental Tools: Environmental Subsidies' (2022), https://
www.alberta.ca/assets/documents/ep-environmental-tools-environmental-subsidies.
pdf.

27. Water Supply and Sanitation Collaborative Council, 'Public Funding for Sanitation—the
Many Faces of Sanitation Subsidies' (2009), https://www.susana.org/en/knowledge-hub/
resources-and-publications/library/details/2010.

28. World Bank, 'Doing More with Less—Smarter Subsidies for Water Supply and Sanitation' (2019), https://www.worldbank.org/en/topic/water/publication/smarter-subsidies-for-water-supply-and-sanitation.
29. Netherlands Enterprise Agency, 'Environmental Investment Allowance (Mia)', https://english.rvo.nl/subsidies-programmes/mia-and-vamil.
30. 'Environment and Energy List 2021'.
31. Government of Saskatchewan, 'Farm Stewardship Program (Fsp)', https://www.saskatchewan.ca/business/agriculture-natural-resources-and-industry/agribusiness-farmers-and-ranchers/canadian-agricultural-partnership-cap/environmental-sustainability-and-climate-change/farm-stewardship-program-fsp.
32. NDC Partnership, 'Financial Incentives to Enable Clean Energy Deployment: Policy Overview and Good Practices', https://ndcpartnership.org/toolbox/financial-incentives-enable-clean-energy-deployment-policy-overview-and-good-practices.
33. Conservation Ontario, 'Market-Based Instruments within the Green Economy'.
34. US EPA, 'Green Infrastructure Municipal Handbook'.
35. NDC Partnership, 'Financial Incentives to Enable Clean Energy Deployment: Policy Overview and Good Practices'.
36. Illinois Environmental Protection Agency, 'Green Infrastructure Grant Opportunities', https://www2.illinois.gov/epa/topics/grants-loans/water-financial-assistance/Pages/gigo.aspx.
37. City of Tucson, 'Gray Water Rebate', https://www.tucsonaz.gov/water/gray-water-rebate.
38. City of Guelph, 'Stormwater Service Credits for Business', https://guelph.ca/living/environment/water/rebates/stormwater-service-fee-credit-program/.
39. City of Toronto, 'Industrial Water Rate Program', https://www.toronto.ca/services-payments/water-environment/how-to-use-less-water/water-efficiency-for-business/industrial-water-rate-program/.
40. 'Capacity Buyback Program', https://www.toronto.ca/services-payments/water-environment/how-to-use-less-water/water-efficiency-for-business/capacity-buyback-program/.

9

Public–Private Partnerships Financing Water Security and Green Growth

Introduction

Water is an infrastructure-intensive sector, requiring significant investments to improve access and service quality. Water is also crucial for food security and is impacted by climate change. However, in many countries, the water sector is underfunded and inefficient. In this context, Public–private partnerships (PPPs) can be a mechanism to help governments fund needed investment and improve technology and efficiency in the water sector. In particular, PPPs are long-term integrated contracts that provide water services, including water and wastewater treatment plants and green infrastructure, to achieve water security and green growth. Since the 1990s, both developed and developing countries have utilized PPPs for many reasons. For instance, PPPs have been utilized to expand the range of service providers beyond traditional public sector monopolies, provide infrastructure and associated services more efficiently, provide cost-effective infrastructure, and drive local economic growth.[1,2,3,4] This chapter will first discuss the concept of PPPs and their financing. The chapter will then discuss PPPs in the context of water resources management. Finally, the chapter will review irrigation-specific and community-based PPPs for green infrastructure.

Public–Private Partnerships

The goal of PPPs is 'to exploit synergies in the joint innovative use of resources and the application of knowledge, with optimal attainment of the goals of all parties involved, where these goals could not be attained to the same extent without the other parties'.[5] However, there is no widely recognized definition of PPPs. In particular, there is no internationally recognized definition of

Financing Water Security and Green Growth. Robert C. Brears, Oxford University Press. © Robert C. Brears (2023). DOI: 10.1093/oso/9780192847843.003.0009

what does and does not constitute a PPP. As such, the term PPP is often used to describe a wide range of arrangements, including the following:

- It is an arrangement between two or more entities that enables them to work cooperatively towards shared or compatible objectives. There is some degree of shared authority and responsibility, a joint investment of resources, shared risk-taking, and mutual benefit.
- It is an ongoing agreement between the government and private sector organizations. The private sector partner participates in the decision-making and production of a public good or service tradition-ally provided by the public sector. In this arrangement, the private sector shares the risk of production.
- It is a legally binding contract between the government and business for the provision of assets and the delivery of services that allocates responsibility and business risks among the various partners.
- It bundles investment and service provision into a single long-term con-tract. Throughout the contract, which could be 20–30 years long, the concessionaire will manage and control the assets, usually in exchange for user fees, which are its compensation for the investment and other costs.
- It could be a contractual arrangement, alliance, cooperative agreement, or collaborative activity used for policy development, programme sup-port, and delivery of government programmes and services.
- It consists of shared and/or compatible objectives and an acknowledged distribution of specific roles and responsibilities among the participants, which can be formal or informal, contractual, or obligatory, between two or more parties. Under this type of PPP, there is a cooperative investment of resources and, therefore, joint risk-taking, sharing of authority, and benefits for all partners.
- It involves the sharing of power, work, support, and/or information with others for the achievement of joint goals and/or mutual benefit.[6]

Irrespective of the type of arrangement a PPP has, they all have the following core attributes:

- A long-term agreement between a government entity and a private sector organization, such as a business, non-profit, institutional, or aca-demic organization, under which the private organization provides or contributes to the provision of a public service.

- The private sector organization receives a revenue stream, which may be from government budget allocations, user charges, or a combination of the two. The agreement, therefore, transfers risk from the government entity to the private sector organization, including service availability or demand risk.
- The private sector organization generally invests in the venture, even if it is limited, such as to working capital.
- In addition to budget allocations, the government may make further contributions, such as providing or enabling access to land, contributing existing assets, or providing debt or equity finance to cover capital expenditures. The government also may provide various types of guarantees that enable risk to be shared effectively between the government and the private sector partner.
- At the end of the PPP contract, the associated asset reverts to government ownership.[7]

Usage of Public–Private Partnerships

There is a range of reasons as to why public authorities would use a PPP, including the following:

- It is the most appropriate route to meet the need for an improved quality of public services, new services not previously provided by the government, or different methods of providing services, which could be driven by public demand, political imperative, or the need to comply with legislative requirements.
- It could be utilized when the current service has reached a crisis or where there is a need for a fresh start in service management.
- It is the only way to finance the project due to fiscal budget constraints.
- It is likely to bring specific financial benefits, such as reduced cost of service, improvement in income collection, more effective use of public assets, and the offloading of residual liabilities from the public sector to the private sector.[8]

Roles of Public–Private Partnership Actors

There are four main parties to a PPP: Public sector, service providers (it could be a consortium), lenders, and end-users. The roles of each actor may vary according to the particular form of PPP transaction. Nevertheless, the overall principle is that any role should be allocated to the party best able to undertake it. In a PPP, the roles of each actor are generally the following:

- *Public sector*: The public sector is responsible for defining, through the service specification and contract conditions, the scope, performance standards, timing, and any requirements regarding the methods of service delivery. It often sets the price that it will pay for the service received. The public sector actor also monitors the outcomes delivered by the service provider and enforce standards.
- *Service provider*: The primary role of the service provider is to manage the investment of the PPP, implement the agreement, such as design, construct, operate, and maintain the asset. It uses the asset to deliver the service, which is the subject of the PPP. For a PPP to represent value for money for the public sector and be profitable for the private sector, it usually means lower operating costs and/or more effective income collection.
- *Lenders*: The key role of lenders is to provide finance for the transactions. They also ensure that the private sector service provider delivers the service agreed in the contract and therefore gets paid for it, as without these receipts, the service providers will not be able to repay their borrowings.
- *End-users*: These are the end-users of the services the PPP provides. While they may not have been integral in the decision to initiate the PPP, there are three roles they can play to ensure their needs are addressed in the PPP process:
  - End users should be asked to provide input to the formulation of the contract documentation.
  - End users should be asked to provide input to the partner selection process in different ways, such as representation on the evaluation panel, assisting with checking the track record of potential suppliers or assessing the cultural fit between the potential suppliers and the public authority.
  - End users can be a source of information that acts as inputs to the monitoring of contract outcomes from the user perspective.

Stakeholder Communication

Those affected by a PPP are broader than the public officials directly responsible for procurement decisions and the private sector partner. Employees, public end-users, internal customers, the press, conservation organizations, and other third-party interest groups will have opinions and agendas about a PPP outcome. As far as possible, their needs should be accommodated.

As such, part of the planning for a PPP should be a communication strategy. It is essential to communicate openly with stakeholders to minimize potential resistance to establishing a PPP. It is possible to be open on many matters in the contract strategy and consult on them, such as the shortlisting and award criteria, the design of the service specification, and setting performance standards.[9]

Financing of Public–Private Partnerships

There are two main types of funds that can be raised for financing PPPs:

- *Equity*: Equity for PPPs can be in the form of:
  - *Capital shares*: A contractor/industrial developer interested in construction and/or the operation and maintenance aspect of the asset may purchase shares in the PPP. On some occasions, the government may invest in equity shares, acting as a project partner.
  - *Junior or subordinated debt, mezzanine debt*: This is usually provided by industrial developer/contractor shareholders, or it may be provided by third-party financial investors, including the government, on some occasion.
- *Debt*: Debt for PPPs can be in the form of:
  - *Loans (bridging loans/short term or long-term loans)*: Usually, commercial banks and investment banks provide debt financing. Other sources can include:
    - Multilateral/regional development banks (World Bank, International Finance Corporation, Asian Development Bank, etc.)
    - Export credit agencies and/or bilateral development banks
    - National development banks or national financial agencies
    - Institutional investors, such as pension funds, insurance companies, and sovereign funds
    - Shadow lenders and debt funds.
  - *Bonds or project bonds*: Bonds as an instrument for debt mainly come from capital markets, i.e., institutional investors (pension funds, insurance companies, and sovereign funds), investors, or through an initial public offering.[10]

Special Purpose Vehicles

In a PPP, the private sector partner, or consortium of private firms, undertaking the project usually establish a specific project company called a special purpose vehicle (SPV). The SPV independently signs the PPP contract with a public entity to undertake a specific project. The SPV acts as a legally distinct entity, reducing the liability to the parent company, and generally finances stand-alone projects off the corporate balance sheet. The company owners of the SPV will not usually finance all project requirements themselves; instead, they will provide a proportion as equity and either borrow the rest from financial institutions or place debt securities in the capital market.[11]

Compensation of the Project Company

In PPPs where the private sector partner finances the building and operation of a project, it may be compensated with a combination of user fees and government payments:

- *User fees*: User fees are efficient and link compensation directly to the level of service provided. An example of a user fee would be a water tariff. User fees should be fair and equitable, provide incentives for efficiency, ensure cost-recovery/return on investment, and be understandable and straightforward. Where access to a similar service has historically been provided free of charge or for a minimum charge, the effect of introducing fees should be assessed in consultation with the affected people, helping to ensure user fees do not undermine the efficiency and viability of the project
- *Government support*: Governments may subsidize the private sector party under a PPP agreement. This can take many forms, including debt or equity finance, grants, cash subsidies, revenue guarantees, access to cheap capital, in-kind grants, land acquisitions, and tax exemptions. Grant financing of PPPs is one of the most common forms of support. The public sector usually employs them to realize infrastructure requirements that are not financially viable to other sources of financing (due to risk, viability, or scale issues) or where social characteristics require them to remain in the public domain.[12,13]

Measuring Performance

Monitoring the performance of the private sector partner and checking it against the contract requirements is crucial for ensuring the success of a PPP. The selection of appropriate performance measures, and the targets for them, is an important activity that needs to be undertaken at the planning phase of the PPP. They signal to the bidder what is expected and will form part of the lenders' assessment about the risks associated with the transaction, specifically, the likelihood that the service provider will fail to deliver its obligations and therefore be unable to meet its financing obligations. The performance measures should be manageable. There should be a realistic number of measures to focus priorities on and make the private sector partner performance monitoring manageable.

Meanwhile, the targets for the performance measures should:

- Be appropriate in that they encourage improved performance, both in the short and long term.
- Be evidence-based (derived from performance levels on other comparable contracts).
- Have an agreed future target date for achieving and sustaining any significant improvement on existing performance.
- Be clear on what is and what is not acceptable performance.[14]

Public–Private Partnership Project Lifecycle

The complete lifecycle of a PPP consists of four phases:

1. *Project selection*: The government agency identifies and selects a project for development as a PPP in the selection phase. The selection stage aims to determine which projects appear more suitable for delivery via PPP and then prioritize those projects. Projects should be evaluated and screened based on the strength of the underlying rationale for the project, institutional readiness to implement the project, project readiness, and PPP suitability. The government then should prioritize the potential projects, in view of its development priorities and capacity, including resource constraints, in terms of staffing and funding, that may limit the number of PPPs that can be pursued at one time.
2. *Project development*: In this phase, the government agency undertakes a comprehensive feasibility study to assess the project's viability (technical, economic, financial, fiscal, environmental, social, legal, risk allocation, etc.). This stage may involve significant revisions to the project as more information becomes known. The feasibility study findings may change the project's size, scope, structure, and financing and funding mechanisms. The government agency should appoint a project manager to supervise and manage the PPP project daily. Furthermore, project preparation and development need to involve the

community, those directly affected by the project and those less immediate, the poor, women, and disenfranchised groups. This stage should
also involve consulting the market to understand project structures that
meet market requirements and market appetite for certain projects

3. *Procurement and award*: In this phase, the government agency con-
   ducts an open, competitive procurement process to select a private
   partner to realize the project. The process should be governed by local
   or national procurement laws and regulations. At this stage, the government agency will likely require external assistance in preparing the
   tender documents (i.e., requests for qualification and proposals and the
   draft PPP agreement) and with evaluating bids and negotiating the final
   PPP agreement with the preferred bidder

4. *Implementation*: During the implementation phase, the project is constructed, the private sector begins operations, and services are delivered. The government agency's role in this phase consists of contract
   management and monitoring the performance of the private sector
   partner. Therefore, on project implementation, the project manager
   should be replaced by a contract manager to act as the primary point of
   contact of the government agency with the private sector partner. The
   contract manager is generally responsible for:

   a. Monitoring the performance of the private sector partner and check-
      ing it against the contract requirements.
   b. Budgeting and settling payments due from the government agency
      under the PPP contract.
   c. Handling contract events according to the provision of the PPP
      contract, for example, changes in law, contract amendments,
      non-compliance with performance.
   d. Reporting on the performance of the PPP to the government agency
      and stakeholders.
   e. Preparing for the handover of the project's residual assets from the
      private sector partner to the government agency, in accordance with
      and on the conclusion of the PPP agreement.[15]

Water Service Public–Private Partnerships

Traditionally, the dominant model for providing water services is public,
with the water systems owned and operated by local governments through
their public works department and public utility commissions. An alternative is the use of PPPs that combine the strengths of the public and private

sectors to deliver water services on a project or programme basis. Both developed and developing countries are using water service PPPs to exploit the knowledge and financial capital of the private sector to improve value and accountability to taxpayers and water users. When effectively structured and employed, PPPs can contribute solutions to various challenges facing water delivery while offering additional sources of capital, improving operational efficiencies and cost savings, and providing clear paths of accountability and remedy. Table 9.1 summarizes a range of benefits that well-structured water service PPPs can provide.[16,17] Overall, a range of considerations needs accounting for to ensure water service PPPs make water delivery more cost-effective, sustainable, and accountable to the public, as summarized in Table 9.2.[18]

Water Service Public–Private Partnership Agreements

PPPs in water and sanitation utilize a range of agreements that outline the relationships and responsibilities between various stakeholders, including the following.

Projects Involving Existing Assets

For projects that use existing assets (no new build), the main form of contracts are:

- *Management contract*: The operator manages assets and any existing staff in return for a fee. There may be a performance incentive added in the form of a bonus or penalty. In turn, the authority may raise revenue through tariffs or from the public budget. The operator has limited repair and renewal obligations, and the contracts tend to be for a short period of time (1–5 years).
- *Operation and maintenance contracts*: The operator operates assets in return for a fee. There may be a performance incentive added in the form of a bonus or penalty. Typically, the operator has greater control over operations than under a management contract and may bring in their staff. The authority usually pays the operator fees. In turn, the authority may raise revenue through tariffs or from the public budget. The operator has limited repair and renewal obligations, although they may be more extensive than a management contract. The contracts are usually for a medium period of time (5–10 years).
- *Affermage contract*: This type of contract is used in civil law jurisdictions and is similar to a lease. Under the affermage, the operator 'fermier' has

Table 9.1 Benefits of water service public–private partnerships

Benefit	Description
Additional sources of financing	Water and sewer systems are capital-intensive, and many systems require immediate upgrades from years of underinvestment. When governments are unwilling to, or cannot, increase public debt to meet investment needs, the private sector can supply capital through a PPP without impacting municipal balance sheets
Improved speed and efficiency of procurement	PPPs can speed up procurement (design, construction, and commissioning) of water services compared to the traditional model of separate design and construction phasing
Improved operational efficiency	PPPs can generate operational savings through cross-training staff, reducing staff levels, implementing organizational best practices, and exploiting economies of scale
Highly qualified personnel	Developing and retaining highly qualified staff is critical to private sector companies. Therefore, there is a low probability of underqualified staff being involved in PPP operations
Additional and more specialized governance	PPPs can enable high-level technical and performance governance through management and monitoring systems of the private sector partner
Transfer of risk from the public sector	The public sector can transfer commercial risk and responsibility to the private sector firms that are better equipped to mitigate it
Clear accountability	PPPs create a clear path of responsibility through the partnership agreement
Improved regulatory compliance	Regulatory compliance can significantly improve under a PPP arrangement due to contractual performance obligations of the private sector partner and relief of conflict of interest in the enforcement regime
Protection of the public interest	Thorough PPP contracts will contain provisions for monitoring the compliance of the private partner regularly, providing a feedback loop between objectives and performance that is not clouded by a conflict of interest

delegated to it the obligation to supply customers with potable water in the delegated area as well as operation and maintenance obligations, and a limited obligation to repair and replace (usually only minor parts). Revenue comes from tariffs, and the operator's fee is paid out of revenues. Any revenues collected above the operator's fee are paid to the authority for investment in the scheme. The authority is the owner of the scheme and is responsible for major repairs, renewal, and expansion. Affermage contracts are usually for a medium period of time (3–10 years).

Table 9.2 Considerations for successful water service public–private partnerships

Consideration	Description
Type of PPP	The type of PPP must be appropriate for the situation and customized to the specific strengths and deficiencies of the infrastructure and public partner capabilities
Willingness to change	The public sector's change in role from service provider to contract manager must be philosophically and culturally accepted by the public partner
Clear communication to stakeholders	With PPPs representing a significant change to the traditional model of service delivery, legitimate concerns must be addressed through clear communication of the need and benefits of a proposed PPP
Competitive process	The process for selecting a private sector partner must be transparent to all affected parties, fair, and carefully designed to ensure that the actual needs of the public sector are met
Performance-based agreements	Many of the benefits of PPPs come from the private partner's ability to produce the required outcomes in a way that is different to the status quo of public sector system management. Therefore, PPP agreements must be outcome or performance-based. Furthermore, functional specifications, rather than detailed specifications of how outcomes are to be accomplished, should be used to encourage innovative solutions
Asset protection	Public assets must be protected from neglect during the course of a PPP, ensuring that cost efficiencies are not developed at the cost of asset depletion. This can be ensured by specifying the required condition of assets at the end of the contract, requiring financial guarantees, specifying a minimum operations and maintenance schedule, or specifying periodic independent condition audits
Mutual benefit	Each partner must be willing to accept the motives of the other and work for mutual benefit. The public sector partner needs to accept the need for the private sector partner to make a profit and consider their profitability a success factor. In turn, the private sector partner needs to go beyond the strict terms of the PPP agreement on occasion to support the public sector partner
Major capital investment	Where a PPP encompasses some significant capital investment, it is essential to determine how the partners will handle unforeseen needs and determine financing arrangements, for example, the private sector partner may discover an asset to be in a lower condition than expected

- *Lease contract*: This is a contract under which the operator is granted the right to exploit the assets for a fixed period, usually for a medium period (5–10 years). The operator has more extensive repair and renewal obligations. The operator may also be required to make capital investments.

The operator usually bears extensive revenue risk as it pays a fixed lease fee to the authority out of revenues as well as taking its fee.[19]

Projects Involving New Builds or Expansions

- *Lease contract*: See description above
- *Design-Build-Operate (DBO) contract*: Under a DBO contract, the operator is required to design and build the project and deliver the service. The operator is not required to finance the project. They will typically be paid a lump sum for installation on commissioning of the scheme and then a periodic fee for operations. Responsibility for constructing and operating the system rests with the operator, and the cost rests with the authority. DBO contracts usually have longer terms than the affermage and management agreements (construction period plus operating period of 6–10 years). The authority bears revenue risk.
- *Design-Build-Lease contract*: The operator designs and builds a scheme then sells it to the contracting authority who then leases it back to the operator to operate it (usually for 10–30 years). On the expiry of the lease, the scheme is then transferred back to the authority.
- *Build-Operate-Transfer (BOT) contract*: The operator designs, builds, finances, and operates a system for the contract duration. BOTs are often used for bulk water supply or wastewater treatment plants. The operator owns the asset until termination when the new asset transfers to the authority. The operator is usually remunerated through a volume (produced/treated) based fee paid by the authority.
- *Concession agreements*: In a concession agreement, the operator is granted the right to develop and exploit assets for the duration of the contract and sometimes pays the authority a concession fee in return. This may involve using existing assets and/or the development of new assets. The operator is remunerated from tariffs and usually takes end-user demand and payment risk.[20,21,22]

Case 9.1 Public–Private Partnerships for Water Infrastructure in Saudi Arabia

The Saudi Water Partnership Company (SWPC) has invited developers to submit expressions of interest (EOI) in the project to develop an independent water transmission pipeline (IWTP) from Jubail to Buraydah. The planned IWTP will have a total length of 603 kilometres and a transmission capacity of up to 650,000 cubic metres a day. The successful developer or developer consortium will develop the project on a build, own, operate, and transfer (BOOT) basis. The project company, formed by the developer, will provide the entire water transmission capacity to SWPC under a water transmission agreement (WTA). The WTA will have a total length of 35 years. SWPC has also invited firms to submit an EOI for the Al-Ahsa and Eastern Province water reservoir project. In addition, SWPC is seeking to appoint a developer to deliver the independent strategic water storage project as part of its strategy to increase water storage to seven days of demand by 2030. The project will be developed under a BOOT model and involve the development of both water reservoirs and associated infrastructure and facilities. The successful bidder will form a project company that will operate under a 30-year water storage agreement.[23,24]

Irrigation Public–Private Partnerships

Irrigated agricultural projects, particularly those involving smallholder farmers, are often challenging to fund commercially as they cannot deliver short-term predictable financial returns. Irrigation projects are self-contained investments linked solely to the local off-take, i.e., the viability of the agricultural activities using the water. Therefore, infrastructure providers are exposed to market and commodity risks. As such, there various arrangements that can be initiated between irrigation operators and farmers in PPPs to enhance their financial viability, including:

- *Providing smallholder farmers in the command area the option of becoming outgrowers to a larger commercial farmer*: Engaging farmers as outgrowers involves providing them with seeds and other inputs required to grow a certain crop, training them in growing the crop, specifying quality standards the harvested crops must meet, and purchasing the harvested crops from them at an agreed-upon price.
- *The irrigation operator being responsible for all aspects of operating the irrigation system up to the farm level and maintaining the system up to the tertiary canals*: This means that farmers through their water user associations are responsible for maintaining the tertiary network while the private operator is responsible for operating and maintaining the entire system, with farmers paying a tariff that covers the operating and maintenance costs. The result is that farmers are not responsible for operating and maintaining the irrigation system.

The most used contractual forms of PPP in irrigation are:

- *Operation, management, and maintenance contract*: The private sector is engaged to undertake operation, management, and maintenance of infrastructure services for defined recipients. The private sector provides a service for a fee (either from the government or users). The assets are publicly financed, and this form is common where there is limited scope to raise private capital.

- *Infrastructure concession*: The private sector is engaged to raise commercial finance for infrastructure development and then construct, operate, manage, and maintain the infrastructure. Investment and financing costs are recovered through fees (either from the government or users). Risk can be shared between the public and private sector parties with a guarantee on minimum revenue. The investment can be undertaken in whole or in part by the private sector partner where there is grant funding available to cover some of the investment cost.
- *Farm service agreement*: The private sector partner can partner with smallholder farmers and communities for the provision of farm-level service. Services could be on-farm, such as planting, harvesting, and water application, or off-farm, such as storing, processing, and marketing, for example, outgrower services. The farm services will improve the agricultural performance of the water users, which will improve the viability of irrigation infrastructure.
- *Hub farm agreement*: The private sector partner undertakes commercial agricultural production through a land concession or lease, which could be on unoccupied land owned by the government or third parties, or community land held under the collective title and leased in return for a fee or share in commercial operations. Private capital is required for on-farm investments, while irrigation fees can reflect any or all infrastructure costs (operation, management, maintenance, investment, and finance, etc.).[25]

Case 9.2 Pontal—Public–Private Partnership Irrigation Project

The World Bank seeks to establish the Pontal—Public–Private Partnership Irrigation Project for common use irrigation infrastructure in an area of over 7,700 hectares of irrigable land for commercial agriculture in the Pontal region of Brazil, State of Pernanbuco. The private partner would operate, manage, and further develop the common infrastructure (already 70 per cent has been built by the government) to ensure that the area is fully irrigated within six years of the beginning of the contract and that at least 25 per cent of the irrigated land is available for small farmers. The private partner will be remunerated for the sale of water (through user tariffs) and a capacity payment by the government. The contract duration is 25 years.[26]

Community-based Public-Private Partnerships for Green Infrastructure

A community-based public–private partnership (CBP3) is a partnership between a local government and a private entity to implement green infrastructure. The partnership 'provides flexibility, implements advances in technology, addresses dynamic community trends and goals, and instils long-term financial and regulatory commitments for integrating green infrastructure into stormwater management programs'. The standard method used by many local governments in implementing green infrastructure is to evaluate design, construction, and maintenance needs for individual projects. This approach may be sensible for small programmes with a limited number of projects to maintain. However, for larger programmes, such as green infrastructure retrofits across a city, individually based procurement may not be the most efficient process. Instead, communities should decide on the most efficient and least costly procurement. The most cost-effective, large-scale implementation of green infrastructure will require a PPP in which multiple entities are constructing projects through multiple municipal programmes or private sector development projects. Table 9.3 summarizes the main aspects of a CBP3 while some of the main benefits for a local government entering a CBP3 for green infrastructure retrofits include:

- Increasing the ability to leverage public funds while minimizing the impacts on a municipality's debt capacity.
- Accessing advanced, even proprietary, technologies not available through standard procurement approaches.
- Improving asset management and the scientific application of lifecycle cost practices.
- Drawing on private sector expertise and the widest range of private-sector financial resources, including new sources of private capital, therefore, eliminating the need to wait for future budget cycles to pay for infrastructure projects.
- Benefiting local economic development by creating a marketplace for small, minority, and disadvantaged businesses to grow.
- Relieving pressure on internal local government resources by using private sector resources.[27]

Table 9.3 Aspects of community-based public–private partnerships

Aspect	Description
Alignment of goals	Common goals among the public and private partners in CBP3s create shared results
Accountability	CBP3 partners share responsibilities for project governance and major decisions, but the primary partner is responsible for the performance-based implementation
Transparency	CBP3 private sector partners operate under a fixed performance fee. The partnership is managed through adaptive management by regular partner meetings where major decisions necessary to achieve the project's intended goals are governed
Sustainability	All excess cash flow from savings or efficiencies in CBP3s are reinvested into the project or returned to the local government
Efficient use of funds	Use of private capital, expertise, and efficiencies leverages public investment in CBP3s, with efficient long-term operational cost savings being reinvested into the project
Commitment	The private partner in a CBP3 is committed to the local community through community stewardship and economic development of small and disadvantaged businesses
Value-driven	In a CBP3, the public sector bases its selection of a private partner on qualifications and long-term value versus price

Case 9.3 Stormwater Authority of Chester's Community-based Public–Private Partnership

The Stormwater Authority of Chester has created a CBP3 to plan, finance, build, and maintain up to $50 million in green stormwater infrastructure (GSI) over the next 20–30 years on around 350 acres to address significant pollution and flooding issues, improve neighbourhood quality of life, assist small, minority-owned businesses, drive economic growth, and make cost savings to water and other public and private capital improvement efforts (for example, streets, housing, economic development, and education) in the region. In particular, the GSI is expected to reduce costs by 30–50 per cent over this period. The CBP3 involves:

- US Environmental Protection Agency (EPA) providing more than $150,000 in technical and planning assistance, including how to design and develop the CBP3, enabling greater infrastructure investments and efficiencies.
- PENNVEST, Pennsylvania's infrastructure investment authority, providing a $1 million planning/pre-construction grant to support the initial $11–15 million green street projects in Chester.
- The water quality programme being planned by the Stormwater Authority of the City of Chester and its private partner, Corvias.
- The Chester Water Authority matching the EPA technical and planning assistance funds with a $50,000 grant.

Overall, Chester aims to become a regional hub for the stormwater industry sector. By being a 'living lab' of GSI applications and large-scale infrastructure investments, other communities in the region will seek Chester's companies and professionals for their own GSI and integrated infrastructure re-development programmes.[28]

Notes

1. Marlies Hueskes, Koen Verhoest, and Thomas Block, 'Governing public–private partnerships for sustainability: An analysis of procurement and governance practices of PPP infrastructure projects', *International Journal of Project Management* 35, no. 6 (2017/08/01/ 2017), https://doi.org/https://doi.org/10.1016/j.ijproman.2017.02.020, https://www.sciencedirect.com/science/article/pii/S0263786317302557.
2. Åse Johannessen et al., 'Strategies for building resilience to hazards in water, sanitation and hygiene (WASH) systems: The role of public private partnerships', *International Journal of Disaster Risk Reduction* 10 (2014/12/01/ 2014), https://doi.org/https://doi.org/10.1016/j.ijdrr.2014.07.002, http://www.sciencedirect.com/science/article/pii/S2212420914000557.
3. Radies Kusprihanto Purbo, Christine Smith, and Robert Bianchi, 'Lessons Learned from Public–Private Partnerships in Indonesia's Water Sector', *Bulletin of Indonesian Economic Studies* 55, no. 2 (2019), https://doi.org/10.1080/00074918.2018.1550250, https://dx.doi.org/10.1080/00074918.2018.1550250.
4. 'Water and Sanitation Agreements', 2022, https://ppp.worldbank.org/public-private-partnership/sector/water-sanitation/water-agreements.
5. Anis Chowdhury Jomo KS, Krishnan Sharma, Daniel Platz, 'Public–Private Partnerships and the 2030 Agenda for Sustainable Development: Fit for purpose?' (2016). https://www.un.org/en/desa/public-private-partnerships-and-2030-agenda-sustainable-development-fit-purpose.
6. Jomo KS, 'Public–Private Partnerships and the 2030 Agenda for Sustainable Development: Fit for Purpose?'.
7. Jomo KS, 'Public–Private Partnerships and the 2030 Agenda for Sustainable Development: Fit for Purpose?'.
8. M. Burnett, *Public-Private Partnerships: A Decision Maker's Guide* (European Institute of Public Administration, 2007). https://books.google.co.nz/books?id=ZjfKIQAACAAJ.
9. 'Stakeholder Communication and Engagement', 2022, accessed 6 January 2022, https://pppknowledgelab.org/guide/sections/39-stakeholder-communication-and-engagement.
10. 'PPP Certification Program Guide', 2022, accessed 6 January 2022, https://ppp-certification.com/ppp-certification-guide/about-ppp-guide.
11. Laura Turley and Abby Semple, 'Financing Sustainable Public–Private Partnerships' (2013). https://www.iisd.org/system/files/publications/ppp_financing.pdf.
12. Laura Turley and Abby Semple, 'Financing Sustainable Public–Private Partnerships'.
13. European Commission, 'Guidelines for Successful Public–Private Partnerships' (2003). https://ec.europa.eu/regional_policy/sources/docgener/guides/ppp_en.pdf.
14. Burnett, *Public-Private Partnerships: A Decision Maker's Guide*.
15. World Bank, 'Municipal Public–Private Partnership Framework' (2020). https://openknowledge.worldbank.org/handle/10986/33572.

16. The Canadian Council for Public Private Partnerships, 'Benefits of Water Service Public–Private Partnerships' (2001). http://www.archives.gov.on.ca/en/e_records/walkerton/part2info/publicsubmissions/pdf/benefitsofwaternew.pdf.

17. Sónia Lima, Ana Brochado, and Rui Cunha Marques, 'Public–Private Partnerships in the Water Sector: A Review', *Utilities Policy* 69 (2021/04/01/ 2021), https://doi.org/https://doi.org/10.1016/j.jup.2021.101182, https://www.sciencedirect.com/science/article/pii/S0957178721000163.

18. The Canadian Council for Public Private Partnerships, 'Benefits of Water Service Public-Private Partnerships'.

19. World Bank, 'Structuring Private-Sector Participation (PSP) Contracts for Small Scale Water Projects' (2014). https://library.pppknowledgelab.org/documents/4129/download.

20. World Bank, 'Structuring Private-Sector Participation (PSP) Contracts for Small Scale Water Projects'.

21. Congressional Budget Office, 'Public–Private Partnerships for Transportation and Water Infrastructure' (2020). https://www.cbo.gov/publication/56003.

22. Tong Yang et al., 'Application of the Public–Private Partnership Model to Urban Sewage Treatment', *Journal of Cleaner Production* 142 (2017/01/20/ 2017), https://doi.org/https://doi.org/10.1016/j.jclepro.2016.04.152, https://www.sciencedirect.com/science/article/pii/S0959652616304413.

23. 'Saudi Arabia Invites Interest in Fourth PPP Water Transmission Scheme', 2021, https://energy-utilities.com/saudi-arabia-invites-interest-in-fourth-ppp-water-news114584.html.

24. 'Saudi Arabia Invites Interest in PPP Water Reservoir Projects', 2021, accessed 6 January 2022, https://energy-utilities.com/saudi-arabia-invites-interest-in-ppp-water-news115751.html.

25. 'PPPs in Irrigation', 2022, accessed 6 January 2022, https://ppp.worldbank.org/public-private-partnership/ppp-sector/water-sanitation/ppps-irrigation.

26. 'Pontal—Public–Private Partnership Irrigation Project', 2021, accessed 6 January 2022, https://ppp.worldbank.org/public-private-partnership/library/pontal-public-private-partnership-irrigation-project.

27. US EPA, 'Community Based Public Private Partnerships (CBP3s) and Alternative Market-Based Tools for Integrated Green Stormwater Infrastructure' (2015). https://www.epa.gov/sites/production/files/2015-12/documents/gi_cb_p3_guide_epa_r3_final_042115_508.pdf.

28. Chester Water Authority, 'A New Model for Urban Renewal: Stormwater Authority of Chester's Community-Based Public–Private Partnership' (2017). https://www.chestercity.com/wp-content/uploads/2017/05/Chester_CCBP3_Announce_FactSheet_v5.pdf.

10

Biodiversity Offsets Financing Water Security and Green Growth

Introduction

Infrastructure development results in biodiversity loss due to loss and fragmentation of species' habitats and land use and land cover changes. Biodiversity loss is an environmental challenge of global concern as biodiversity, and associated ecosystems, provide a range of invaluable services to society that underpins human health and well-being, security, and economic growth. These services include clean water and flood protection. As a result, there has been a growing interest in biodiversity offsetting as a policy instrument for financing biodiversity conservation on the ground or in the water during the past decade. Biodiversity offsetting aims to compensate for the biodiversity losses that occur in one place from economic activities by requiring the developers to fund the costs of environmental protection or restoration activities there or somewhere else. It is estimated that policies for offsetting biodiversity losses are used in over 30 countries and have cumulatively restored over eight million hectares of land. The main drivers of biodiversity offsets are legislation and policies encouraging compensation by national governments and international agreements, global financial institutions that require biodiversity offsets to be considered a condition of being granted funding, and voluntary commitments from corporations pre-emptively managing business risks.[1,2,3,4,5] This chapter will first define the concept of biodiversity offsets. The chapter will then review how their performance and success can be enhanced, followed by a review on how to ensure their financial sustainability. Finally, the chapter will provide a framework for preparing and implementing biodiversity offsets on the ground or in the water.

Biodiversity Offsets

The International Finance Corporation defines biodiversity offsets as 'measurable outcomes resulting from actions designed to compensate for

Financing Water Security and Green Growth. Robert C. Brears, Oxford University Press. © Robert C. Brears (2023).
DOI: 10.1093/oso/9780192847843.003.0010

significant residual adverse biodiversity impacts arising from project development and persisting after appropriate avoidance, minimization, and restoration measures have been taken'. The goal of biodiversity offsets is to achieve No Net Loss and preferably Net Gain of biodiversity on the ground or in the water, compared to the baseline situation before the original project is implemented. Biodiversity offsets can include securing or setting aside land or water areas for conservation, enhanced management of habitat or species, and other defined activities. They can be used to:

- Create, expand, or buffer existing protected areas
- Enhance, link, or restore habitats
- Protect or manage species of conservation interest (either within a designated conservation area or more broadly across the landscape or aquatic habitat where the species occurs).[6]

Biodiversity offsets differ from other types of conservation activities in two main ways:

1. *They link to damage from another project*: Biodiversity offsets are explicitly linked to one or more development projects that are causing some loss of biodiversity, for example, the elimination or degradation of a patch of natural habitat.
2. *They focus on No Net Loss or Net Gain*: Biodiversity offsets are expected to fully compensate for specified adverse residual impacts—to the level of No Net Loss or preferably Net Gain—in a way that is measurable or verifiable, long-term, and additional to any other ongoing or planned conservation measures.[7]

Types of Biodiversity Offsets

There are two main types of biodiversity offsets:

- *Voluntary biodiversity offsets*: A developer undertakes a biodiversity offset where there is no legal requirement to do so as they perceive a business advantage, such as:
  - *Licence to operate and regulatory goodwill, managing risk and liability, or strengthening reputation*: Designing a high-quality biodiversity offset can help companies work effectively with local, national, and international stakeholders. Adopting best practices helps streamline

permit approval, lowering the risk of project delay and significant unanticipated start-up and operational costs.

- ○ *Operational efficiency and cost savings*: Biodiversity offsets may provide a more cost-effective solution focusing solely on onsite mitigation measures. Companies may reduce overall costs by working through the mitigation hierarchy while achieving greater conservation results. Also, companies with good relations with regulators and communities can achieve financial benefits of operational efficiency, avoiding the costs associated with revoked licenses or blockaded facilities.
- ○ *Access to finance*: Companies seeking project finance from banks subscribed to the Equator Principles are encouraged to consider biodiversity offsets. Applying best practices can help developers secure credit and investment.
- ○ *Competitive advantage*: Companies that voluntarily adopt biodiversity offsets may win concessions, attract finance, and gain market share.
- ○ *Pre-empt regulations*: There is a business case for developers to undertake voluntary offsets to pre-empt future mandatory requirements. The rewards are a 'first-mover' competitive advantage that could open up the possibility of companies influencing emerging environmental regulation and also contribute to the international adoption of policies that work well for business.
- • *Regulatory biodiversity offsets*: Under regulatory approaches, biodiversity offsets are mandatory for certain defined activities or impacts. The regulatory requirement for biodiversity offsets is usually integrated into the development approval processes, including environmental impact assessments, land-use planning laws, and legislation covering permitting for specific industry sectors. The availability of an offset should not be seen as an automatic green light of approval.[8,9]

Mitigation Hierarchy

In many jurisdictions, developers are first required to avoid biodiversity impacts, then minimize the impacts that cannot be avoided. Then, if there are any residual impacts, offset these through actions that generate an equivalent biodiversity gain elsewhere. The actions of (i) avoiding, then (ii) reducing, and finally, (iii) offsetting impacts are known as the mitigation hierarchy. In this hierarchy, avoidance can be achieved by either locating the project area away from sites of high biodiversity conservation value, carefully locating infrastructure within the designated project area, avoiding the use of certain technologies or techniques, or avoiding or curtailing certain types of problematic activities during specific times of the year, such as during the migration or breeding periods of species of conservation interest. When adverse impacts cannot be avoided entirely, they can be minimized by applying the approaches mentioned above used for avoidance or through other adjustments in project construction or operation.

Nonetheless, in many projects, all feasible efforts to avoid or minimize biodiversity losses or restore biodiversity onsite will not be enough to prevent significant adverse impacts on biodiversity. Therefore, well-designed and adequately implemented biodiversity offsets can compensate for significant residual impacts. Overall, the result of the biodiversity offset should be No Net Loss of biodiversity or even a Net Gain. Table 10.1 outlines the core principles for ensuring biodiversity offsets are successful.[10,11,12,13,14]

Biodiversity Offset Currency

The choice of metric for measuring the success of biodiversity offsets is complex and directly associated with the multidimensional nature of biodiversity. The choice of metric will influence how gains and losses are accounted for and how equivalence and No Net Loss are met. In early offset projects, the area was the currency used: the area impacted was offset by at least an equal area elsewhere. However, as our understanding of ecosystems grew, area by itself is no longer an adequate metric. Table 10.2 provides examples of metrics used by biodiversity offset schemes.[15]

Selecting Biodiversity Offset Sites

Offset site selection and how selected sites sit within the broader landscape are essential aspects of offset design. Biodiversity offsets can be delivered in the vicinity of the area impacted. The reasoning is that it increases the chances of contributing to the conservation and integrity of the same ecosystem and the needs of the local people. Nevertheless, in certain circumstances, more significant environmental benefits can be achieved when offsets are aligned with landscape or regional conservation goals, such as the potential for securing the protection of non-statutory sites of local biodiversity importance or biodiversity offset schemes being a source of conservation funding for biodiversity conservation initiatives.[16]

Table 10.1 Principles for ensuring success of biodiversity offsets

Principle	Description
Additionality	The biodiversity offset should prove additionality, which refers to the conservation benefit or gains produced due to delivering an offset that would not have arisen in the absence of the compensation action. Additionality can be achieved through two main types of biodiversity offsets: • *Restoration offsets*: These involve actions to restore an ecosystem, habitat, or species population (outside the footprint of the original development project) and thereby improving its biodiversity conservation status or value, for example, the improvement of ecological functioning and biodiversity value of a wetland by increasing its available water supply. • *Preservation offsets*: Also known as protective or averted loss offsets, they involve intentionally protecting an ecosystem, habitat, or species population (outside the original project's footprint) that is already in good condition or otherwise of a high biodiversity value but lacks sufficient legal or on-the-ground protection. The assumption is that the designated offset area (or species of concern) would eventually be diminished, degraded, or lost if it was not explicitly protected through the conservation support provided by the biodiversity offset.
Equivalence	Biodiversity offsets should conserve the same biodiversity values (species, habitats, ecosystems, or ecological functions) as those lost to the original project. It should be like-for-like. In some cases, the biodiversity offset area may be ecologically different from the original project area, but with an ecosystem type or species composition acknowledged as a higher conservation priority than the biodiversity to be lost under the original project. This approach is known as trading-up.

Permanence	Biodiversity offsets are typically expected to persist for as long as the adverse biodiversity impacts from the original project. Practically this means in perpetuity. Biodiversity offset planners can ensure this by having key features in place:
	
	• *Formal legal protection of the land, water area, or species involved, as needed for a successful conservation outcome. Legal protection might be in the form of*:
	  a. National/sub-national/local government laws or regulations
	  b. By-laws of organized communities
	  c. On-the-ground protection and management, such as zoning, prohibited uses, the physical presence of conservation staff, or conservation incentive payments to landholders.
	
	• *Financial sustainability*: Financing needs to take into account up-front as well as recurrent costs.

Table 10.2 Common metrics used by biodiversity offset schemes

Focus	Examples of metrics used
Ecosystem structure	• Habitat area • Fragmentation
Ecosystem function	• Net primary production • Nitrogen content • Soil pH
Species traits	• Survival rate • Emigration rate • Dispersal distance
Species populations	• Vegetation per cent cover • Number of trees per size/age class
Community composition	• Species diversity

Aggregated Biodiversity Offsets

Aggregated biodiversity offsets are 'conservation outcomes from compensation activities carried out to offset the residual impacts of more than one project, usually in a specific area or ecoregion'. They differ from individual offsets by compensating for the residual adverse effects of more than one development project while delivering multiple benefits (Table 10.3). There is a range of contexts in which aggregated biodiversity offsets may be appropriate, including the following:

- The same ecosystem or ecoregion is exposed to cumulative impacts from several operators, particularly those in the same sector, in the same general time period.
- There are several small scale developments that are individually insignificant but which may have significant cumulative impacts (and individual offsets are not justified or have high transaction costs).
- Effective coalitions have developed or evolved in/around particular locations, with the involvement of companies, government, communities, or non-governmental organizations.

Table 10.3 Benefits of aggregated biodiversity offsets

Benefit	Description
Reduced transaction costs	Successful biodiversity offsets usually involve high transaction costs, with multiple stakeholders and various legal, political, or social impediments that need to be overcome. Under an aggregated offsets system, transaction costs can be reduced as each biodiversity offset does not need to be designed from scratch
Increased developer participation	A governmental framework that promotes or requires offsets under specified circumstances would likely result in participation by a higher proportion of private sector and public works agencies than a regulatory environment that lacks clear procedures or strict legal requirements. The result is increased funding of biodiversity conservation from the private sector or through public sector infrastructure projects
Addressing cumulative impacts	Private or public sector project developers' increased participation in supporting biodiversity offsets would address the cumulative impacts of multiple development projects. A government offsets framework could identify large, ecologically valuable offset areas that could compensate for the cumulative impacts of multiple projects
Optimizing site selection	Improved land-use planning would enable biodiversity offset sites to be selected according to conservation priorities at a national or sub-national level rather than in an ad hoc, project-by-project manner. This would result in reduced project-specific costs and delays associated with verifying the feasibility of proposed offset locations
Improved land-use planning	A governmental framework for biodiversity offsets that pre-selects potential biodiversity offset sites will help ensure that high-value conservation areas are not mistakenly allocated to incompatible forms of development

- Individual developers do not have the skills or resources necessary to deliver effective biodiversity offsets, but collaborating and pooling resources would make biodiversity offsets achievable.
- There are many developers in the same sector and area of operation with a common set of international certification requirements and/or financing conditions to be met
- There are reputable or certified organizations willing and able to supply the necessary conservation services.

- Legislation and planning frameworks are enabling, for example, there is an established conservation plan for the affected area with clear priorities supported by reliable information on biodiversity.[17,18]

Implementing Biodiversity Offsets

There are three main ways of implementing biodiversity offsets:

- *Developer-initiated*: In this approach, the government has a policy that encourages or requires biodiversity offsets, but the onus rests on the developers to find their offsets. However, this approach is generally unpopular as:
  - Identifying and securing appropriate offset areas is usually outside the core expertise of developers, particularly smaller companies. It can be time- and resource-consuming.
  - Projects or companies may move on before an appropriate offset has been located or implemented.
  - Lack of government oversight can lead to inefficient, fragmented, and un-strategic offsets.
- *In lieu fees*: Under this system, a government agency stipulates payment from the developer, intending to deploy the funds later to find a suitable offset. This approach is favourable to developers as their offset requirements can be resolved quickly and with certainty through a single payment. In lieu fees allow aggregation of individual offsets into larger, more beneficial areas.
- *Market mechanisms*: A way of implementing biodiversity offsets is to use market mechanisms such as conservation banking and the generation and sale of biodiversity credits. A developer can provide their biodiversity offset, for example, on land the developer owns, or enter into an arrangement with a third party to provide the required offset. These arrangements are usually made by purchasing biodiversity credits from a conservation bank (an area of land where biodiversity credits are established in advance of any actual trading of credits for offsets) or from individuals and organizations that can provide biodiversity credits to the requisite standard: the developer pays the third party an agreed price in return for the requisite number and type of biodiversity credits that comprise the offset. In this context, 'credits' are quantified gains in biodiversity generated by actions that increase the extent, quality or security of habitat or species.[19]

Improving Biodiversity Offset Performance and Success

There is a range of initiatives that can be undertaken to improve the performance and success of biodiversity offsets, including:

- *Effective policy*: The government's position on biodiversity offsetting needs to be unambiguous as possible. The biodiversity offsetting policy needs to contextualize offsetting within the broader development policy context, clearly articulate the offsetting objective in addressing the ecological deficit, clarify definitions, reiterate the importance of the mitigation sequence, and place offsetting as a legitimate and supported option in the mitigation sequence. The biodiversity offsetting policy also needs to clarify that certain landscapes, ecosystems, or elements of ecological infrastructure are irreplaceable and cannot be offset and must be protected and maintained. Furthermore, the policy should be clear that offsets can be used to protect and maintain these irreplaceable elements.
- *Capacity building and maintenance interventions*: By mainstreaming offsetting into the current work of competent authorities, capacity should already be in place as part of the mitigation sequence. For the efficient and effective implementation of biodiversity offsetting, competent authorities must have developed and be able to implement standard operating procedures and systems for the design, evaluation, monitoring, and reporting of offsets.
- *Research and development*: Biodiversity offsets will need to be driven by research, experimentation, pilot project implementation, baseline assessments, improved measurements and measurement metrics, long-term reporting, and environmental improvement practices. Research interest will be increased with the publication of an offsetting policy and the increased use of offsetting as a component of the mitigation sequence.[20]

Financial Sustainability of Biodiversity Offsets

Biodiversity offsets involve recurrent costs for the protection, management, and monitoring of ecosystems and species. These recurrent costs can include salaries, supplies, incentive payments to landowners, and field support to volunteers. As biodiversity offsets should be designed for perpetuity, they should be designed to mobilize sufficient funding to cover at least some of their long-term recurrent costs. The standard options for meeting the recurrent cost needs of biodiversity offsets are listed in Table 10.4.[21]

Table 10.4 Options for meeting recurrent cost needs of biodiversity offsets

Financing option	Description
Regular operating budget	Most protected areas with recurrent costs receive some type of annual support, which usually comes from national or local government funding for protected areas or their landowners in the case of private protected areas
Donor-funded projects	Conservation projects funded by international donors, including multilateral and bilateral development agencies and conservation non-governmental organizations, usually cover up-front investment costs. They also usually provide some support for recurring costs, but not usually over the long term
Self-generated revenues	Some protected areas generate revenues within their boundaries through tourism activities or fees. Typically, these fees are not sufficient to cover their total operating costs
Private philanthropy	Some conservation areas, potentially including biodiversity offset areas, have their recurrent costs of protection met, wholly or in part, by corporate or individual sponsors
Carbon offset payments	Biodiversity offsets often establish or strengthen protected areas, many of which contain ecosystems with high levels of carbon stored in their biomass and/or soils. Carbon offset payments can be used to cover some of the protection and management costs of forests or other high-carbon ecosystems being conserved and/or restored under a biodiversity offset
Project-specific revenue transfers	Conservation areas established or strengthened as biodiversity offsets can be sustained through dedicated revenue transfers from specific infrastructure projects. Water infrastructure projects and other revenue-generating infrastructure projects can support the recurring costs of associated biodiversity offsets because maintaining the offset can be part of the infrastructure project's regular operating costs
Conservation trust funds	Conservation trust funds (CTF) enable development project sponsors to set money aside up-front to support the recurring costs of maintaining the biodiversity offset. If enough money is set aside, the CTF can serve as an endowment fund that generates a sustainable annual income stream to be used for conservation expenditures

Framework for Preparing and Implementing Biodiversity Offsets

Biodiversity offsets can involve a diverse range of activities for enhancing the conservation of habitats and species off-site from the original project area. Four steps should be followed to ensure biodiversity offsets, whether for a public or private sector development project, is successful in achieving No Net Loss and preferably Net Gain of biodiversity on the ground or in the water:

- *Step 1: Estimate residual biodiversity losses from the original project*: It is necessary to estimate the likely biodiversity losses if the original infrastructure, extractive, or other development project were to proceed as planned, considering other available measures in the mitigation hierarchy:

  1. The main instrument to determine the biodiversity information needed is the Environmental and Social Impact Assessment (ESIA) or Environmental Impact Assessment (EIA). ESIAs or EIAs should specify the following:
     a. *Ecosystem types affected*: The ESIA or EIA should estimate the total area of each habitat type that is expected to be converted (lost) or modified (including degraded) as a direct or indirect impact of the original development project.
     b. *Species of conservation interest*: The ESIA or EIA should indicate which species of global or national conservation interest (Critically Endangered, Endangered, Vulnerable, or Near Threatened or any others with small global ranges) are likely to be adversely affected and to what extent.
     c. *Special biodiversity values*: The ESIA or EIA should describe the other ways in which the project area may be of biodiversity interest, for example, having high species or habitat diversity or have existing recognition as a Ramsay Wetland of International Importance.
     d. *Protection status*: The ESIA or EIA should indicate whether the project area has any kind of protected status.
     e. *Site ownership and control*: The ESIA or EIA should indicate which individual, corporation, community, government, or other entity legally owns the land and/or water rights and which entity has legal or *de facto* management control over the area and its natural resources.
     f. *Baseline threats*: The ESIA or EIA should seek to quantify ongoing baseline rates of habitat loss or degradation (if any) within the project area. It should describe existing and likely future threats.

g. *Significance of residual adverse impacts*: The ESIA or EIA should assess and explain the significance of the proposed project's expected residual impacts on biodiversity, including both direct and indirect impacts. Establishing the significance of the expected adverse biodiversity impacts is a crucial input to deciding whether a biodiversity offset may be needed.

h. *Precautionary principle*: Where scientific data is lacking, the precautionary principle should be considered to ensure the proposed project avoids causing significant, irreversible harm.

2. *Apply the mitigation hierarchy*: As per the mitigation hierarchy, biodiversity offsets are considered a last resort after the other mitigation approaches (avoid, minimize, and restore) have all been feasibly applied. The need for a biodiversity offset is based on the type and severity of adverse residual impacts that would remain after using the other mitigation approaches.

3. *Assess the feasibility of offsetting*: If the full application of the pre-offset mitigation hierarchy (avoid, minimize, restore) still leaves significant adverse residual impacts, then a biodiversity offset may be the best solution. Two questions are required to be answered to determine whether a biodiversity offset is feasible:

a. *Could the damage from the original project be feasibly offset?* At times, certain adverse residual impacts cannot be easily offset, for instance, the affected area is unique or irreplaceable from a biodiversity point of view.

b. *Could the proposed conservation offset activities be feasibly implemented?* A suitable biodiversity offset might not be feasible to implement or have a low likelihood of success due to land tenure, political, socioeconomic, security, or other constraints.

- *Step 2: Select the biodiversity offset activities and conservation site(s)*: Depending on the local context, expected biodiversity impacts, and desired outcomes (No Net Loss or ideally a Net Gain), a variety of offset activities may be chosen, including a combination of the following options:

1. *New or expanded protected areas*: Protected areas, including governmental, community, and private conservation areas, can be

created or expanded to offset the biodiversity losses from the original project.

2. *Improved management or habitat enhancement*: The management of existing protected areas could be strengthened, if additionality can be demonstrated.

3. *Habitat restoration or enhancement*: Species habitat could be established, restored, or enhanced, particularly in areas with some degree of long-term protection.

4. *Livelihood or community support*: Biodiversity offsets should include support for addressing livelihood or community development issues in the vicinity of conservation areas to help build local support and mitigate any negative socioeconomic impacts from newly restricted access to natural resources.

5. *Species-specific interventions*: Biodiversity offsets can support measures to reduce other non-project threats to species.

6. *Financial support*: All types of biodiversity offset activities require some level of funding. However, in some cases, the sponsor of the development project may provide additional support to an aggregate, large-scale conservation offset, or even a CTF, that is designed to compensate for the cumulative impact of multiple projects, rather than designing a separate, individual offset from scratch.

- *Step 3: Prepare the biodiversity offset project component*: There are a set of critical provisions that need to be identified in the project documentation to ensure the biodiversity offset project is successful:

  1. *Basic requirements for biodiversity offsets include documenting*:
     a. *Specific activities and inputs*: The inputs for the project need to be identified, such as on-the-ground investments required, habitat restoration or enhancement measures used, community support, and the availability of incentive payments to landholders conditional on conservation results.
     b. *Institutional responsibilities*: The project documentation needs to define the responsibilities of different organizations. Since the organization leading the implementation of the biodiversity offset is usually different from the sponsor of the original development project, inter-institutional coordination mechanisms need to be identified.
     c. *Implementation schedule*: The time frames for implementing biodiversity offset investments or actions should be clearly

defined, including the expected start date and (if not recurrent) the target end date for each planned activity.

d. *Budget*: An adequate budget is required to ensure the effective implementation of any biodiversity offset, with it accounting for both up-front investment costs and long-term recurrent costs.

e. *Funding sources*: Up-front investment costs typically should be met as a defined part of the original project's investment costs since the original project provides the basis for doing the biodiversity off-site in the first place.

2. *Procedures for establishing or upgrading protected areas*: Many biodiversity offsets involve protected area establishment, enlargement, or upgrading of legal status or management. As such, the biodiversity offset project needs to:

a. *Verify the conservation value*: The biodiversity offset proposal should document that the proposed protected area is of high conservation value—adequate to meet the No Net Loss criteria at a minimum.

b. *Verify the land tenure, socioeconomic, and political feasibility*: The offset proposal should indicate who:
   ○ Owns and/or claims the land (and associated water area) comprising the new or expanded protected area.
   ○ Has any concessions, leases, or other legally recognized land rights.
   ○ Is currently occupying or using the land or natural resources in any way.

c. *Select the management category*: Protected area management categories vary in terms of their emphasis on different conservation and management objectives.

d. *Delineate the boundaries*: The offset proposal should include a detailed map showing the planned protected area boundaries.

e. *Stakeholder consultation*: Consultations should be carried out with the full range of interested stakeholders, including local communities and resource users, regarding the proposed new or expanded protected area and its planned boundaries and management category.

f. *Prepare the legal and supporting documents*: Getting the new or expanded protected area legally established (gazetted) typically will require drafting a new law, regulation, or executive or ministerial decree for public (government-owned) protected areas or new by-laws, contracts, trust agreements, easements, or other legally binding documents for private protected areas. In addition to these key legal documents, a variety of supporting technical documents (including maps) will usually need to be prepared.

- *Step 4: Monitoring implementation of the biodiversity offset activities and results:* Biodiversity offsets require significant investment in the monitoring of implementation and outcomes and involve:

  1. *Implementation monitoring:* Diligent monitoring of implementation by the responsible entity is essential for achieving the desired outcomes on the ground.
  2. *Environmental rules for contractors:* These are needed to help ensure that contractors and construction workers do not cause undue damage while working in sensitive natural areas.
  3. *Outcome monitoring:* To verify that a biodiversity offset has achieved its No Net Loss objective, field-based outcome monitoring is needed, which is an essential part of adaptive management: If the biodiversity offset is not achieving its goals, monitoring can provide the information needed to adjust project implementation to improve on-the-ground outcomes effectively. The scope, duration, frequency, and budget for outcome monitoring activities should be defined as part of preparing a biodiversity offset. Overall, outcome monitoring activities should be designed to:
     a. Be feasible to carry out in the field.
     b. Obtain much-needed information.
     c. Avoid unnecessary complexity, for example, using too many indicators.[22]

Case 10.1 Auckland Council's Healthy Waters Biodiversity Offset Bank

Auckland Council's Healthy Waters Biodiversity Offset Bank programme allows developers to purchase credits to offset the environmental impacts of their developments on waterways. The programme:

1. Calculates how many credits a developer needs to meet offset requirements.
2. Sells the credits to the developer.
3. Contributes the income towards funding ecological enhancement projects in Auckland.
4. Delivers the ecological project (when fully funded).

Developers can use the programme if they have already tried to avoid, remedy, and mitigate the adverse environmental impacts of their developments. A credit is based on the relevant Stream Ecological Value (SEV) for the proposed ecological enhancement project, where the number of credits is determined by a calculation of the predicted increase in the SEV score and the size of the stream bed.

Meanwhile, landowners can suggest sites on their properties as potential projects for the council's Connect and Enhance programmes:

- *Connect*: The Connect programme matches farmers and landowners with certified suppliers. The supplier will identify, and design waterway planting projects focused on restoring and rehabilitating degraded waterways. If the project meets the council's approval, the council will fund a supplier to deliver it. All connect projects must achieve additional ecological benefits.
- *Enhance*: The city council delivers the Enhance projects. Most of the projects are on council land and focus on restoring and rehabilitating degraded waterways.[23]

Case 10.2 The Scottish Borders Biodiversity Offsets Scheme

The Scottish Borders contains biodiversity of international and national value. Nevertheless, the region has seen a significant amount of renewable energy development, particularly wind energy, with more wind farm proposals currently in the planning process. National and local planning policy supports renewable energy development while minimizing adverse impacts on wildlife. However, the Local Plan policy in the area allows the reasons in favour of development to sometimes outweigh the desirability of retaining particular habitat features on a development site. The Scottish Borders Council, with stakeholders, has developed a biodiversity offset scheme that aims to account for the residual impacts of renewable energy and mineral development on black grouse, on blanket bog, and other upland habitats. The implementation of 11 individual schemes in the Scottish Borders enables the mainstreaming of biodiversity into the planning process by seeking biodiversity benefits at the landscape scale while benefiting ecosystem services, including flood protection, water quality, carbon storage, and recreation.

One example of an individual scheme is the Langhope Rig—Biodiversity Offset, which was secured by Scottish Borders Council from the developer SSE Renewables. The scheme, facilitated through the Langhope Rig Wind Farm development, funds two biodiversity conservation projects:

- *Upper Teviot native and riparian woodland planting project*: This is in its fifth year (2021/2022). It is run in conjunction with the Hawick Flood Scheme objectives of reducing the impact of flooding downstream. Over the past year, Tweed Forum has worked with farmers and landowners to help facilitate a further 40 hectares of native tree planting in the headwaters of the River Teviot. If the planting is successful, it will add to the 80 hectares already planted.

- *Ale Wetlands grant scheme*: This project is now complete with ten new wildlife ponds created in the Central Borders area. Open water is a rare habitat in the Scottish Borders, as centuries of drainage works have seen the bulk of the ponds and wetlands being drained for agricultural improvement. This project has helped create habitat for a range of wetland wildlife, including frogs, toads, newts, drag-onflies, and ducks such as teal.[24,25]

Case 10.3 Wisconsin's Wetland Compensatory Mitigation

Wetlands provide many ecosystem services, including flood control, water quality, fish and wildlife habitat, and water for rivers and streams. Wisconsin law requires mitiga-tion for wetland impacts approved under wetland individual permits and some projects authorized under the nonfederal wetland exemption. There are three ways of satisfying compensatory mitigation requirements:

- *Wetland mitigation banking*: A wetland individual permit applicant or exempt project proponent can purchase credits from an approved and open mitigation bank. Mitigation banking is divided into 12 watersheds that serve as the areas where banks may sell credits and be considered 'in service area'. Any individual or entity may establish and operate a wetland mitigation bank in Wisconsin. Wet-land mitigation banks are regulated by the US Army Corps of Engineers (USACE) and the Department of Natural Resources.
- *In-lieu fee programme*: A wetland individual permit applicant or exempt project proponent can purchase credits from the Department of Natural Resources Wis-consin Wetland Conservation Trust (WWCT). The WWCT has been operating since 2014 and sells wetland credits to permittees needing to offset authorized wet-land impacts. As of June 2021, the WWCT has allocated $18 million to 14 different mitigation projects and has completed over 500 acres of construction across nine sites
- *Permittee responsible mitigation*: If no mitigation credits are available for pur-chase or if preferred, an individual permit applicant or a nonfederal exempt project proponent may satisfy mitigation requirements through the completion of a wetland mitigation project. While the Department of Natural Resources does not prefer this option, a wetland individual permit applicant can satisfy their compensatory requirement by completing a mitigation project in the same watershed service area or within a half-mile of the permitted wetland impact. A nonfederal exempt project proponent can complete a mitigation project within

the same compensation search area, the county, and within a 20-mile radius of the impacted wetland. The process for projects is:

1. *Meeting*: For nonfederal exemptions requiring mitigation and individual permit applicants, applicants should meet with their local wetland specialist before submitting a request to the Department of Natural Resources. The purpose of the meeting is to discuss the proposed project purpose and need, the project alternatives to avoid and minimize wetland impacts, the options for wetland mitigation, and the information requirements for the application submittal.

2. *Contact with the USACE*: Individual permit applicants are also encouraged to contact the USACE to determine whether USACE requires a permit and compensatory mitigation for the intended activity.

3. *Instruction to satisfy responsibility*: After the application has been submitted and the Department of Natural Resources Water Management Specialist has made a preliminary determination of the amount of approvable wetland impact, the Department of Natural Resources Wetland Mitigation Coordinator will notify the applicant of their mitigation requirement after determining which of the available compensatory mitigation options best replaces the wetland functions lost due to the project.[26]

Notes

1. Juan David Quintero and Aradhna Mathur, 'Biodiversity Offsets and Infrastructure', *Conservation Biology* 25, no. 6 (2011), http://www.jstor.org.ezproxy.canterbury.ac.nz/stable/41315406.

2. OECD, 'Biodiversity Offsets: Effective Design and Implementation' (2016). https://www.oecd.org/environment/resources/Policy-Highlights-Biodiversity-Offsets-web.pdf.

3. Niak Sian Koh, Thomas Hahn, and Wiebren J. Boonstra, 'How Much of a Market Is Involved in a Biodiversity Offset? A Typology of Biodiversity Offset Policies', *Journal of Environmental Management* 232 (2019/02/15/ 2019), https://doi.org/https://doi.org/10.1016/j.jenvman.2018.11.080, https://www.sciencedirect.com/science/article/pii/S0301479718313458.

4. Carsten Mann, 'Strategies for Sustainable Policy Design: Constructive Assessment of Biodiversity Offsets and Banking', *Ecosystem Services* 16 (2015/12/01/ 2015), https://doi.org/https://doi.org/10.1016/j.ecoser.2015.07.001, https://www.sciencedirect.com/science/article/pii/S2212041615300127.

5. Sophus Olav Sven Emil zu Ermgassen et al., 'The Role of "No Net Loss" Policies in Conserving Biodiversity Threatened by the Global Infrastructure Boom', *One Earth* 1, no. 3 (2019/11/22/ 2019), https://doi.org/https://doi.org/10.1016/j.oneear.2019.10.019, http://www.sciencedirect.com/science/article/pii/S2590332219301332.

6. World Bank, 'Biodiversity Offsets: A User Guide' (2016). https://openknowledge.worldbank.org/handle/10986/25758.
7. World Bank, 'Biodiversity Offsets: A User Guide'.
8. IUCN, 'Biodiversity Offsets: Policy Options for Governments' (2014). https://portals.iucn.org/library/sites/library/files/documents/2014-028.pdf
9. Sarah Benabou, 'Making Up for Lost Nature?: A Critical Review of the International Development of Voluntary Biodiversity Offsets', *Environment & Society* 5 (2014), http://www.jstor.org/stable/43297071.
10. Fabien Quétier and Sandra Lavorel, 'Assessing Ecological Equivalence in Biodiversity Offset Schemes: Key Issues and Solutions', *Biological Conservation* 144, no. 12 (2011), https://doi.org/10.1016/j.biocon.2011.09.002, https://dx.doi.org/10.1016/j.biocon.2011.09.002.
11. Lucie Bezombes, Christian Kerbiriou, and Thomas Spiegelberger, 'Do Biodiversity Offsets Achieve No Net Loss? An Evaluation of Offsets in a French Department', *Biological Conservation* 231 (2019/03/01/ 2019), https://doi.org/https://doi.org/10.1016/j.biocon.2019.01.004, https://www.sciencedirect.com/science/article/pii/S0006320718306098.
12. Bárbara Gonçalves et al., 'Biodiversity Offsets: From Current Challenges to Harmonized Metrics', *Current Opinion in Environmental Sustainability* 14 (2015), https://doi.org/10.1016/j.cosust.2015.03.008, https://dx.doi.org/10.1016/j.cosust.2015.03.008.
13. World Bank, 'Biodiversity Offsets: A User Guide'.
14. Toby A. Gardner et al., 'Biodiversity Offsets and the Challenge of Achieving No Net Loss', *Conservation Biology* 27, no. 6 (2013), http://www.jstor.org/stable/24480255.
15. Gonçalves et al., 'Biodiversity Offsets: From Current Challenges to Harmonized Metrics'.
16. Gonçalves et al., 'Biodiversity Offsets: From Current Challenges to Harmonized Metrics'.
17. World Bank, 'Biodiversity Offsets: A User Guide'.
18. IUCN, 'Biodiversity Offsets: Policy Options for Governments'.
19. IUCN, 'Biodiversity Offsets: Policy Options for Governments'.
20. Peter Lukey et al., 'Making Biodiversity Offsets Work in South Africa—A Governance Perspective', *Ecosystem Services* 27 (2017/10/01/ 2017), https://doi.org/https://doi.org/10.1016/j.ecoser.2017.05.001, https://www.sciencedirect.com/science/article/pii/S2212041617303017.
21. World Bank, 'Biodiversity Offsets: A User Guide'.
22. World Bank, 'Biodiversity Offsets: A User Guide'.
23. 'Healthy Waters Biodiversity Offset Bank', 2022, accessed 7 January 2022, https://www.aucklandcouncil.govt.nz/environment/looking-after-aucklands-water/Pages/healthy-waters-biodiversity-offset-bank.aspx.
24. NatureScot, 'The Scottish Borders Biodiversity Offsets Scheme' (2017). https://www.nature.scot/sites/default/files/2017-10/A2394889-Biodiversity-Duty-local-authority-case-studies-The-Scottish-Borders-Biodiversity-Offsets-Scheme.pdf.
25. 'Langhope Rig—Biodiversity Offset Conservation Projects', 2022, accessed 7 January 2022, https://tweedforum.org/our-work/projects/langhope-rig-biodiversity-offset-conservation-projects/.
26. 'Wetland Compensatory Mitigation', 2022, accessed 7 January 2022, https://dnr.wisconsin.gov/topic/Wetlands/mitigation.

11
Tradable Permits Financing Water Security and Green Growth

Introduction

Tradable permit schemes have been implemented in environmental policy since the 1970s and are commonly used to reduce greenhouse gas emissions. They have also been implemented in a broader spectrum of fields, including water resources management.[1] Tradable permit schemes are one of the most efficient market-based instruments for allocating water resources and for mitigating the pollution of water resources.[2] This chapter will first discuss the concept of tradable permit schemes before discussing tradable water rights and water quality trading (WQT). The chapter will then review the concept of urban water trading and stormwater volume credit trading. Following this, the chapter will discuss groundwater trading and the acquiring of water for the environment.

Tradable Permit Schemes

Tradable permits are marketable rights that allow the use of a common resource or the emission of polluting substances. Every tradable permit scheme is based on permits (or rights) granted by a regulatory authority to participants in the scheme, who are usually companies that wish to exploit resources or emit polluting substances. Permits can be traded (or transferred) between participants who pay the most to gain the right to exploit resources or pollute.[3] Tradable permit schemes are implemented to manage the use of a common resource that may be overexploited or depleted if there is no regulatory protection, for example, the over-exploitation of surface water, or curb the quantity of pollutants emitted, for example, water pollution. As such, a tradable permit may provide the right to emit a predetermined quantity of pollution (water pollution) or the right to use a predetermined quantity of a common resource (water rights).

Financing Water Security and Green Growth. Robert C. Brears, Oxford University Press. © Robert C. Brears (2023).
DOI: 10.1093/oso/9780192847843.003.0011

Table 11.1 Types of tradable permit schemes

Name of the permit	Credit trading Credits	Cap-and-trade Allowances
Emission target	Standard/baseline for individual unit (resource depleting or polluting installation)	Global standard/cap for a collectivity of units (industry sector), divided into a number of allowances
Environmental effectiveness	Upper limit for each unit: However, if the number of units increases, total emissions also increase	Upper aggregate limit: Total amount of emissions or resource use cannot be exceeded within the scheme
Flexibility of scheme	Emissions/resource use above the standard/baseline for individual units is possible through the purchase of credits from over-complying units	Emission/resource use above the aggregate standard is prohibited. Individual units can buy/sell as many allowances as they want
Generation and allocation of permits	Credits are granted to individual units for over-compliance compared to the baseline (the baseline could be a technological standard or 'without-measures scenario')	Allowances are generated by legal authority and distributed to units based on historical production volume or emissions (grandfathering), auctions, first-come-first-served

Types of Tradable Permit Schemes

There are two types of tradable permit schemes available: credit trading programmes and cap-and-trade schemes, as summarized in Table 11.1.[4]

Designing Tradable Permit Schemes

Designing a tradable permit scheme involves a sequential decision-making process as follows:

1. *Defining objectives*: The objectives of the tradable permit system and its basic characteristics need defining, such as the physical basis of permits, usage rights, conditions under which transfer of credits/allowances can be exercised, and legal status of the credits/allowances.
2. *Determining the initial allocation of credits/allowances*: Criteria should be developed on the price of credits/allowances, market mechanisms used for their distribution, what auction methods should be used, for

credits, how a benchmark should be determined for acceptable levels of emissions/use of the resource, and how reliable monitoring can be ensured.

3. *Encouraging flexibility*: The tradable permit scheme should be designed to provide temporal and spatial flexibility and which flexibility options, such as banking, borrowing, etc., are suitable.

4. *Organizing trade*: Trading rules need to be developed that identifies who can make trades, such as whether trading of permits/allowances can be done within an entity ('intra-firm trades'), bilaterally between two entities, through brokers, or carried out under the auspices of an administrative authority.

5. *Effective monitoring*: Reliable and cost-effective systems for monitoring pollutant emissions and/or resource abstraction, such as performance tracking systems and information disclosure, need to be developed to establish the credibility of the scheme.

6. *Encouraging compliance*: There need to be tools available to encourage participants to comply with the requirements and not to exceed emission or abstraction levels beyond what is allowed in their permit, such as the enforcement of penalties and fines, verification of emission reduction performance.

7. *Promoting participation*: There need to be the means available to promote participation by agents and ensure that the programme runs smoothly and fairly.

8. *Combining tradable permit schemes with other instruments*: Tradable permit schemes can be combined with taxation if the extent of pollution abatement costs and environmental damage is uncertain and when authorities want to have both guarantees of physical environmental performance and avoid exposing participants to excessive economic costs. Tradable permit schemes can also be linked with voluntary agreements.[5]

Tradable Water Rights

In most countries where water is scarce or costly to access, systems of rights for water use have evolved through customs or bodies of law and regulations (or both). These water rights specify how much surface water is divided between sectors, such as agriculture, industry, and domestic water

Table 11.2 Types of water rights

Type	Description
Riparian rights	Under this system, anyone who possesses land next to a flowing river or stream may take its water as long as enough is left for downstream users. Diversions of water to locations not adjoining the river or stream are prohibited. These systems usually occur in areas where water is relatively abundant and where the strict definition of rights is not crucial
Prior rights	These rights are based on the appropriation doctrine, where the water right is acquired by actual use over time. Diversions of water are permitted, and quotas are allocated to specified parties on a first-come, first-served basis and are subject to the 'use it or lose it' rule. The traditional elements of a valid appropriation are: • The intention to apply the water to a beneficial use • The actual diversion of water from a natural source • The application of the water to beneficial use within a reasonable period
Public allocation	This system involves the publicly administered distribution of water. Public authorities decide how to allocate water using guidelines or laws establishing priorities and often specify the uses to which the water can be put. Although there is often a charge for water use, the water rights themselves are obtained without charge

supply, and between individual water users within a sector. Water rights are usually based on a variant or combination of three systems, as detailed in Table 11.2.[6,7]

Water rights can be traded informally, where individuals or groups of water rights holders sell water to other users at freely negotiated prices. However, while these markets can help solve water shortages, they are not supported by existing laws, limiting transactions to spot sales of water or the sale (lease) of water for a single year rather than permanent sales of water rights. The lack of long-term secure access to water under such a system also discourages investment in activities that require access to large quantities of water.[8]

In contrast, some countries have implemented legislation that permits secure and well-defined tradable water rights. Under this system, a regulatory authority sets the water consumption cap (the maximum amount of water abstraction allowed in the hydrographic basin) and allocates the corresponding abstraction rights among the basin users, who can then exchange them according to their present and/or future expected water consumption needs. Water users who use water more efficiently can sell the rights that are no longer needed once they manage to lower their water consumption. The water rights are acquired by being recorded in a public registry as either consumptive or non-consumptive, temporary or permanent. Permanent consumptive rights are defined in volumetric terms and temporary consumptive rights can only be honoured if all permanent consumptive rights have been met. Non-consumptive rights, used for electricity generation, grant the owner the use of water if it is returned to its source at a specified location and quality. Consumptive uses are those where the water use results in water not being available for other beneficial use. Examples of this include water consumed by a crop.

Tradable water rights allow the price of water to reflect the value of its alternative uses, creating an incentive for it to be put to the most productive use. Under a tradable water rights regime, the water charge should equal the operation and maintenance cost of the infrastructure while the price of the water rights is the market price for the right to use the water.[9,10] Table 11.3 summarizes the various public policy benefits of water trading.[11]

Table 11.3 Public policy benefits of water trading

Benefit	Description
Conflict mitigation	The seller and buyer both benefit from transfers, and any potential conflicts can be resolved through direct negotiation
Flexibility	Sellers and buyers can find mutually agreeable ways in which the water can be transferred, which can vary depending on hydrologic conditions or adapt to other management needs
Allocation of water to new users	Transfers reallocate water to meet emerging water demands, and prices compensate sellers for making water available to buyers
Decentralized decision-making	Resource decisions are made by participants so that local conditions and needs are accommodated
Economic incentives for water conservation	Prices established in water trading markets provide an incentive for water users to lower their consumption, invest in water-efficient technology, and implement other water-saving practices
Encourages investment	Prices will increase with increased demand for water, supporting investment in water conservation, improved water resource management, and new infrastructure required to implement water transfers

Case 11.1 Wheatley Watersource Trading in the United Kingdom

In the United Kingdom, Wheatley Solutions launched on 1 December 2020, Wheatley Watersource, enabling users to see market information in the pilot water catchment areas and facilitating the trade of water in the Suffolk East water catchment region. The concept was developed at Innovate East, an annual festival of innovation in the water industry hosted by Anglian Water and Essex & Suffolk Water and in association with Water Resources East. Wheatley Watersource allows the communication necessary to broker and track the trade or sharing of water between water abstraction licence holders and others interested in an alternative water source, for example, golf courses. Users can advertise their need for water or the availability of surplus water, using a map to show geographic proximity and automated alerts to other users of new activity relevant to them. The uniqueness of Wheatley Watersource is that it was developed in consultation with the Environment Agency (EA) and uses EA rules and data to provide an immediate assessment of the trade opportunity. Wheatley Watersource identifies:

- If a trade/sharing can take place without referral to the EA (a 'fast trade'); or
- If a trade/sharing requires a referral. If a referral is required, Wheatley Watersource can facilitate a pre-application to the EA for a variation to a licence, new licence, or trade in water rights.[12]

Case 11.2 Water Markets and Trade in the Murray-Darling River Basin

Water in the Murray-Darling River Basin in Australia can be bought and sold, either permanently or temporarily. This water is traded on markets, within catchments, between catchments, or along river systems. The New South Wales, Queensland, South Australian, and Victorian state governments are primarily responsible for managing water markets, with each state having its process and rules for allocating water. Water trading allows water holders to decide whether they need to buy or sell water at a particular time. There are two types of trades available:

- *Permanent trade*: This is the trade of water entitlements ('entitlement trade'). Specifically, an entitlement holder sells their water entitlement permanently.
- *Temporary trade*: This is the annual trade of water allocations ('allocation trade'). Specifically, an entitlement holder can trade their allocation in any season, based on their business model.

Meanwhile, Table 11.4 summarizes water entitlements, water allocations, and water usage definitions in the Murray-Darling River Basin.[13]

Table 11.4 Water entitlements, water allocations, and water usage definitions

Definition	Description
Water entitlements	• These are rights to an ongoing share of water within a system • The water market determines the financial value of a water entitlement
Water allocations	• This is the amount of water distributed to users (water entitlement holders) in a given year • Allocations against entitlements change according to rainfall, inflows into storage, and how much water is already stored • Allocations can increase throughout the year in response to changes in the system
Water usage	• This is how much water is used from the water that is allocated. When water is allocated to an entitlement holder, they use it as needed • The amount used is an individual business decision, where entitlement holders consider climate and rainfall, their cropping cycle, and their business plan

Water Quality Trading

WQT is a market-based approach for reducing or controlling water pollution. It allows permitted dischargers in a watershed to trade water quality credits or pollution allowances to meet water quality standards. Instead of being based on an actual physical commodity, WQT is based on trading a license or a permit to pollute. The main objective of WQT is to reduce the costs of water pollution control, usually following the imposition of a cap on pollutant emissions by regulators. In most WQT schemes, a cap is put on water pollutants. The cap is referred to as a Total Maximum Daily Load (TMDL), which represents the maximum amount of pollutant that a watershed can assimilate without exceeding water quality standards.

Three types of WQT schemes exist: among point sources, among non-point sources, or among point and non-point sources. WQT between point sources is the most common, with credits traded among industries discharging pollutants into the water as part of a TMDL. Alternatively, TMDL is taken to establish an overall cap for a water body, which is then directly distributed to different parties in the form of proportionate allowances. Finally, some WQT schemes include non-point sources where point sources receive credits from a regulatory authority for funding non-point source pollution reduction projects.[14]

Water Quality Trading Monitoring

WQT schemes need to ensure that credit generating practices are routinely monitored or inspected to ensure pollutant reductions continue to occur as expected. WQT schemes need to specify how and when emitters are monitored and whether discharges are monitored in advance (ex-ante control) or once they have occurred (ex-post monitoring). The method of determining emissions for regulatory compliance is crucial for the environmental integrity of the system:

- *Ex-ante monitoring*: This is typically used to prevent non-compliance, with participants who change discharge levels having to first submit an estimation before any approval can be given. However, this approach increases transaction costs and decreases trading efficiency.
- *Ex-post monitoring*: This usually requires participants to self-report their discharges, and compliance is established periodically (often annually) after any changes and trades have taken place. This system allows participants to trade freely. However, this type of system is expensive to set up as it requires the establishment of models or systems that robustly estimate discharges using the supplied data.[15,16]

Conditions for Successful Water Quality Trading Schemes

A series of minimum conditions are necessary for the creation and successful operation of a WQT scheme, as detailed in Table 11.5.[17]

Table 11.5 Conditions for successful water quality trading schemes

	Condition	Description
Necessary conditions	Presence of a regulator	There needs to be the presence of a regulator to set a cap on pollutants, monitor pollution, and verify the legitimacy of water quality credits that are created
	The ability of polluters to improve water quality	Polluters need to have the ability to create water quality improvements or reduce pollutant discharge through technology or management. Furthermore, regulators need to be able to verify these reductions are actual and likely to last

	Appropriate legal framework	WQT schemes require a legal environment that will uphold the rights of buyers and sellers. Some basics include: • A legal system that recognizes agreements must be kept • Legal remedies to enforce contract rights in cases of non-compliance with contract obligations • General respect for the rule of law
Enabling conditions	Effective regulator	The regulator must have the authority to set discharge limits to protect waterways and have the power to issue meaningful fines for non-compliance
	Demand for water quality credits	Demand is the first and foremost enabling condition for trading to take place. Demand is created by a strong regulatory or non-regulatory drive, such as creating goodwill with local communities
	Willingness to engage in trade	There needs to be willing buyers and sellers to engage in WQT schemes. This willingness is dependent on regulators understanding that while they can create markets, they can also destroy them due to regulatory uncertainty
	Trading across political and administrative boundaries	Many important watersheds extend across multiple states or international boundaries. When trading can only take place within a single state or country, it reduces the potential for trading and water quality improvements

Case 11.3 Maryland's Water Quality Trading Program

Maryland's WQT Program creates a public market for nitrogen, phosphorous, and sediment reductions. The voluntary programme is a collaborative effort between the Maryland Department of the Environment (MDE) and the Maryland Department of Agriculture to enhance the restoration and protection of the Chesapeake Bay and local waters by increasing the pace and reducing the costs of implementation efforts. Credits (where credit is defined as one pound pollutant reduction for one year) can be generated through the following process:

1. Meet baseline requirements for the applicant's sector (including stormwater and wastewater).
2. Implement a best management practice (BMP).
3. Demonstrate a load reduction below the established baseline.
4. Submit a Credit Certification and Registration Form to MDE.
5. MDE reviews the documentation and determines certification.
6. Certified credits are published on Maryland's Trading Registry to be purchased.

Table 11.6 Credit verification timelines for alternative best management practices

Best management practice	Credit duration
Impervious urban to pervious	5 years
Impervious urban to forest	5 years
Regenerative step pool storm conveyance	3 years
Urban stream restoration	3 years
Outfall stabilization	3 years
Shoreline management	3 years

Wastewater treatment plants can participate in the WQT Program if they use enhanced nutrient reduction treatment technology and purchase credits from outside of the wastewater sector. The credits are not valid or tradable until verified and placed on the Registry. The Credit Certification and Registration Form must include the identification of the location and segmentshed where the BMP is being implemented and a map identifying the location and boundaries of the BMP, documentation of ownership or permission from the landowner, a description of the BMP, how credits were calculated, and any other supporting documentation. The credits are verified annually through Discharge Monitoring Reports, as required by the facility's National Pollutant Discharge Elimination System.

Non-governmental organizations, such as private citizens, aggregators, etc., non-Municipal Separate Storm Sewer Systems, and any permittee who has fully met their permit restoration requirement can generate credits through the implementation of stormwater and alternative urban BMPs for the WQT Program. A practice can usually start generating credits as soon as installed. The BMP(s) need to be verified by a qualified person, with the number of stormwater point source and non-regulated source credits generated calculated using assessment tools, such as the Stormwater Credit Calculator. Verification of the stormwater practices lasts up to three years, with most alternative BMPs requiring annual verification, except for the practices listed in Table 11.6. Furthermore, a maintenance plan must be in place during the lifespan of credit, which can be transferred to the buyer.[18]

Urban Water Trading

In urban settings, hybrid water systems incorporate alternative water sources that supplement the mains water supply. Specifically, a range of alternative water sources, including rainwater and stormwater, groundwater, treated or untreated greywater, and treated blackwater, can be utilized in hybrid water systems. These systems can be used as a smart water grid to facilitate micro-trading, where households act as prosumers, producing and selling water within a peer-to-peer network. For example, a household could generate water through rainwater harvesting, putting water back on the grid by pumping it into the non-potable water infrastructure system for selling or purchasing water from neighbours with alternative water source systems installed. Micro-trading can generate multiple benefits, including lowering the volume of water requiring treatment and reducing energy use and emissions in treating water and wastewater. In the energy sector, micro-trading is well established, with households generating energy through photovoltaic cells, storing energy in batteries, and selling excess energy to other users through the existing power distribution infrastructure.[19,20]

Case 11.4 Rainwater Trading in China

China has traded rainwater for the first time involving two local private companies and the local government in Changsha, the provincial capital of Hunan. First, the Hunan Yuchuang Environmental Protection Engineering Company bought 20,000 cubic metres of rainwater collected by a local residential property management firm over the next three years at 0.7 yuan ($0.11) per cubic metre. Hunan Yuchuang Environmental Protection Engineering Company then sold 12,000 cubic metres of that rainwater to an urban landscaping company affiliated with the city government for 3.85 yuan ($0.60) per cubic metre for three years to replace the use of potable water for urban greenery and street cleaning. Despite this being a 450 per cent mark-up in the price paid by the government-affiliated company, 3.85 yuan per cubic metre is still 20 per cent cheaper than the local tap water. The rainwater is collected via equipment installed on residential buildings, with the rights belonging to the residential property management firm. Once the rainwater is purchased, it is disinfected and maintained by the purchaser.[21]

Stormwater Volume Credit Trading

Stormwater volume credit trading provides an offsite compliance option for developers and property owners subject to stormwater management regulations. For example, in many cities, regulations include onsite retention or detention requirements for new developments and redevelopment projects above a specific size. A credit trading programme enables these developers or property owners to meet a portion of their requirements offsite by buying volume-based stormwater credits. The credits are generated from installing and maintaining blue-green infrastructure (BGI) located offsite. Credits can be generated by:

1. Property owners or third parties voluntarily implementing BGI retrofits on properties not subject to post-construction stormwater management requirements.
2. Developers and property owners who are subject to post-construction stormwater management requirements building BGI projects that exceed minimum stormwater requirements.

A stormwater volume credit trading programme requires a local entity to oversee and manage the trading marketplace and ensure that the BGI projects behind the credits are properly maintained over time. The entity could be either a city stormwater agency or an independent entity created or retained as a programme administrator. Stormwater volume credit trading programmes provide a range of benefits for participants, including:

- *Flexibility*: Post-construction stormwater trading provides flexibility for property owners and developers subject to post-construction stormwater management requirements. They can buy credits from an offsite provider when it is cheaper/easier than managing stormwater onsite.
- *Community acceptance*: Stormwater volume credit trading programmes do not involve adopting a new stormwater fee or tax. Instead, trading can provide an optional pathway for developers and property owners to achieve regulatory compliance.
- *Improved water quality and stormwater control*: A trading programme can improve overall water quality/stormwater control compared to standards that require developers to manage stormwater onsite. Communities can capture more volume over time through multiple BGI practices with a smaller capacity than one BGI practice with a larger capacity due to most storms generating a small amount of runoff. Municipalities can also incentivize credit generation in areas that will generate the most benefits, rather than gaining additional stormwater control when new development/redevelopment happens to occur.

Designing Successful Stormwater Volume Credit Trading Programmes

A range of design elements need considering to ensure stormwater volume credit trading programmes are successful:

- *Trading boundaries*: The credit trading programme should not result in adverse water quality impacts relative to a baseline condition. Trading boundaries covering a large geographic area can increase the risk of localized flooding, erosion, or water quality impacts, particularly when the programme allows trades outside of the local sewershed. Watershed boundaries used in credit trading should be defined to match local conditions. Furthermore, it is recommended that offsite compliance should occur in the same watershed.
- *Flexibility in meeting regulatory requirements*: Conditions that allow property owners to meet a portion of their stormwater management requirements offsite should not be overly restrictive. A more flexible programme can increase the size of the stormwater credit trading market.
- *In-lieu fee programme*: An in-lieu fee programme allows developers to pay a fee to the local municipality when it is not feasible to implement stormwater controls onsite. The municipality uses the revenue collected to build stormwater control projects that offset landowners' requirements. The programme allows city agencies to aggregate projects to install BGI in the public right-of-way or other public property. Also, an in-lieu fee can be used to set the price ceiling for a credit trading programme: if it is cheaper for developers to purchase credits from the market than to pay the in-lieu fee, then the in-lieu fee will serve as the price ceiling.
- *Credit currency and duration*: A stormwater credit trading programme is a market where property owners buy and sell volume-based stormwater credits. Each credit is based on a unit of BGI capacity, or volume managed. As such, each credit reflects a volume based on the design capacity of the credit-generating BGI. Credits should be measured in gallons, litres, or cubic feet. Another design consideration is related to the period over which credits are valid. The first option is to set a short 'lifespan' for credits. After several years, credit-generators could re-certify their credits by passing a municipality inspection and applying for recertification. Alternatively, the programme could require credit generators to sell credits for a much more extended period (for example, 30–50 years) or for the life of the development to which they are selling the credits.
- *Design guidelines, maintenance obligations, and credit certification*: Guidelines should be developed to ensure that BGI construction, post-construction certification, and ongoing maintenance meet the city's design standards. These provisions ensure that the voluntary BGI built on the private property meet the city's regulatory requirements.

The design and construction guidelines can take the form of a manual explaining which BGI systems are eligible for accreditation and how they should be built and maintained. During the lifetime of a credit, owners should commit to maintaining the BGI and allow site inspections to confirm BGI functionality. Certification usually includes a methodology to process BGI credit applications to ensure that the projects meet design, construction, and maintenance standards before the credits can be sold.

- *Community engagement*: The process of designing and developing a stormwater volume credit trading programme that the public supports is crucial to its success. Municipalities should invite local stakeholders, such as local businesses, trade groups, advisory groups, residents, and community and environmental organizations, to participate in developing and implementing the programme. Community acceptance can be enhanced through a comprehensive outreach and marketing plan to increase the likelihood of success, develop partnerships, and ensure a smooth transition to the programme.[22,23,24]

Case 11.5 Washington DC's Stormwater Retention Credit Trading Program

Washington, DC's Department of Energy and Environment (DOEE) runs the Stormwater Retention Credit (SRC) Trading Program, enabling property owners and developers to earn revenue for projects that reduce stormwater runoff by installing green infrastructure or removing impervious surfaces. The SRC Price Lock Program enables SRC generators to sell SRCs to DOEE at fixed prices, creating a price floor in the SRC market and offering certainty about the revenue from an SRC-generating project. If participants sell to another buyer, DOEE also pays a portion of the purchase price (the fixed price of the SRC Price Lock Program) on behalf of the buyer. Furthermore, DOEE offers SRC Aggregator Startup Grants of up to $75,000 to support SRC-generating businesses. The grant can be used to evaluate sites for the feasibility of green infrastructure retrofits. In addition, the funds can be used to support technical and outreach work to identify and aggregate SRCs from green infrastructure projects in the Municipal Separate Storm Sewer System, typically across multiple sites. Through the technical and outreach work funded by the grant, businesses can identify a pool of suitable projects to generate SRCs and participate in the SRC Price Lock Program. Overall, it is expected that the SRC Price Lock Program and the SRC Aggregator Startup Grants will make it easier to generate SRCs on land owned by non-profits, such as churches, cemeteries, schools, and similar institutions with DOEE prioritizing funding for these projects.[25]

Groundwater Trading

Groundwater resources are an important water source for agricultural irrigation and urban users. Nonetheless, there is often little control or planning involved with its management resulting in frequent overuse. Over-abstraction of groundwater is associated with various negative externalities, including water drawdown and groundwater depletion; reduced dilution and assimilation of contaminants; increased salinity; pollution; seawater intrusion in coastal aquifers; and land subsidence effects. There are also environmental costs of over-abstraction of groundwater, including drying wetlands and springs, streamflow reduction and declining lake levels, and the loss of vegetation and groundwater-dependent ecosystems.[26,27,28,29]

Groundwater Trading Structures

Groundwater trading does not usually involve the physical exchange of water itself. Instead, it is the right to extract water that is exchanged. An effective groundwater trading scheme that addresses economic and environmental impacts of over-abstraction requires the following, while Table 11.7 details the various groundwater trading structures available:

- That water use be capped or limited, therefore, imposing the need to trade.
- That usage volumes are measured.
- That there are secure and tradable water use entitlements.
- That third-party effects be managed.[30,31]

Ensuring Success of Groundwater Trading Schemes

Groundwater trading schemes should be designed and managed with sensitivity to hydrological conditions and our evolving understanding and knowledge of these conditions. Successful groundwater trading schemes need to:

- *Establish boundaries*: The boundaries of the aquifer system at the ground-surface level need to be defined. Without an understanding of these boundaries, water managers will not know which users' groundwater extraction is drawing from the same resource, and therefore which users should be subject to the same cap on resource use and should

Table 11.7 Groundwater trading structures

Trading Structure	Description	Administrator	Participant Costs
Bilateral contracts	• The most common form of water transaction worldwide • No form of trading mechanism exists • Participants mainly learn of one another through word of mouth	None (informal and decentralized)	• No third-party fees • High search and transaction costs
Brokerage	Representation of a buyer or seller in a water rights transaction	Private sector	Brokerage fee
Bulletin boards	A physical or electronic board where interested parties can list information about their water rights for others to get in contact with them	Private sector, regulatory agencies	• No third-party fees • Moderate search and transaction costs
Auction and reverse auction	A physical or electronic system where buyers outbid one another (auction) or sellers undercut one another (reverse auction) to trade water	Private sector, regulatory agencies	Auction fees if privately run
Electronic clearinghouse	Leverages the power of computer optimization and a tailor-made algorithm to match participants within the trading rules and by price points	Private sector, regulatory agencies	Trading fee, if privately run

have shares in a given consumptive pool (the quantity of water from a specified resource that can be made available for consumptive use).

• *Determine sustainable yield*: The overall volume of permitted water use needs determining. The size of the consumptive pool in terms of the volume of water available is usually based on some estimate of the annual sustainable yield of a system. One approach is to define the consumptive pool as the available net recharge of the aquifer. This could be the gross recharge, less outflow to the ocean or leakage to other aquifers, with a volumetric allocation reserved for environmental needs. The sustainable yield may have to be calculated annually to consider previous rainfall recharge and water level responses. Development of the consumptive pool model using sustainable yield leads to a range of hydrological information and monitoring requirements, including:

○ Knowledge of the hydrogeology of the groundwater system and the interconnectedness of aquifers.
○ Knowledge of the water balance to allow an estimate of net recharge, sustainable yield, and consumptive pool volumes.
○ An understanding of the third-party impacts of abstraction levels and the likely spatial relationships between impacts and points of extraction.

• *Set trading limits*: One method for limiting the impacts of concentration of use is to limit the water available for trade as a proportion of the total water extracted within a management area over a given period. Limiting tradable water would restrict the potential scale of associated impacts. Another option is to use concentration limits according to location. Trading rules could limit the potential for concentration of use at specific distances from a sensitive area. Also, localized allocation limits could be developed if there is limited information on whether recharge is evenly distributed across a large system or on how quickly that recharge and the sub-surface flow will equalize impacts from pumping.[32]

Case 11.6 Fox Canyon Water Market Reducing Groundwater Pumping

Ventura County, California, generates around $2.1 billion from agriculture. It also faces population pressure, with nearly 450 people per square mile, which is about five times the average population density of the United States. Both agriculture and infrastructure are dependent on the availability of water, resulting in rapidly diminishing groundwater reserves in California. In 2014, the state passed the Sustainable Groundwater Management Act (SGMA) to ensure the future sustainability of groundwater supplies. Following the passage of SGMA, The Nature Conservancy (TNC) applied for and received a $1.8 million Conservation Innovation Grant from the US Department of Agriculture's Natural Resources Conservation Service to develop the Fox Canyon Water Market. The grant helped TNC provide support for Fox Canyon Groundwater Management Agency and project partner California Lutheran University in their effort to establish a market-driven and producer-led approach to reducing groundwater pumping. Under this cap-and-trade type system, agricultural producers in the Fox Canyon area are subject to fixed groundwater allocations based on historical use. Producers can purchase additional allocations or sell any unused allocation. The market is online, anonymous, and uses an algorithm-driven matching platform, creating a level playing field and a fairer deal for farming operations of all sizes. In March 2020, the market exchange opened, and while it is still in a pilot phase, the market has already had 58-acre feet of pumping allocations change hands.[33]

Environmental Water Buyback

In many river basins, environmental flows have been severely affected by increased water extraction for irrigation, industry, and domestic use. In response, water managers are implementing strategies to acquire water for the environment, including purchasing water rights from water-intensive sectors, particularly agriculture, and reallocating this to the environment to restore environmental flows.[34]

Case 11.7 Instream Buybacks in Colorado

Instream Buybacks are the purchase of water rights to leave the water instream to restore natural flows and supply. Colorado has established instream flow rights on over 8,500 miles of stream and 486 natural lakes. The instream flow rights and natural lake rights provide legal protection for the natural environment through a reach of stream, not just at a bypass point. The instream water rights protect riparian zones, wildlife habitats, and fisheries. The Colorado Water Conservation Board (CWCB) can acquire water, water rights, or interests in water to preserve or improve the natural environment. Its Water Acquisitions Program is a voluntary programme that allows owners of water rights to donate, sell, lease, or loan existing decreed water rights to the CWCB on a permanent or temporary basis. Some examples of projects include the following:

- TNC has made several donations to the CWCB over the years, including a 300 cubic feet per second senior water right to protect flows through 29 miles of Gunnison River.
- The City of Boulder donated senior water rights to the CWCB to maintain instream flows in Boulder Creek through the city.
- The Colorado Water Trust, a private non-profit conservation group, purchased and conveyed a water right to the CWCB to preserve and improve the natural environment of Boulder Creek and the Blue River.[35,36]

Notes

1. Öko-Institut e.V., 'Tradable Permit Schemes in Environmental Management: Evolution Patterns of an Expanding Policy Instrument' (2008). https://www.oeko.de/oekodoc/977/2008-317-en.pdf.
2. R.C. Brears, *Water Resources Management: Innovative and Green Solutions* (De Gruyter, 2021).
3. Öko-Institut e.V., 'Tradable Permit Schemes in Environmental Management: Evolution Patterns of an Expanding Policy Instrument'.
4. Öko-Institut e.V., 'Tradable Permit Schemes in Environmental Management: Evolution Patterns of an Expanding Policy Instrument'.
5. OECD, 'Domestic Transferable Permits for Environmental Management: Design and Implementation' (2001). https://www.oecd-ilibrary.org/environment/domestic-transferable-permits-for-environmental-management_9789264192638-en.
6. Paul Holden and Mateen Thobani, 'Tradable Water Rights: A Property Rights Approach to Improving Water Use and Promoting Investment', *Cuadernos de Economía* 32, no. 97 (1995), http://www.jstor.org/stable/41951282.
7. FAO, 'Modern Water Rights: Theory and Practice' (2006). http://www.fao.org/3/a-a0864e.pdf.
8. World Bank, 'Tradable Water Rights: A Property Rights Approach to Resolving Water Shortages and Promoting Investment' (1996). https://documents1.worldbank.org/curated/en/941411468761706580/pdf/multi-page.pdf.
9. Holden and Thobani, 'Tradable Water Rights: A Property Rights Approach to Improving Water Use and Promoting Investment'.
10. Simone Borghesi, 'Water Tradable Permits: A Review of Theoretical and Case Studies', *Journal of Environmental Planning and Management* 57, no. 9 (2014/09/02 2014), https://doi.org/10.1080/09640568.2013.820175, https://doi.org/10.1080/09640568.2013.820175.
11. Western Governors' Association, 'Water Transfers in the West: Projects, Trends, and Leading Practices in Voluntary Water Trading' (2012). http://www.westernstateswater.org/wp-content/uploads/2012/12/Water_Transfers_in_the_West_2012.pdf.
12. 'Water Trade Pilot Launches', 2022, accessed 6 January 2022, https://www.wheatleysolutions.co.uk/2020/12/01/water-catchment-data-hub-for-sharing-and-brokering-water-ready-to-pilot-in-the-east-anglia/.
13. 'Water Markets and Trade', 2022, accessed 6 January 2022, https://www.mdba.gov.au/water-management/managing-water/water-markets-trade.
14. Öko-Institut e.V., 'Tradable Permit Schemes in Environmental Management: Evolution Patterns of an Expanding Policy Instrument'.
15. Minnesota Pollution Control Agency, 'Water Quality Trading Guidance', (2021). https://www.pca.state.mn.us/sites/default/files/wq-gen1-15.pdf.
16. Motu Economic and Public Policy Research, 'Trading Efficiency in Water Quality Trading Markets: An Assessment of Trade-Offs' (2011). https://www.motu.nz/our-research/environment-and-resources/nutrient-trading-and-water-quality/trading-efficiency-in-water-quality-trading-markets-an-assessment-of-trade-offs/.
17. Pacific Institute, 'Incentive-Based Instruments for Water Management' (2015). https://pacinst.org/wp-content/uploads/2016/02/issuelab_23697.pdf

18. 'Water Quality Trading Program Home', 2022, accessed 6 January 2022, https://mde.maryland.gov/programs/Water/WQT/Pages/index.aspx.

19. Mario Schmack et al., 'Urban Water Trading—Hybrid Water Systems and Niche Opportunities in the Urban Water Market—a literature review', *Environmental Technology Reviews* 8, no. 1 (2019/01/01 2019), https://doi.org/10.1080/21622515.2019.1647292, https://doi.org/10.1080/21622515.2019.1647292.

20. Elizabeth Ramsey et al., 'A Smart Water Grid for Micro-Trading Rainwater: Hydraulic Feasibility Analysis', *Water* 12, no. 11 (2020), https://doi.org/10.3390/w12113075.

21. 'China Trades Rainwater for First Time, But Analysts Say Unstable Trading System Is Far from Being Market-Driven', 2020, accessed 6 January 2022, https://www.scmp.com/economy/china-economy/article/3114375/china-trades-rainwater-first-time-analysts-say-unstable.

22. American Rivers, ed., *Stormwater Currency: Establishing a Stormwater Volume Credit Trading Program* (2019). Accessed at https://www.americanrivers.org/wp-content/uploads/2019/09/AR_StormwaterVolumeCreditTrading_Final.pdf

23. NRDC, 'How to: Stormwater Credit Trading Programs' (2018). https://www.nrdc.org/sites/default/files/stormwater-credit-trading-programs-ib.pdf.

24. US EPA, 'Off-Site Stormwater Crediting: Lessons from Wetland Mitigation' (2018). https://www.epa.gov/sites/default/files/2018-10/documents/off-site_stormwater_crediting_lessons_from_wetland_mitigation-2018-04.pdf.

25. 'Stormwater Retention Credit Trading Program', 2020, accessed 5 May 2020, https://doee.dc.gov/src.

26. Amanda Palazzo and Nicholas Brozović, 'The Role of Groundwater Trading in spatial water management', 145 (2014), https://doi.org/10.1016/j.agwat.2014.03.004, https://dx.doi.org/10.1016/j.agwat.2014.03.004.

27. Sarah Ann Wheeler, Karina Schoengold, and Henning Bjornlund, 'Lessons to Be Learned from Groundwater Trading in Australia and the United States' (Springer International Publishing, 2016).

28. Tamara Boyd and John Brumley, 'Groundwater Trading in Australia: A Preliminary Analysis and Research Agenda', *Australasian Journal of Water Resources* 7, no. 1 (2003/01/01 2003), https://doi.org/10.1080/13241583.2003.11465229, https://doi.org/10.1080/13241583.2003.11465229.

29. James H. Skurray, E. J. Roberts, and David J. Pannell, 'Hydrological Challenges to Groundwater Trading: Lessons from South-West Western Australia', *Journal of Hydrology* 412 (2012), https://doi.org/10.1016/j.jhydrol.2011.05.034.

30. Skurray, Roberts, and Pannell, 'Hydrological Challenges to Groundwater Trading: Lessons from South-West Western Australia.'

31. Environmental Defense Fund, 'Groundwater Trading as a Tool for Implementing California's Sustainable Groundwater Management Act' (2017). https://www.edf.org/sites/default/files/documents/water-markets.pdf.

32. Skurray, Roberts, and Pannell, 'Hydrological challenges to Groundwater Trading: Lessons from South-West Western Australia.'

33. 'The Fox Canyon Water Market: A Market-Based Tool for Groundwater Conservation Goes Live', 2021, accessed 6 January 2022, https://www.usda.gov/media/blog/2020/05/08/fox-canyon-water-market-market-based-tool-groundwater-conservation-goes-live.

34. M. S. Iftekhar, J. G. Tisdell, and J. D. Connor, 'Effects of Competition on Environmental Water Buyback Auctions', *Agricultural Water Management* 127 (2013/09/01/ 2013), https://doi.org/https://doi.org/10.1016/j.agwat.2013.05.015,   https://www.sciencedirect.com/science/article/pii/S0378377413001340.

35. Delaware Riverkeeper Network, 'Values of Large Scale Watershed Protection' (2021). https://delawareriverkeeper.org/sites/default/files/Large%20Scale%20Watershed%20Protection%20Infographic.pdf.

36. 'Instream Flow Water Acquisitions', 2021, accessed 9 December 2021, https://cwcb.colorado.gov/instream-flow-water-acquisitions.

12
Best Practices and Conclusion

Introduction

From the case studies of locations of differing climates, lifestyles, and income levels applying a range of innovative financial instruments and approaches to achieve water security and green growth, a range of best practices have been identified for other regions aiming to create climate-resilient water supplies, reduce water–energy–food nexus pressures, encourage water conservation and efficiency, increase water reliability, decrease the costs and pollution associated with wastewater disposal, utilize natural processes to improve water quality, manage water quantity by restoring the hydrologic function of the landscape, and improve overall water governance.

Green Bonds and Green Loans

In the context of water security and green growth, green bonds can be issued to construct grey infrastructure, green infrastructure, and hybrid infrastructure. Environmental impact bonds (EIBs) are typically used for green infrastructure projects such as stream and floodplain restoration, stormwater planters in right-of-ways, and constructed wetlands. Green loans are any loan instrument made available to exclusively finance or refinance, in whole or part, new and/or existing eligible green projects, including projects that focus on sustainable water resources management. From the case studies of locations applying green bonds, EIBs, and green loans to implement and mainstream water security and green growth projects, a variety of best practices have been identified for other locations.

Green Bonds Funding Green Infrastructure Projects

Green bonds can be leveraged with zero-interest loans to fund green infrastructure projects and upgrade sewer systems and drinking water treatment

Financing Water Security and Green Growth. Robert C. Brears, Oxford University Press. © Robert C. Brears (2023).
DOI: 10.1093/oso/9780192847843.003.0012

and distribution systems, creating direct construction jobs. For instance, green bonds can be used to:

- Reduce combined sewer overflows by installing green infrastructure and increasing wet weather treatment capacity
- Construct advanced wastewater treatment facilities
- Upgrade sewage treatment plants to generate biogas to meet treatment facility power needs

Green Bonds Used to Meet Water Utility Environmental Objectives

Water utilities can use green bonds to meet various environmental objectives, in addition to pollution prevention and control, such as using the proceeds for climate change mitigation and adaptation, natural resource conservation, and biodiversity conservation projects.

Multilateral Agencies Using Green Bonds to Meet Priorities

Multilateral agencies can utilize green bonds to promote their priorities in climate change mitigation, climate and disaster resilience, and environmental sustainability, including water infrastructure and services projects. They can also invest in green bonds issued by water utilities to upgrade water supply and sanitation and implement renewable energy projects.

Environmental Impact Bonds Financing Green Infrastructure

EIBs can be publicly issued by city agencies and water utilities to finance green infrastructure in areas of cities frequently impacted by polluted stormwater runoff and flooding. The EIB can implement green stormwater infrastructure to mitigate localized flooding while generating multiple co-benefits, including improving stream health, providing access to green space, improving air quality, providing public environmental education, restoring native habitat, and creating green jobs. The EIB's performance structure can be based on the volume of stormwater captured or detained, as volume:

- Is a simple metric that can be applied to and aggregated across all project types and geography.

- Reflects both flood reduction and water quality improvement.
- Is easy for investors to understand.
- Allows consistent prediction and measurement of results.

Commercial Green Loans for Green Initiatives

Commercial banks can launch green loan programmes that reward cus-tomers with a special low rate when they borrow for a green initiative, such as installing rainwater tanks, greywater treatment systems, solar hot water systems, or purchasing water-efficient goods and appliances.

Government Green Loan Guarantees

Government agencies can provide loan guarantee programmes to help pri-vate lenders provide affordable financing to qualified borrowers to improve access to clean, reliable water for households and businesses in rural areas. Lenders could be state or national government savings or loan agencies, farm credit banks, or credit unions, while eligible borrowers could be public bodies or non-profit organizations.

Green Loans Supporting Production of Water Technologies

Governments can develop green technology financing schemes to support the uptake of green technologies. For example, the government agency in charge can provide soft loans to participating financial institutions who then offer green loans to finance the production of and investments in green tech-nology, such as advanced water treatment technology, leakage monitoring and minimization, recycling and reuse of water, and efficient water treatment plants.

Debt-for-Nature Swaps

Many developing countries have large international (public sector) debts and debt servicing absorbs a significant proportion of total budget expen-diture. The large scale of the debt contributes significantly to environ-mental degradation and the deterioration of the natural resource base. Furthermore, post-COVID-19 economic recovery costs could deplete the financial resources needed to address environmental degradation. As such, debt-for-nature (DFN) swaps can ensure that economic recovery benefits the environment and its ecosystems. From the case study of a location applying a DFN swap to implement and mainstream water security and green growth projects, a variety of best practices have been identified for other locations.

Encouraging Farmers to Protect Water Resources

DFN swap projects can encourage farmers to implement rotational grazing to improve productivity and promote the conservation of biodiversity and forest connectivity in protected wild areas, including the protection of water resources and implementation of conservation practices for water and wetlands in common and fragile ecosystems.

Raising Awareness of Environmental Issues

DFN swap projects can raise awareness and create knowledge, change attitudes, and develop skills in teachers and school children on environmental issues with a special focus on watersheds, biological corridors, protection of forest ecosystems, and conservation of hunted species.

Developing Environmental Workshops for Children

DFN swap projects can develop environmental workshops for school children, involving planting native trees in the schools, cleaning rivers and communities, and eco-tours. Schools can promote outstanding students for their commitment to the environment. Furthermore, free education platforms that contain lessons and interactive environmental education tools linked to basic subjects can be developed.

Developing Indicators to Monitor Freshwater Ecosystems

DFN swap projects can develop indicators and monitoring protocols to measure the 'state of the health' of ecosystems and freshwater populations at the level of the system of protected wildlife areas and, on that basis, to make management decisions.

Constructing Decentralized Wastewater Treatment Systems

DFN swap projects can design and construct decentralized wastewater treatment plants powered by solar photovoltaic systems.

Payments for Watershed Services

Payments for Ecosystem Services schemes are a transparent system for the provision of ecosystem services through conditional payments to voluntary providers. In the context of water resources management, Payments for Watershed Services (PWS) schemes are an instrument for watershed protection and management and have been implemented in both developing and developed countries at different scales worldwide. From the case studies of locations applying PWS to implement and mainstream water security and green growth projects, various best practices have been identified for other locations.

Water Utility-Operated Payments for Watershed Services Schemes

Water utilities can create and operate online PWS markets for nature-based solutions that aim for nutrient neutrality, biodiversity net gain, net-zero carbon, and flood risk management. The use of online trading platforms:

- *Optimizes investments*: The online trading platform can optimize investments and delivery for any environmental improvement measure, such as carbon offsetting, catchment nutrient balancing, nutrient/nitrogen neutrality, source protection, net biodiversity gain, and increasing landscape connectivity and permeability.
- *Encourages the development of new markets*: Online trading platforms can enable an organization, either public or private, to create a marketplace for environmental improvement measures, for example, the planting of cover crops to offset nutrient runoff. The online trading platform could then work with the applicant to define a set of outcomes, a plan to achieve them, and the measurement methodologies required to verify them. Following this, farmers could submit prices for delivering some or all of the measures, with the online trading platform taking payment for the project and holding it in escrow until all the work by the farmers is completed.

- *Utilizes technologies to verify credits*: Online trading platforms can utilize a range of technologies to verify that work has been carried out. For example:

  1. Water utilities could operate an online trading platform for PWS in river catchments to encourage farmers to create projects on-farm to improve water quality and biodiversity.
  2. Buyers, including private companies, public bodies, and private investors, could offer payment to farmers to create nature-based projects that generate a known quantity of environmental benefits or credits.
  3. The credits generated could be verified through remote sensing via satellite

Market-based Instruments

Over the past several decades, market-based instruments (MBIs) have become the preferred environmental policy tool for influencing environmental outcomes for a range of reasons. Those include a new orientation towards markets and deregulation in public policy, an increasing recognition of the limitations of government in general, and of traditional command and control systems of environmental regulation in particular, an increasing concern that regulations may not adequately cope with emerging environmental problems, and a desire to further implement the polluter pays principle and to internalize environmental costs into the prices of goods and services. From the case studies of locations applying MBIs to implement and mainstream water security and green growth projects, various best practices have been identified for other locations.

Pesticide Taxes to Reduce Water Pollution

Pesticide taxes can be implemented to protect well fields. The tax can be a quantity-based tax differentiated according to health and environmental criteria. Therefore, the higher the toxicity, the higher the tax on the individual products. The tax can also provide information about the individual pesticide's human health risks, their toxicity towards non-target organisms, and risk to groundwater.

Water Pricing Based on Full Cost Recovery

Water utilities can set prices that recover the full costs of providing water and wastewater-related services, with water charges covering the supply, treatment, and transfer of water, the collection, treatment, reuse, and disposal of wastewater, maintenance of the water and wastewater distribution system, community water conservation programmes, and environmental contributions.

Volumetric Water Charges for Irrigation Systems

Irrigation water managers can establish volumetric charges based on acre-feet of water delivered. Water usage can be determined by the flow rate multiplied by the duration of the water run. Flow rate can be determined based on predetermined capacities of gates, laterals, and turnouts throughout the distribution system.

Stormwater Fees to Improve Stormwater Quality

City agencies can use stormwater fees to provide a sustainable, dedicated revenue source for maintaining, operating, and improving the stormwater management system, including installing green infrastructure practices to improve stormwater quality. The stormwater fee can be based on the impervious area on a property. Single-family properties can be charged different rates depending on the property's impervious surface area, while non-single-family properties can be billed based on an Equivalent Residential Unit, which can be set at the size of the impervious surface area of the median-sized house in the city: the larger the impervious surface area of the parcel, the higher the stormwater fee for the property.

Tax Deductions for Investments in Water Technologies

Governments can provide tax deductions for companies that invest in various environmental technologies, including rainwater harvesting systems, industrial water-saving technologies, utilizing of wastewater or process water from a nearby company for a company's process, recovery of resources from wastewater, removal plants for micropollutants in water, and underground water storage systems, among others.

Subsidies for Agricultural Best Management Practices

Government agencies can provide subsidies to farmers to implement best management practices (BMPs), including riparian grazing management, improving drainage, and planting permanent foliage, to improve water quality and biodiversity and reduce greenhouse gas emissions.

Grants for Water Quality Improvement Projects

Government agencies can provide grants for green infrastructure projects that prevent, eliminate, or reduce water quality impairments by decreasing stormwater runoff into waterways. Applicants can be encouraged to develop multiple BMPs, such as bioinfiltration, wetland creation, floodplain reconnection, and rainwater harvesting, within the same watershed to increase their effectiveness and efficiency, with eligible projects including:

- Reconnecting streams with their floodplains.
- Treating and controlling stormwater runoff at sites that impact nearby waterways.
- Treating and controlling water generated from impervious surfaces associated with urban development.

Greywater Rebates for Retrofits or New Homes

Water utilities can offer greywater rebates to existing homes and new developments to encourage the uptake of greywater systems that collect wastewater from hand washing sinks, showers, bathtubs, and clothes washing machines for irrigation of landscape plants, fruit trees, and lawns.

Stormwater Credits for Implementing Best Management Practices

Water utilities can offer industrial, commercial, institutional, and multi-residential properties credits on their stormwater bill if they implement a range of BMPs, including installing infiltration galleries, permeable pavement, rainwater cisterns, constructed wetlands, rain gardens, and green roofs, among others.

Discounted Water Rates for Commercial Customers with Water Conservation Plans

Water utilities can offer commercial customers a discounted water rate if they submit a comprehensive water conservation plan. Furthermore, water utilities can offer free water audits to commercial customers and reward participants that implement permanent water-saving measures with a one-time rebate, with the amount dependent on the water saved.

Public–Private Partnerships

Public–private partnerships (PPPs) are long-term integrated contracts that provide water services, including water and wastewater treatment plants and green infrastructure, to achieve water security and green growth. Both developed and developing countries have utilized PPPs for many reasons, including expanding the range of service providers beyond traditional public sector monopolies, providing infrastructure and associated services more efficiently, providing cost-effective infrastructure, and driving local economic growth. From the case studies of locations applying PPPs to implement and mainstream water security and green growth projects, various best practices have been identified for other locations.

Public–Private Partnerships for Traditional Water Infrastructure

Water utilities can develop PPPs for water transmission pipeline projects based on a build, own, operate, and transfer basis. The project company, formed by the developer, can provide the entire water transmission capacity to the water utility under a water transmission agreement. PPPs can also be used to develop strategic water storage facilities.

Public–Private Partnerships for Commercial Irrigation Projects

PPPs can be utilized for commercial irrigation infrastructure projects. The private partner could operate, manage, and develop the infrastructure. In addition, the private partner could be remunerated for the sale of water (through user tariffs) and receive a capacity payment by the government.

Community-based Public–Private Partnerships

Community-based public–private partnerships (CBP3s) can be utilized to plan, finance, build, and maintain green stormwater infrastructure (GSI) to address significant pollution and flooding issues, while improving neighbourhood quality of life, assisting small, minority-owned businesses, driving economic growth, and making cost savings to water and other public and private capital improvement efforts. In addition, the CBP3 can enable locations to become regional hubs for the stormwater industry sector. By being a 'living lab' of GSI applications and large-scale infrastructure investments, other communities in the region are likely to seek the location's companies and professionals for their own GSI and integrated infrastructure re-development programmes.

Biodiversity Offsets

Infrastructure development results in biodiversity loss due to loss and fragmentation of species' habitats and land use and land cover changes. Biodiversity loss is an environmental challenge of global concern as biodiversity, and associated ecosystems provide a range of invaluable services to society that underpins human health and well-being, security, and economic growth. These services include clean water and flood protection. During the past decade, there has been a growing interest in biodiversity offsetting as a policy instrument for financing biodiversity conservation. From the case studies of locations applying biodiversity offsets to implement and mainstream water security and green growth projects, various best practices have been identified for other locations.

Biodiversity Offset Banks for Developers

City agencies can develop biodiversity offset bank programmes to allow developers to purchase credits to offset the environmental impacts of their developments on waterways. The programme could calculate how many credits a developer needs to purchase to meet their offset requirement. The programme could then contribute the income towards funding ecological enhancement projects around the city. Furthermore, landowners could suggest to the programme sites on their properties for potential projects.

Biodiversity Offsets for Renewable Energy Projects Impacting Water

Government agencies could develop biodiversity offset schemes to account for the residual impacts of renewable energy on lands with significant biodiversity. This enables the mainstreaming of biodiversity into the planning process by seeking biodiversity benefits at the landscape scale while benefiting ecosystem services, including flood protection, water quality, carbon storage, and recreation.

Wetland Mitigation Project Options

With wetlands providing many ecosystem services, including flood control, water quality, fish and wildlife habitat, and water for rivers and streams, laws can be put into place that requires mitigation for projects that impact wetlands, with three options available to satisfy compensatory mitigation requirements:

- *Wetland mitigation banking*: A wetland permit applicant could purchase credits from an approved and open mitigation bank.
- *In-lieu fee programme*: A wetland permit applicant could purchase credits from a government agency that sells wetland credits to permittees needing to offset authorized wetland impacts.
- *Permittee responsible mitigation*: If no mitigation credits are available for purchase or if preferred, a permit applicant could satisfy mitigation requirements through the completion of a wetland mitigation project.

Tradable Permits

Tradable permit schemes are efficient for allocating water resources and for mitigating the pollution of water resources. From the case studies of locations applying tradable permits to implement and mainstream water security and green growth projects, various best practices have been identified for other locations.

Water Trading in Catchment Areas

Water trading platforms can be established for individual water catchment areas. The platform could allow the communication necessary to broker and track the trade or sharing of water between water abstraction licence holders and others interested in an alternative water source. In addition, the platform could enable users to advertise their need for water or the availability of surplus water, using a map to show geographic proximity and through automated alerts to other users of new activity relevant to them.

Water Trading in Transboundary River Basins

Water trading in river basins can be established to enable water rights to be bought and sold, either permanently (trade of water entitlements) or temporarily (for example, the annual trade of water allocations). The water could be traded on markets, within catchments, between catchments, or along river systems. If the river basin crosses political boundaries, governments could be responsible for managing water markets, with each government having its process and rules for allocating water. Water trading allows water holders to decide whether they need to buy or sell water at a particular time.

Water Quality Trading Programmes to Reduce Water Pollution

Water Quality Trading (WQT) programmes can be created to reduce nitrogen, phosphorous, and sediment pollution of waterways. Credits could be generated through the following process:

1. The applicant could meet a set of baseline requirements for their particular sector, implement a BMP and demonstrate a load reduction below an established baseline, and then submit a credit certification application to the government agency in charge of the WQT programme.
2. The government agency would then review the documentation and determine certification. The certified credits would then be published on the WQT programme's trading registry for purchase.
3. Credits could be purchased by wastewater treatment plants that already use nutrient reduction treatment technology.

Generating Stormwater Credits for Water Quality Trading Programmes

WQT programmes could allow, for example, non-governmental organizations and companies to generate credits through the implementation of stormwater and alternative urban BMPs. A project could start generating credits as soon as installed, with the number of credits generated calculated using assessment tools. A maintenance plan should be in place during the lifespan of credit.

Urban Rainwater Trading Schemes

Urban water trading systems can be established that allow for rainwater trading. Rainwater could be collected via equipment installed on residential buildings, with the rights belonging to the residential property owner. The collected water could be sold to companies for various non-potable uses, such as irrigation and street cleaning, with the purchaser responsible for disinfecting and maintaining it.

Stormwater Credit Trading

Stormwater credit trading programmes enable developers or property owners to meet a portion of their stormwater management requirements offsite by buying volume-based stormwater credits from property owners and developers who install green infrastructure or remove impervious surfaces. City agencies can incorporate a price lock programme that creates a price floor in the stormwater credit trading market and offers certainty about the revenue from a stormwater credit-generating project. In addition, grants can be disbursed to support stormwater credit-generating businesses, with the grant used for the businesses to evaluate sites for the feasibility of green infrastructure retrofits. Overall, the price lock programme and grants can make it easier to generate stormwater credits on land owned by non-profits, such as churches, schools, and similar institutions.

Groundwater Trading Programmes

Under a cap-and-trade groundwater trading programme, agricultural producers could be subject to fixed groundwater allocations based on historical use. Producers could then purchase additional allocations or sell their unused allocation. The market could be online, anonymous, and use an algorithm-driven matching platform, creating a level playing field and a fairer deal for farming operations of all sizes.

Purchasing of Water Rights to Protect Environmental Flows

Government agencies could acquire water, water rights, or interests in water to preserve or improve the natural environment. For example, a voluntary water acquisitions programme could be established by a government agency where water rights owners donate, sell, lease, or loan existing decreed water rights to the programme on a permanent or temporary basis to protect riparian zones, wildlife habitat, and fisheries.

Conclusion

Achieving water security and green growth worldwide is challenged by various climatic and non-climatic trends, including rapid population growth and urbanization, economic growth and rising income levels, ageing infrastructure, and increased demand for energy and food, impacting water quantity and water quality. As such, there is an expectation that demand for innovative water management solutions will increase, in particular, solutions that enable the more efficient use of available water resources, enhance the quality of water for humans and nature, improve water resource planning to balance rising demand with limited, and often variable, supplies of water, enhance resilience to extreme weather events, and mitigate carbon emissions.

The various innovative policies and technologies available to achieve water security and green growth include demand management, smart digital water management, alternative water supplies, nature-based solutions, and renewable energy and resource recovery. Demand management balances rising demand for limited, and often variable, supplies of water to achieve water security for both humans and nature by making better use of existing water supplies before plans are made to increase supply further. Smart digital water management can facilitate demand management by increasing water efficiency, detecting leaks promptly, and monitoring droughts. Nevertheless, even with successful demand management measures, some locations will require alternative water sources, namely water reuse and water recycling initiatives.

Nature-based solutions involve the use of natural or semi-natural systems that utilize ecosystem services in the management of water resources and associated risks. For example, green infrastructure can help purify polluted water, while the equivalent grey infrastructure solution is wastewater treatment plants. To reduce the impacts of floods, green infrastructure solutions increase the water infiltration and storage capacity of wetlands and soils.

Water managers can also mitigate droughts by releasing water from natural storage features such as lakes and aquifers for human and natural use.

Regarding climate change mitigation and circular economy thinking, the facilities and infrastructure of water and wastewater treatment facilities provide opportunities to generate renewable energy and recover resources from wastewater. In particular, water utilities can implement traditional renewable energy activities on facility-owned buildings and surrounding land. At the same time, numerous resources can be recovered from wastewater to generate new revenue streams for water utilities.

Nonetheless, despite knowledge of the multiple benefits that demand management, smart digital water management, alternative water supplies, nature-based solutions, and renewable energy and resource recovery provide, a key barrier to their wide-spread adoption is a lack of understanding of their financing such as, how can demand management strategies be financed sustainably, what are the best practices for blended finance projects, and who should pay for green infrastructure solutions. Furthermore, there are no one-size-fits-all solutions for financing water infrastructure and services as they are highly context-specific.

However, a failure to invest in innovative policies and technologies available to achieve water security and green growth will lead to significant economic losses, including losses from inadequate water supply and sanitation, urban property flood damage, and water insecurity of existing irrigators. A lack of water security could lead to sustained negative economic growth in parts of the world. As such, it is globally recognized that innovative finance is required to close the financing gap to achieve water security and green growth.

There is an array of financing instruments and approaches available from public, domestic, private, and blended financial sources to achieve water security and green growth, including green bonds and green loans to construct green-grey hybrid infrastructure, DFN swaps that enable countries to swap debt for initiating water security projects, PWS schemes that prevent floods, MBIs such as seasonal water pricing to encourage water conservation, PPPs that involve local governments cooperating with local private sector actors to implement local water security projects, biodiversity offset schemes that protect water resources and related biodiversity, and WQT schemes that reduce or control water pollution.

Bibliography

ADB. 'Asian Water Development Outlook 2016: Strengthening Water Security in Asia and the Pacific' (2016). https://www.adb.org/sites/default/files/publication/189411/awdo-2016.pdf.

ADB. 'Adb to Invest up to $40 Million in Ggu Green Bonds to Upgrade Water, Sanitation in Georgia' (2020). https://www.adb.org/news/adb-invest-40-million-ggu-green-bonds-upgrade-water-sanitation-georgia#:~:text=TBILISI%2C%20GEORGIA%20(27%20July%202020,debt%20of%20renewable%20energy%20and.

ADB. 'Adb Green Bond Newsletter and Impact Report 2021' (2021). https://www.adb.org/publications/adb-green-bonds.

Adhikari, Bhim, and Gemma Boag. 'Designing Payments for Ecosystem Services Schemes: Some Considerations'. *Current Opinion in Environmental Sustainability* 5, no. 1 (2013/03/01/ 2013): 72–7.

Alaerts, J. Guy. 'Financing for Water—Water for Financing: A Global Review of Policy and Practice'. *Sustainability* 11, no. 3 (2019).

Alamdari, Nasrin, David J. Sample, Andrew C. Ross, and Zachary M. Easton. 'Evaluating the Impact of Climate Change on Water Quality and Quantity in an Urban Watershed Using an Ensemble Approach'. *Estuaries and Coasts* 43, no. 1 (2020/01/01 2020): 56–72.

American Rivers, ed. *Stormwater Currency: Establishing a Stormwater Volume Credit Trading Program.* American Rivers, 2019.

American Society of Civil Engineers. 'The Economic Benefits of Investing in Water Infrastructure: How a Failure to Act Would Affect the Us Economic Recovery' (2020). http://www.uswateralliance.org/sites/uswateralliance.org/files/publications/The%20Economic%20Benefits%20of%20Investing%20in%20Water%20Infrastructure_final.pdf

Anglian Water. 'Anglian Water Funds 850 Capital Investment Projects through Green Bonds since 2017' (2020). https://www.anglianwater.co.uk/news/anglian-water-green-bond-investment/#:~:text=Since%20it%20announced%20its%20first,Bonds%20totalling%20%20A3876%20million.&text=Since%20then%2C%20the%20projects%20delivered,company's%202010%20capital%20carbon%20baseline.

APMG International. 'Ppp Certification Program Guide' (2022), accessed 6 January 2022, https://ppp-certification.com/ppp-certification-guide/about-ppp-guide.

Arnell, Nigel W., Sarah J. Halliday, Richard W. Battarbee, Richard A. Skeffington, and Andrew J. Wade. 'The Implications of Climate Change for the Water Environment in England'. *Progress in Physical Geography: Earth and Environment* 39, no. 1 (2015): 93–120.

Auckland Council. 'Healthy Waters Biodiversity Offset Bank' (2022), accessed 7 January 2022, https://www.aucklandcouncil.govt.nz/environment/looking-after-aucklands-water/Pages/healthy-waters-biodiversity-offset-bank.aspx.

Babel, Mukand S., Victor R. Shinde, Devesh Sharma, and Nguyen Mai Dang. 'Measuring Water Security: A Vital Step for Climate Change Adaptation'. *Environmental Research* 185 (2020/06/01/ 2020): 109400.

Baltimore City Department of Public Works. 'Stormwater Fee' (2018). https://publicworks.baltimorecity.gov/stormwater-fee.

Banerjee, Simanti, Silvia Secchi, Joseph Fargione, Stephen Polasky, and Steven Kraft. 'How to Sell Ecosystem Services: A Guide for Designing New Markets'. *Frontiers in Ecology and the Environment* 11, no. 6 (2013): 297–304.

Benabou, Sarah. 'Making Up for Lost Nature?: A Critical Review of the International Development of Voluntary Biodiversity Offsets'. *Environment & Society* 5 (2014): 103–23. http://www.jstor.org/stable/43297071.

Bennett, Drew E., Hannah Gosnell, Susan Lurie, and Sally Duncan. 'Utility Engagement with Payments for Watershed Services in the United States'. *Ecosystem Services* 8 (2014/06/01/ 2014): 56–64.

Bezombes, Lucie, Christian Kerbiriou, and Thomas Spiegelberger. 'Do Biodiversity Offsets Achieve No Net Loss? An Evaluation of Offsets in a French Department'. *Biological Conservation* 231 (2019/03/01/ 2019): 24–9. https://doi.org/https://doi.org/10.1016/j.biocon.2019.01.004. https://www.sciencedirect.com/science/article/pii/S0006320718306098.

Blöschl, Günter, Julia Hall, Alberto Viglione, Rui A. P. Perdigão, Juraj Parajka, Bruno Merz, David Lun, et al. 'Changing Climate Both Increases and Decreases European River Floods'. *Nature* 573, no. 7772 (2019/09/01 2019): 108–11.

Boisvert, Valérie, Philippe Méral, and Géraldine Froger. 'Market-Based Instruments for Ecosystem Services: Institutional Innovation or Renovation?'. *Society & Natural Resources* 26, no. 10 (2013): 1122–36.

Border Bank. 'Green Loan'. https://www.borderbank.com.au/loans/green-loan/.

Boretti, Alberto, and Lorenzo Rosa. 'Reassessing the Projections of the World Water Development Report'. *npj Clean Water* 2, no. 1 (2019/07/31 2019): 15.

Borghesi, Simone. 'Water Tradable Permits: A Review of Theoretical and Case Studies'. *Journal of Environmental Planning and Management* 57, no. 9 (2014/09/02 2014): 1305–32. https://doi.org/10.1080/09640568.2013.820175.

Bösch, Matthias, Peter Elsasser, and Sven Wunder. 'Why Do Payments for Watershed Services Emerge? A Cross-Country Analysis of Adoption Contexts'. *World Development* 119 (2019/07/01/ 2019): 111–19.

Bottazzi, Patrick, Emma Wiik, David Crespo, and Julia P. G. Jones. 'Payment for Environmental 'Self-Service': Exploring the Links between Farmers' Motivation and Additionality in a Conservation Incentive Programme in the Bolivian Andes'. *Ecological Economics* 150 (2018/08/01/ 2018): 11–23.

Boyd, Tamara, and John Brumley. 'Groundwater Trading in Australia: A Preliminary Analysis and Research Agenda'. *Australasian Journal of Water Resources* 7, no. 1 (2003/01/01 2003): 57–63. https://doi.org/10.1080/13241583.2003.11465229.

Boyer, Christopher N., Damian C. Adams, Tatiana Borisova, and Christopher D. Clark. 'Factors Driving Water Utility Rate Structure Choice: Evidence from Four Southern U.S. States'. *Water Resources Management* 26, no. 10 (2012/08/01 2012): 2747–60.

Brears, Robert C. *Urban Water Security*. Chichester, UK; Hoboken, NJ: John Wiley & Sons, 2016.

Brears, Robert C. *The Green Economy and the Water-Energy-Food Nexus*. London: Palgrave Macmillan UK, 2017.

Brears, Robert C. *Blue and Green Cities: The Role of Blue-Green Infrastructure in Managing Urban Water Resources*. Palgrave Macmillan UK, 2018.

Brears, Robert C. *Climate Resilient Water Resources Management*. Cham, Switzerland: Palgrave Macmillan, 2018.

Brears, Robert C. *Developing the Circular Water Economy*. Cham, Switzerland: Palgrave Macmillan, 2020.

Brears, Robert C. *Nature-Based Solutions to 21st Century Challenges*. Oxfordshire, UK: Routledge, 2020.

Brears, Robert C. *Regional Water Security*. Wiley, 2021.

Brears, Robert C. *Water Resources Management: Innovative and Green Solutions*. De Gruyter, 2021.

Brownson, Katherine, and Laurie Fowler. 'Evaluating How We Evaluate Success: Monitoring, Evaluation and Adaptive Management in Payments for Watershed Services Programs'. *Land Use Policy* 94 (2020/05/01/ 2020): 104505.

Burnett, M. *Public-Private Partnerships: A Decision Maker's Guide*. European Institute of Public Administration, 2007. https://books.google.co.nz/books?id=ZjfKIQAACAAJ.

Burt, Charles M. 'Volumetric Irrigation Water Pricing Considerations'. *Irrigation and Drainage Systems* 21, no. 2 (2007/05/01 2007): 133–44.

Campanhão, Ligia Maria Barrios, and Victor Eduardo Lima Ranieri. 'Guideline Framework for Effective Targeting of Payments for Watershed Services'. *Forest Policy and Economics* 104 (2019/07/01/ 2019): 93–109.

Canadian Council for Public Private Partnerships, The. 'Benefits of Water Service Public-Private Partnerships' (2001). http://www.archives.gov.on.ca/en/e_records/walkerton/part2info/publicsubmissions/pdf/benefitsofwaternew.pdf.

Cassimon, Danny, Martin Prowse, and Dennis Essers. 'The Pitfalls and Potential of Debt-for-Nature Swaps: A Us-Indonesian Case Study'. *Global Environmental Change* 21, no. 1 (2011/02/01/ 2011): 93–102.

CBD. 'Debt-for-Nature Swaps' (2001). https://www.cbd.int/doc/nbsap/finance/Guide_Debt_Nov2001.pdf

CBD. 'Investing in Nature for Sustainable Development' (2010). https://www.cbd.int/financial/debtnature/costarica-naturalsolutions.pdf.

Center for International Forestry Research. 'Payments for Ecosystem Services (Pes): A Practical Guide to Assessing the Feasibility of Pes Projects' (2014). https://www.cifor.org/publications/pdf_files/Books/BFripp1401.pdf.

Chester Water Authority. 'A New Model for Urban Renewal: Stormwater Authority of Chester's Community-Based Public-Private Partnership' (2017). https://www.chestercity.com/wp-content/uploads/2017/05/Chester_CCBP3_Announce_FactSheet_v5.pdf.

Chicago Metropolitan Agency for Planning. 'Full-Cost Water Pricing Guidebook for Sustainable Community Water Systems' (2012).

City of Atlanta Department of Watershed Management. 'Environmental Impact Bond (Eib) for Green Infrastructure in Proctor Creek Watershed' (2020). https://www.atlantawatershed.org/environmental-impact-bond/.

City of Guelph. 'Stormwater Service Credits for Business' (2022). https://guelph.ca/living/environment/water/rebates/stormwater-service-fee-credit-program/.

City of Toronto. 'Capacity Buyback Program' (2022). https://www.toronto.ca/services-payments/water-environment/how-to-use-less-water/water-efficiency-for-business/capacity-buyback-program/.

City of Toronto 'Industrial Water Rate Program' (2022). https://www.toronto.ca/services-payments/water-environment/how-to-use-less-water/water-efficiency-for-business/industrial-water-rate-program/.

City of Tucson. 'Gray Water Rebate' (2022). https://www.tucsonaz.gov/water/gray-water-rebate.

Climate Bonds Initiative. 'Summary of Faqs: Guide for Issuers on Green Bonds for Climate Resilience' (2020). https://www.climatebonds.net/files/files/Summary%20of%20FAQs_Green%20Bonds%20for%20Climate%20Resilience.pdf.

Climate Bonds Initiative. 'Water Infrastructure Criteria under the Climate Bonds Standard' (2021). https://www.climatebonds.net/files/files/Water%20Criteria%20Document%20Final_17Jan21.pdf

Colorado Water Conservation Board. 'Instream Flow Water Acquisitions' (2021), accessed 9 December 2021, https://cwcb.colorado.gov/instream-flow-water-acquisitions.

Congressional Budget Office. 'Public-Private Partnerships for Transportation and Water Infrastructure' (2020). https://www.cbo.gov/publication/56003.

Conservation Ontario. 'Market-Based Instruments within the Green Economy' (2013). https://conservationontario.ca/fileadmin/pdf/policy-priorities_section/GreenEconomy_Literature_Review.pdf.

Convergence. 'Blending with Technical Assistance' (2019). https://assets.ctfassets.net/4cgqlwde6qy0/3RZClckJliqSyQVy5zkxaT/d3154bf0a55836bd3ec26fb07258a913/Technical_Assistance_Brief_vFinal.pdf.

Cook, Christina, and Karen Bakker. 'Water Security: Debating an Emerging Paradigm.' *Global Environmental Change* 22, no. 1 (2012/02/01/ 2012): 94–102.

CPIC. 'Conservation Investment Blueprint: Environmental Impact Bond for Green Infrastructure' (2019). http://cpicfinance.com/wp-content/uploads/2019/01/CPIC-Blueprint-Environmental-Impact-Bond-for-Green-Infrastructure.pdf.

Delaware Riverkeeper Network. 'Values of Large Scale Watershed Protection' (2021). https://delawareriverkeeper.org/sites/default/files/Large%20Scale%20Watershed%20Protection%20Infographic.pdf.

Delpla, I., A. V. Jung, E. Baures, M. Clement, and O. Thomas. 'Impacts of Climate Change on Surface Water Quality in Relation to Drinking Water Production.' *Environment International* 35, no. 8 (2009/11/01/ 2009): 1225–33.

Department of Energy & Environment. 'Stormwater Retention Credit Trading Program.' 2020, accessed 5 May 2020, https://doee.dc.gov/src.

Deschryver, Pauline, and Frederic de Mariz. 'What Future for the Green Bond Market? How Can Policymakers, Companies, and Investors Unlock the Potential of the Green Bond Market?'. *Journal of Risk and Financial Management* 13, no. 3 (2020).

Dogsé, P., and B. von Droste. *Debt-for-Nature Exchanges and Biosphere Reserves: Experiences and Potential.* Unesco, 1990.

EcoAgriculture Partners. 'Innovations in Market-Based Watershed Conservation in the United States: Payments for Watershed Services for Agricultural and Forest Landowners' (2011). https://ecoagriculture.org/publication/innovations-in-market-based-watershed-conservation-in-the-united-states/.

EEA. 'Environmental Taxes: Implementation and Environmental Effectiveness' (1996). https://www.eea.europa.eu/publications/92-9167-000-6/download.

EEA. 'Assessment of Cost Recovery through Water Pricing' (2013). https://www.eea.europa.eu/publications/assessment-of-full-cost-recovery.

EnTrade. 'A New Deal for the Natural Environment' (2022). https://www.entrade.co.uk.

Environmental Defense Fund. 'Groundwater Trading as a Tool for Implementing California's Sustainable Groundwater Management Act' (2017). https://www.edf.org/sites/default/files/documents/water-markets.pdf.

European Commission. 'Guidelines for Successful Public–Private Partnerships' (2003). https://ec.europa.eu/regional_policy/sources/docgener/guides/ppp_en.pdf.

European Commission. 'Water–Energy Nexus in Europe' (2019). https://publications.jrc.ec.europa.eu/repository/bitstream/JRC115853/online_ecj095x_policy_report_interactive_4.pdf.

FAO. 'Debt for Nature Swaps to Promote Natural Resource Conservation' (1993). http://www.fao.org/3/T0670E/T0670E00.htm#cont.

FAO. 'Control of Water Pollution from Agriculture' (1996). http://www.fao.org/3/w2598e/w2598e00.htm#Contents.

FAO. 'Modern Water Rights: Theory and Practice' (2006). http://www.fao.org/3/a-a0864e.pdf.

FAO. 'Towards a Water and Food Secure Future: Critical Perspectives for Policy-Makers' (2015). http://www.fao.org/3/a-i4560e.pdf.

FAO. 'More People, More Food, Worse Water? A Global Review of Water Pollution from Agriculture' (2018). http://www.fao.org/3/ca0146en/CA0146EN.pdf

FAO. 'The State of Food and Agriculture 2020' (2020). http://www.fao.org/documents/card/en/c/cb1447en/.

Flammer, Caroline. 'Corporate Green Bonds'. *Journal of Financial Economics* (2021/01/31/2021).

Flörke, Martina, Christof Schneider, and Robert I. McDonald. 'Water Competition between Cities and Agriculture Driven by Climate Change and Urban Growth'. *Nature Sustainability* 1, no. 1 (2018/01/01 2018): 51–8.

Forever Costa Rica Association. 'I Debt-for-Nature Swap' (2021). https://costaricaporsiempre.org/en/programas/i-canje-de-deuda-por-naturaleza/.

Fox, Sam, Will Shepherd, Richard Collins, and Joby Boxall. 'Experimental Quantification of Contaminant Ingress into a Buried Leaking Pipe During Transient Events'. *Journal of Hydraulic Engineering* 142, no. 1 (2016): 04015036.

Freeburn, Lloyd, and Ian Ramsay. 'Green Bonds: Legal and Policy Issues'. *Capital Markets Law Journal* 15, no. 4 (2020): 418–42.

Gallego Valero, Leticia, Encarnación Moral Pajares, and Isabel M. Román Sánchez. 'The Tax Burden on Wastewater and the Protection of Water Ecosystems in Eu Countries'. *Sustainability* 10, no. 1 (2018).

Gardner, Toby A., Amrei Von Hase, Susie Brownlie, Jonathan M. M. Ekstrom, John D. Pilgrim, Conrad E. Savy, R. T. Theo Stephens, et al. 'Biodiversity Offsets and the Challenge of Achieving No Net Loss'. *Conservation Biology* 27, no. 6 (2013): 1254–64. http://www.jstor.org/stable/24480255.

Garrick, Dustin, Lucia De Stefano, Winston Yu, Isabel Jorgensen, Erin O'Donnell, Laura Turley, Ismael Aguilar-Barajas, et al. 'Rural Water for Thirsty Cities: A Systematic Review of Water Reallocation from Rural to Urban Regions'. *Environmental Research Letters* 14, no. 4 (2019/04/10 2019): 043003.

Glen R. Behrend, P.E., Amanda Hallauer, and David Bell, PWS. 'Atlanta's Environmental Impact Bond for Green Infrastructure'. In *National Watershed and Stormwater Conference*. Charleston, South Carolina 2019.

Global Water Partnership. 'Water as a Social and Economic Good: How to Put the Principle into Practice' (1998). https://www.ircwash.org/resources/water-social-and-economic-good-how-put-principle-practice.

Gonçalves, Bárbara, Alexandra Marques, Amadeu Mortágua Velho Da Maia Soares, and Henrique Miguel Pereira. 'Biodiversity Offsets: From Current Challenges to Harmonized Metrics'. *Current Opinion in Environmental Sustainability* 14 (2015): 61–7. https://doi.org/10.1016/j.cosust.2015.03.008. https://dx.doi.org/10.1016/j.cosust.2015.03.008.

Government of Alberta. 'Environmental Tools: Environmental Subsidies' (2022). https://www.alberta.ca/assets/documents/ep-environmental-tools-environmental-subsidies.pdf.

Government of Saskatchewan. 'Farm Stewardship Program (Fsp)' (2022). https://www.saskatchewan.ca/business/agriculture-natural-resources-and-industry/agribusiness-farmers-and-ranchers/canadian-agricultural-partnership-cap/environmental-sustainability-and-climate-change/farm-stewardship-program-fsp.

Greer, Robert A. 'A Review of Public Water Infrastructure Financing in the United States'. *WIREs Water* 7, no. 5 (2020).

Greiner, Romy, and Allyson Lankester. 'Supporting on-Farm Biodiversity Conservation through Debt-for-Conservation Swaps: Concept and Critique'. *Land Use Policy* 24, no. 2 (2007/04/01/ 2007): 458–71.

Grigg, Neil S. 'Stormwater Programs: Organization, Finance, and Prospects'. *Public Works Management & Policy* 18, no. 1 (2013/01/01 2012): 5–22.

GWP. 'Water Demand Management: The Mediterranean Experience' (2012). http://www.gwp.org/Global/ToolBox/Publications/Technical%20Focus%20Papers/01%20Water%20Demand%20Management%20-%20The%20Mediterranean%20Experience%20(2012)%20English.pdf.

GWP. 'Water in the Green Economy' (2012). http://www.gwp.org/Global/ToolBox/Publications/Perspective%20Papers/03%20Water%20in%20the%20Green%20Economy%20(2012).pdf.

GWW. 'Charges Explained' (2022). https://www.gww.com.au/accounts-billing/prices-charges/prices-charges-explained

Hahm, Hongjoo. 'Current Trends in Private Financing of Water and Sanitation in Asia and the Pacific'. *Asia-Pacific Sustainable Development Journal* 26, no. 1 (2019): 67–83.

Hallauer, Amanda Medori, Aditya Tyagi, Glen Behrend, David Bell, and Benjamin Cohen. 'Environmental Impact Bond: An Innovative Financing Mechanism for Enhancing Resilience in the City of Atlanta through Green Infrastructure'. Paper presented at the World Environmental and Water Resources Congress 2019, Pittsburgh, Pennsylvania, 2019.

Hamlin, Timothy B. 'Debt-for-Nature Swaps: A New Strategy for Protecting Environmental Interests in Developing Nations'. *Ecology Law Quarterly* 16, no. 4 (1989): 1065–88.

Hansen, Stein. 'Debt for Nature Swaps—Overview and Discussion of Key Issues'. *Ecological Economics* 1, no. 1 (1989/02/01/ 1989): 77–93.

Harlan, Sharon L., Scott T. Yabiku, Larissa Larsen, and Anthony J. Brazel. 'Household Water Consumption in an Arid City: Affluence, Affordance, and Attitudes'. *Society & Natural Resources* 22, no. 8 (2009/08/11 2009): 691–709.

Havemann, Tanja, Christine Negra, and Fred Werneck. 'Water Infrastructure and Investment' (2015). https://sustainabledevelopment.un.org/content/documents/hlpwater/08-WaterInfrastInvest.pdf.

Havemann, Tanja, Christine Negra, and Fred Werneck. 'Blended Finance for Agriculture: Exploring the Constraints and Possibilities of Combining Financial Instruments for Sustainable Transitions'. *Agriculture and Human Values* (2020/07/27 2020).

Herrera, Diego, Shannon Cunniff, Carolyn DuPont, Benjamin Cohen, Dakota Gangi, Devyani Kar, Natalie Peyronnin Snider, et al. 'Designing an Environmental Impact Bond for Wetland Restoration in Louisiana'. *Ecosystem Services* 35 (2019/02/01/ 2019): 260–76.

High Level Panel on Water. 'Making Every Drop Count: An Agenda for Water Action' (2018). https://sustainabledevelopment.un.org/content/documents/17825HLPW_Outcome.pdf.

Holden, Paul, and Mateen Thobani. 'Tradable Water Rights: A Property Rights Approach to Improving Water Use and Promoting Investment'. *Cuadernos de Economía* 32, no. 97 (1995): 263–89. http://www.jstor.org/stable/41951282.

Huber-Stearns, Heidi R., Joshua H. Goldstein, and Esther A. Duke. 'Intermediary Roles and Payments for Ecosystem Services: A Typology and Program Feasibility Application in Panama'. *Ecosystem Services* 6 (2013/12/01/ 2013): 104–16.

Hueskes, Marlies, Koen Verhoest, and Thomas Block. 'Governing Public–Private Partnerships for Sustainability: An Analysis of Procurement and Governance Practices of Ppp Infrastructure Projects'. *International Journal of Project Management* 35, no. 6 (2017/0801/ 2017): 1184–95. https://doi.org/https://doi.org/10.1016/j.ijproman.2017.02.020. https://www.sciencedirect.com/science/article/pii/S0263786317302557.

Humphreys, Elena, Andrea van der Kerk, and Catarina Fonseca. 'Public Finance for Water Infrastructure Development and Its Practical Challenges for Small Towns'. *Water Policy* 20, no. S1 (2018): 100–11.

IDB. 'Transforming Green Bond Markets: Using Financial Innovation and Technology to Expand Green Bond Issuance in Latin America and the Caribbean' (2019). https://publications.iadb.org/en/transforming-green-bond-markets-using-financial-innovation-and-technology-expand-green-bond

IDFC. 'Idfc Blended Finance: A Brief Overview' (2019). https://www.idfc.org/wp-content/uploads/2019/10/blended-finance-a-brief-overview-october-2019_final.pdf.

IEA. 'Weo-2016 Special Report: Water-Energy Nexus' (2016). https://webstore.iea.org/weo-2016-special-report-water-energy-nexus.

IEA. 'Water-Energy Nexus: World Energy Outlook Special Report' (2017). https://www.iea.org/reports/water-energy-nexus.

IEA. 'Introduction to the Water-Energy Nexus' (2020). https://www.iea.org/articles/introduction-to-the-water-energy-nexus

Iftekhar, M. S., J. G. Tisdell, and J. D. Connor. 'Effects of Competition on Environmental Water Buyback Auctions'. *Agricultural Water Management* 127 (2013/09/01/ 2013): 59–73. https://doi.org/https://doi.org/10.1016/j.agwat.2013.05.015. https://www.sciencedirect.com/science/article/pii/S0378377413001340.

Illinois Environmental Protection Agency. 'Green Infrastructure Grant Opportunities'. https://www2.illinois.gov/epa/topics/grants-loans/water-financial-assistance/Pages/gigo.aspx#:~:text=The%20new%20Green%20Infrastructure%20Grant,rivers%2C%20streams%2C%20and%20lakes.

IMCA. 'Green Bond Principles'. 'Suggested Impact Reporting Metrics for Sustainable Water and Wastewater Management Projects' (2017). https://www.icmagroup.org/assets/documents/Regulatory/Green-Bonds/Water-Wastewater-Impact-Reporting-Final-8-June-2017-130617.pdf

IMCA. 'Green Bond Principles' (2021). https://www.icmagroup.org/assets/documents/Sustainable-finance/2021-updates/Green-Bond-Principles-June-2021-140621.pdf.

Informa. 'Saudi Arabia Invites Interest in Fourth Ppp Water Transmission Scheme' (2021). https://energy-utilities.com/saudi-arabia-invites-interest-in-fourth-ppp-water-news114584.html.

Informa. 'Saudi Arabia Invites Interest in Ppp Water Reservoir Projects' (2021), accessed 6 January 2022, https://energy-utilities.com/saudi-arabia-invites-interest-in-ppp-water-news115751.html.

Institute for Governance & Sustainable Development. 'Debt-for-Climate Swaps' (2020). http://www.igsd.org/wp-content/uploads/2020/08/Background-Note-on-Debt-Swaps-11Aug20.pdf

International Resource Panel. 'Global Resources Outlook 2019: Natural Resources for the Future We Want' (2019). https://www.resourcepanel.org/reports/global-resources-outlook

International Labor Organization. 'Innovative Finance: Putting Your Money to (Decent) Work'. (2018). https://www.ilo.org/wcmsp5/groups/public/—ed_emp/documents/publication/wcms_654680.pdf.

IPCC. 'Summary for Policymakers' (2018). https://www.ipcc.ch/site/assets/uploads/sites/2/2019/05/SR15_SPM_version_report_LR.pdf

IUCN. 'Pay: Establishing Payments for Watershed Services' (2006). https://www.iucn.org/content/pay-establishing-payments-watershed-services.

IUCN. 'Biodiversity Offsets: Policy Options for Governments' (2014). https://portals.iucn.org/library/sites/library/files/documents/2014-028.pdf

Johannessen, Åse, Arno Rosemarin, Frank Thomalla, Åsa Gerger Swartling, Thor Axel Stenström, and Gregor Vulturius. 'Strategies for Building Resilience to Hazards in Water, Sanitation and Hygiene (Wash) Systems: The Role of Public Private Partnerships'. *International Journal of Disaster Risk Reduction* 10 (2014/12/01/ 2014): 102–15. https://

doi.org/https://doi.org/10.1016/j.ijdrr.2014.07.002. http://www.sciencedirect.com/science/article/pii/S2212420914000557.

Jomo KS, Anis Chowdhury, Krishnan Sharma, Daniel Platz,. 'Public–Private Partnerships and the 2030 Agenda for Sustainable Development: Fit for Purpose?' (2016). https://www.un.org/en/desa/public-private-partnerships-and-2030-agenda-sustainable-development-fit-purpose.

Jones, Ryan, Tom Baker, Katherine Huet, Laurence Murphy, and Nick Lewis. 'Treating Ecological Deficit with Debt: The Practical and Political Concerns with Green Bonds'. *Geoforum* 114 (2020/08/01/ 2020): 49–58.

Kearney, John. 'Food Consumption Trends and Drivers'. *Philosophical Transactions of the Royal Society of London. Series B, Biological Sciences* 365, no. 1554 (2010): 2793–2807.

Koh, Niak Sian, Thomas Hahn, and Wiebren J. Boonstra. 'How Much of a Market Is Involved in a Biodiversity Offset? A Typology of Biodiversity Offset Policies'. *Journal of Environmental Management* 232 (2019/02/15/ 2019): 679–91. https://doi.org/https://doi.org/10.1016/j.jenvman.2018.11.080. https://www.sciencedirect.com/science/article/pii/S0301479718313458.

Küblböck, Karin, and Hannes Grohs. 'Blended Finance and Its Potential for Development Cooperation' (2019). https://www.econstor.eu/handle/10419/200507.

Li, Zhenghui, Gaoke Liao, Zhenzhen Wang, and Zhehao Huang. 'Green Loan and Subsidy for Promoting Clean Production Innovation'. *Journal of Cleaner Production* 187 (2018/06/20/ 2018): 421–31.

Lima, Sónia, Ana Brochado, and Rui Cunha Marques. 'Public–Private Partnerships in the Water Sector: A Review'. *Utilities Policy* 69 (2021/04/01/ 2021): 101182. https://doi.org/https://doi.org/10.1016/j.jup.2021.101182. https://www.sciencedirect.com/science/article/pii/S0957178721000163.

Loan Market Association. 'Green Loan Principles. Supporting Environmentally Sustainable Economic Activity' (2018). https://www.lma.eu.com/application/files/9115/4452/5458/741_LM_Green_Loan_Principles_Booklet_V8.pdf.

Lu, Yan, and Tian He. 'Assessing the Effects of Regional Payment for Watershed Services Program on Water Quality Using an Intervention Analysis Model'. *Science of The Total Environment* 493 (2014/09/15/ 2014): 1056–64.

Lukey, Peter, Tracey Cumming, Sukie Paras, Ida Kubiszewski, and Samuel Lloyd. 'Making Biodiversity Offsets Work in South Africa—a Governance Perspective'. *Ecosystem Services* 27 (2017/10/01/ 2017): 281–90. https://doi.org/https://doi.org/10.1016/j.ecoser.2017.05.001. https://www.sciencedirect.com/science/article/pii/S2212041617303017.

Malaysian Green Technology Corporation. 'What Sector Can Be Funded?' (2022). https://www.mgtc.gov.my/our-services/green-technology-financing-scheme/

Mann, Carsten. 'Strategies for Sustainable Policy Design: Constructive Assessment of Biodiversity Offsets and Banking'. *Ecosystem Services* 16 (2015/12/01/ 2015): 266–74. https://doi.org/https://doi.org/10.1016/j.ecoser.2015.07.001. https://www.sciencedirect.com/science/article/pii/S2212041615300127.

Maryland Department of the Environment. 'Water Quality Trading Program Home' (2022), accessed 6 January 2022, https://mde.maryland.gov/programs/Water/WQT/Pages/index.aspx.

McDonald, Robert I., Katherine Weber, Julie Padowski, Martina Flörke, Christof Schneider, Pamela A. Green, Thomas Gleeson, et al. 'Water on an Urban Planet: Urbanization and the Reach of Urban Water Infrastructure'. *Global Environmental Change* 27 (2014): 96–105.

McDonald, Robert I., Katherine F. Weber, Julie Padowski, Tim Boucher, and Daniel Shemie. 'Estimating Watershed Degradation over the Last Century and Its Impact on Water-Treatment Costs for the World's Large Cities'. *Proceedings of the National Academy of Sciences* 113, no. 32 (2016): 9117–22.

McGowan, Jennifer, Rob Weary, Leah Carriere, Edward T. Game, Joanna L. Smith, Melissa Garvey, and Hugh P. Possingham. 'Prioritizing Debt Conversion Opportunities for Marine Conservation'. *Conservation Biology* 34, no. 5 (2020/10/01 2020): 1065–75.

Ministry for the Environment. 'Market-Based Approaches to Marine Environmental Regulation: Stage 2: Instrument Assessment Framework and Case Study' (2006). https://environment.govt.nz/publications/market-based-approaches-to-marine-environmental-regulation-stage-2-instrument-assessment-framework-and-case-study/.

Ministry of the Environment. 'Green Bond Guidelines: Green Loan and Sustainability Linked Loan Guidelines' (2020). https://www.env.go.jp/policy/guidelines_set_version_with%20cover.pdf

Ministry of Environment and Food of Denmark. 'Pesticides and Gene Technology' (2017). https://www.ohchr.org/Documents/Issues/ToxicWaste/PesticidesRtoFood/Denmark.pdf.

Minnesota Pollution Control Agency. 'Water Quality Trading Guidance' (2021). https://www.pca.state.mn.us/sites/default/files/wq-gen1-15.pdf.

Motu Economic and Public Policy Research. 'Trading Efficiency in Water Quality Trading Markets: An Assessment of Trade-Offs' (2011). https://www.motu.nz/our-research/environment-and-resources/nutrient-trading-and-water-quality/trading-efficiency-in-water-quality-trading-markets-an-assessment-of-trade-offs/.

Muñoz Escobar, Marcela, Robert Hollaender, and Camilo Pineda Weffer. 'Institutional Durability of Payments for Watershed Ecosystem Services: Lessons from Two Case Studies from Colombia and Germany'. *Ecosystem Services* 6 (2013/12/01/ 2013): 46–53.

Murray-Darling Basin Authority. 'Water Markets and Trade' (2022), accessed 6 January 2022, https://www.mdba.gov.au/water-management/managing-water/water-markets-trade.

NASA. 'Carbon Emissions Could Dramatically Increase Risk of U.S. Megadroughts'. https://climate.nasa.gov/news/2238/carbon-emissions-could-dramatically-increase-risk-of-us-megadroughts/.

NatureScot. 'The Scottish Borders Biodiversity Offsets Scheme' (2017). https://www.nature.scot/sites/default/files/2017-10/A2394889-Biodiversity-Duty-local-authority-case-studies-The-Scottish-Borders-Biodiversity-Offsets-Scheme.pdf.

NDC Partnership. 'Financial Incentives to Enable Clean Energy Deployment: Policy Overview and Good Practices' (2022). https://ndcpartnership.org/toolbox/financial-incentives-enable-clean-energy-deployment-policy-overview-and-good-practices.

Netherlands Enterprise Agency 'Environmental Investment Allowance (Mia)' (2021). https://english.rvo.nl/subsidies-programmes/mia-and-vamil.

Netherlands Enterprise Agency. 'Environment and Energy List 2021' (2022).

New Jersey Environmental Digital Library. 'Murphy Administration Invests $386m in Water Infrastructure, Creating 4,600+ Construction Jobs' (2022). https://njedl.rutgers.edu/news/murphy-administration-invests-386m-water-infrastructure-creating-4600-construction-jobs.

NRDC. 'How To: Stormwater Credit Trading Programs' (2018). https://www.nrdc.org/sites/default/files/stormwater-credit-trading-programs-ib.pdf.

Nycander, Gunnel Axelsson. 'Blended Finance: Finding Its Right Place' (2020). https://www.svenskakyrkan.se/filer/8333_SK19489_blended_finance_final.pdf.

ODI. 'Climate Change and Water Finance Needs to Flood Not Drip' (2018). https://odi.org/en/publications/climate-change-and-water-finance-needs-to-flood-not-drip/.

OECD. 'Domestic Transferable Permits for Environmental Management: Design and Implementation' (2001). https://www.oecd-ilibrary.org/environment/domestic-transferable-permits-for-environmental-management_9789264192638-en.

OECD. 'Debt-for-Environment Swap in Georgia: Pre-Feasibility Study and Institutional Options' (2006). https://www.oecd.org/env/outreach/35178696.pdf.

OECD. 'Lessons Learnt from Experience with Debt-for-Environment Swaps in Economies in Transition' (2007). https://www.oecd.org/env/outreach/39352290.pdf.

OECD. 'Biodiversity Offsets: Effective Design and Implementation' (2016). https://www.oecd.org/environment/resources/Policy-Highlights-Biodiversity-Offsets-web.pdf.

OECD 'Water, Growth and Finance' (2016). https://www.oecd.org/environment/resources/Water-Growth-and-Finance-policy-perspectives.pdf.

OECD. 'Mobilising Bond Markets for a Low-Carbon Transition, Green Finance and Investment' (2017). https://www.oecd.org/env/mobilising-bond-markets-for-a-low-carbon-transition-9789264272323-en.htm.

OECD. 'Policy Instruments for the Environment' (2017). https://www.oecd.org/env/indicators-modelling-outlooks/policy-instrument-database/.

OECD. 'Financing Water: Investing in Sustainable Growth' (2018). https://www.oecd.org/water/Policy-Paper-Financing-Water-Investing-in-Sustainable-Growth.pdf.

OECD. 'Making Blended Finance Work for the Sustainable Development Goals' (2018). https://www.oecd.org/development/making-blended-finance-work-for-the-sustainable-development-goals-9789264288768-en.htm.

OECD. 'Blended Finance in the Least Developed Countries 2019' (2019). https://www.oecd.org/finance/blended-finance-in-the-least-developed-countries-2019-1c142aae-en.htm

OECD. 'Making Blended Finance Work for Water and Sanitation: Unlocking Commercial Finance for Sdg 6' (2019). https://www.oecd.org/environment/resources/making-blended-finance-work-for-sdg-6-5efc8950-en.htm.

OECD. 'Development Finance Institutions and Private Sector Development' (2022). https://www.oecd.org/development/development-finance-institutions-private-sector-development.htm.

Öko-Institut e.V. 'Tradable Permit Schemes in Environmental Management: Evolution Patterns of an Expanding Policy Instrument' (2008). https://www.oeko.de/oekodoc/977/2008-317-en.pdf.

Oxfam. 'Blended Finance: What It Is, How It Works and How It Is Used' (2017). https://www-cdn.oxfam.org/s3fs-public/file_attachments/rr-blended-finance-130217-en.pdf.

Pacific Institute. 'Incentive-Based Instruments for Water Management' (2015). https://pacinst.org/wp-content/uploads/2016/02/issuelab_23697.pdf

Palazzo, Amanda, and Nicholas Brozović. 'The Role of Groundwater Trading in Spatial Water Management'. 145 (2014): 50–60. https://doi.org/10.1016/j.agwat.2014.03.004. https://dx.doi.org/10.1016/j.agwat.2014.03.004.

Partridge, Candace, and Francesca Romana Medda. 'The Evolution of Pricing Performance of Green Municipal Bonds'. *Journal of Sustainable Finance & Investment* 10, no. 1 (2020): 44–64.

Pervaze A. Sheikh. 'Debt-for-Nature Initiatives and the Tropical Forest Conservation Act (Tfca): Status and Implementation' (2018). https://fas.org/sgp/crs/misc/RL31286.pdf.

Pfleiderer, Peter, Carl-Friedrich Schleussner, Kai Kornhuber, and Dim Coumou. 'Summer Weather Becomes More Persistent in a 2 °C World'. *Nature Climate Change* 9, no. 9 (2019/09/01 2019): 666–71.

Primer Canje de Deuda por Naturaleza. 'What Is the 1st Us Debt Swap - Cr?' (2022). https://primercanjedeuda.org/que-es-el-i-canje-de-deuda/.

Purbo, Radies Kusprihanto, Christine Smith, and Robert Bianchi. 'Lessons Learned from Public–Private Partnerships in Indonesia's Water Sector'. *Bulletin of Indonesian Economic Studies* 55, no. 2 (2019): 193–212. https://doi.org/10.1080/00074918.2018.1550250.

PwC. 'The World in 2050: Will the Shift in Global Economic Power Continue?' (2015). http://www.pwc.com/gx/en/issues/the-economy/assets/world-in-2050-february-2015.pdf.

Quantified Ventures. 'Atlanta: First Publicly Offered Environmental Impact Bond' (2022). https://www.quantifiedventures.com/atlanta-eib.

Quétier, Fabien, and Sandra Lavorel. 'Assessing Ecological Equivalence in Biodiversity Offset Schemes: Key Issues and Solutions'. *Biological Conservation* 144, no. 12 (2011): 2991–99. https://doi.org/10.1016/j.biocon.2011.09.002.

Quintero, Juan David, and Aradhna Mathur. 'Biodiversity Offsets and Infrastructure'. *Conservation Biology* 25, no. 6 (2011): 1121–23. http://www.jstor.org.ezproxy.canterbury.ac.nz/stable/41315406.

Ramsey, Elizabeth, Jorge Pesantez, Mohammad A. Fasaee, Morgan DiCarlo, Jacob Monroe, and Emily Z. Berglund. 'A Smart Water Grid for Micro-Trading Rainwater: Hydraulic Feasibility Analysis'. *Water* 12, no. 11 (2020). https://doi.org/10.3390/w12113075.

Reed, M. S., K. Allen, A. Attlee, A. J. Dougill, K. L. Evans, J. O. Kenter, J. Hoy, et al. 'A Place-Based Approach to Payments for Ecosystem Services'. *Global Environmental Change* 43 (2017/03/01/ 2017): 92–106.

Rode, Julian, Alexandra Pinzon, Marcelo C. C. Stabile, Johannes Pirker, Simone Bauch, Alvaro Iribarrem, Paul Sammon, et al. 'Why "Blended Finance" Could Help Transitions to Sustainable Landscapes: Lessons from the Unlocking Forest Finance Project'. *Ecosystem Services* 37 (2019/06/01/ 2019): 100917.

Sattler, Claudia, and Bettina Matzdorf. 'Pes in a Nutshell: From Definitions and Origins to Pes in Practice—Approaches, Design Process and Innovative Aspects'. *Ecosystem Services* 6 (2013/12/01/ 2013): 2–11.

Säve-Söderbergh, Melle, John Bylund, Annika Malm, Magnus Simonsson, and Jonas Toljander. 'Gastrointestinal Illness Linked to Incidents in Drinking Water Distribution Networks in Sweden'. *Water Research* 122 (2017/10/01/ 2017): 503–11.

Schmack, Mario, Martin Anda, Stewart Dallas, and Roberta Fornarelli. 'Urban Water Trading—Hybrid Water Systems and Niche Opportunities in the Urban Water Market—a Literature Review'. *Environmental Technology Reviews* 8, no. 1 (2019/01/01 2019): 65–81. https://doi.org/10.1080/21622515.2019.1647292.

Schmitt, Robert. 'Pursuing Innovative Finance Models to Enable Beneficial Energy and Water Infrastructure and Systems'. *The Electricity Journal* 33, no. 1 (2020/01/01/ 2020): 106688.

Schomers, Sarah, and Bettina Matzdorf. 'Payments for Ecosystem Services: A Review and Comparison of Developing and Industrialised Countries'. *Ecosystem Services* 6 (2013/12/01/ 2013): 16–30.

Shandra, John M., Michael Restivo, Eric Shircliff, and Bruce London. 'Do Commercial Debt-for-Nature Swaps Matter for Forests? A Cross-National Test of World Polity Theory1'. *Sociological Forum* 26, no. 2 (2011/06/01 2011): 381–410.

Skurray, James H., E. J. Roberts, and David J. Pannell. 'Hydrological Challenges to Groundwater Trading: Lessons from South-West Western Australia'. *Journal of Hydrology* 412 (2012): 256–68. https://doi.org/10.1016/j.jhydrol.2011.05.034.

Somerset Catchment Market. 'About the Somerset Catchment Market' (2022). https://www.somersetcatchmentmarket.org.uk/about.

South China Morning Post. 'China Trades Rainwater for First Time, but Analysts Say Unstable Trading System Is Far from Being Market-Driven' (2020), accessed 6 January 2022, https://www.scmp.com/economy/china-economy/article/3114375/china-trades-rainwater-first-time-analysts-say-unstable.

South San Joaquin Irrigation District. 'Billing and Customer Service' (2021). https://www.ssid.com/district-services/billing-and-customer-service/.

Speight, Vanessa L. 'Innovation in the Water Industry: Barriers and Opportunities for US and UK Utilities'. *Wiley Interdisciplinary Reviews: Water* 2, no. 4 (2015/07/01 2015): 301–13.

Steele, Paul, and Sejal Patel. 'Tackling the Triple Crisis: Using Debt Swaps to Address Debt, Climate and Nature Loss Post-Covid-19' (2020). https://pubs.iied.org/sites/default/files/pdfs/migrate/16674IIED.pdf

Stein Hansen. 'Debt for Nature Swaps: Overview and Discussion of Key Issues' (1988). http://documents1.worldbank.org/curated/en/823691493257754828/pdf/Debt-for-nature-swaps-overview-and-discussion-of-key-issues.pdf.

Sun, Jian, Zhiliang Dang, and Shaokui Zheng. 'Development of Payment Standards for Ecosystem Services in the Largest Interbasin Water Transfer Projects in the World'. *Agricultural Water Management* 182 (2017/03/01/ 2017): 158–64.

Swain, D. L., O. E. J. Wing, P. D. Bates, J. M. Done, K. A. Johnson, and D. R. Cameron. 'Increased Flood Exposure Due to Climate Change and Population Growth in the United States'. *Earth's Future* 8, no. 11 (2020/11/01 2020): e2020EF001778.

System of Environmental Economic Accounting. 'Economy-Wide Material Flow Accounts and the Sustainable Use of Natural Resources in the Economy' (2021). https://seea.un.org/zh/news/economy-wide-material-flow-accounts-and-sustainable-use-natural-resources-economy.

Tabari, Hossein. 'Climate Change Impact on Flood and Extreme Precipitation Increases with Water Availability'. *Scientific Reports* 10, no. 1 (2020/08/13 2020): 13768.

Tasca, F. A., L. B. Assunção, and A. R. Finotti. 'International Experiences in Stormwater Fee'. *Water Science and Technology* 2017, no. 1 (2018): 287–99.

Tasca, Fabiane Andressa, Alexandra Rodrigues Finotti, and Roberto Fabris Goerl. 'A Stormwater User Fee Model for Operations and Maintenance in Small Cities'. *Water Science and Technology* 79, no. 2 (2019): 278–90.

Taylor, Katherine Selena. 'Australian Water Security Framings across Administrative Levels'. *Water Security* 12 (2021/04/01/ 2021): 100083.

Turley, Laura, and Abby Semple. 'Financing Sustainable Public–Private Partnerships' (2013). https://www.iisd.org/system/files/publications/ppp_financing.pdf.

Tweed Forum. 'Langhope Rig – Biodiversity Offset Conservation Projects' (2022), accessed 7 January 2022, https://tweedforum.org/our-work/projects/langhope-rig-biodiversity-offset-conservation-projects/.

UN Department of Economic and Social Affairs, Population Division. '2018 Revision of World Urbanization Prospects' (2018). https://www.un.org/development/desa/publications/2018-revision-of-world-urbanization-prospects.html.

UNDP. 'Debt for Nature Swaps' (2017). https://www.sdfinance.undp.org/content/sdfinance/en/home/solutions/debt-for-nature-swaps.html.

UNDP. 'Taxes on Pesticides and Chemical Fertilizers' (2017). https://www.undp.org/content/dam/sdfinance/doc/Taxes%20on%20pesticides%20and%20chemical%20fertilizers%20_%20UNDP.pdf.

UNEP. 'State of Finance for Nature' (2021). https://www.unep.org/resources/state-finance-nature.

UNESCO. 'Managing Water under Uncertainty and Risk' (2012). http://www.unesco.org/new/fileadmin/MULTIMEDIA/HQ/SC/pdf/WWDR4%20Volume%201-Managing%20Water%20under%20Uncertainty%20and%20Risk.pdf.

UNESCO. 2018 'Un World Water Development Report, Nature-Based Solutions for Water' (2018). http://www.unesco.org/new/en/natural-sciences/environment/water/wwap/wwdr/2018-nature-based-solutions/.

UNESCO World Water Assessment Programme. 'Un World Water Development Report 2021: Water and Climate Change' (2021). https://www.unwater.org/publications/un-world-water-development-report-2021/.

United Nations Department of Economic and Social Affairs. 'World Population Prospects 2019: Highlights' (2019). https://population.un.org/wpp/Publications/Files/WPP2019_Highlights.pdf.

UN-Water. 'Water Security & the Global Water Agenda' (2013). https://www.unwater.org/publications/water-security-global-water-agenda/#:~:text=The%20Brief%2C%20produced%20by%20UN,the%20umbrella%20of%20water%20security.

UN-Water. 'Partnerships for Improving Water and Energy Access, Efficiency and Sustainability' (2014). http://www.un.org/waterforlifedecade/water_and_energy_2014/pdf/water_and_energy_2014_final_report.pdf.

USDA. 'Water & Waste Disposal Loan Guarantees' (2020). https://www.rd.usda.gov/programs-services/water-environmental-programs/water-waste-disposal-loan-guarantees.

USDA. 'Fox Canyon Water Market, The: A Market-Based Tool for Groundwater Conservation Goes Live' (2021), accessed 6 January 2022, https://www.usda.gov/media/blog/2020/05/08/fox-canyon-water-market-market-based-tool-groundwater-conservation-goes-live.

US EPA. 'Water and Wastewater Pricing: An Informational Overview' (2003). https://nepis.epa.gov/Exe/ZyNET.exe/901U1200.txt?ZyActionD=ZyDocument&Client=EPA&Index=2000%20Thru%202005&Docs=&Query=&Time=&EndTime=&SearchMethod=1&TocRestrict=n&Toc=&TocEntry=&QField=&QFieldYear=&QFieldMonth=&QFieldDay=&UseQField=&IntQFieldOp=0&ExtQFieldOp=0&XmlQuery=&File=D%3A%5CZYFILES%5CINDEX%20DATA%5C00THRU05%5CTXT%5C00000011%5C901U1200.txt&User=ANONYMOUS&Password=anonymous&SortMethod=h%7C-&MaximumDocuments=1&FuzzyDegree=0&ImageQuality=r75g8/r75g8/x150y150g16/i425&Display=hpfr&DefSeekPage=x&SearchBack=ZyActionL&Back=ZyActionS&BackDesc=Results%20page&MaximumPages=1&ZyEntry=2#.

US EPA. 'Setting Small Drinking Water System Rates for a Sustainable Future: One of the Simple Tools for Effective Performance (Step) Guide Series' (2006). https://www.ircwash.org/resources/setting-small-drinking-water-system-rates-sustainable-future-one-simple-tools-effective.

US EPA. 'Green Infrastructure Municipal Handbook' (2008). https://www.epa.gov/green-infrastruct**ure/green-infrastructu**re-municipal-handbook.

US EPA. 'Community Based Public Private Partnerships (Cbp3s) and Alternative Market-Based Tools for Integrated Green Stormwater Infrastructure' (2015). https://www.epa.gov/sites/production/files/2015-12/documents/gi_cb_p3_guide_epa_r3_final_042115_508.pdf.

US EPA. 'Off-Site Stormwater Crediting: Lessons from Wetland Mitigation' (2018). https://www.epa.gov/sites/default/files/2018-10/documents/off-site_stormwater_crediting_lessons_from_wetland_mitigation-2018-04.pdf.

US EPA. 'Economic Incentives' (2022). https://www.epa.gov/environmental-economics/economic-incentives#subsidies.

US EPA. 'Water Security' (2022). https://www.epa.gov/emergency-response-research/water-security.

USGS. 'Urbanization and Water Quality' (2018). https://www.usgs.gov/special-topic/water-science-school/science/urbanization-and-water-quality?qt-science_center_objects=0#qt-science_center_objects.

Varady, Robert G., Tamee R. Albrecht, Andrea K. Gerlak, Margaret O. Wilder, Brian M. Mayer, Adriana Zuniga-Teran, Kacey C. Ernst, and Maria Carmen Lemos. 'The Exigencies of Transboundary Water Security: Insights on Community Resilience'. *Current Opinion in Environmental Sustainability* 44 (2020/06/01/ 2020): 74–84.

Varady, Robert G., Adriana A. Zuniga-Teran, Gregg M. Garfin, Facundo Martín, and Sebastián Vicuña. 'Adaptive Management and Water Security in a Global Context: Definitions, Concepts, and Examples'. *Current Opinion in Environmental Sustainability* 21 (2016/08/01/ 2016): 70–77.

Vörösmarty, Charles J., Vanesa Rodríguez Osuna, Anthony D. Cak, Anik Bhaduri, Stuart E. Bunn, Fabio Corsi, Jorge Gastelumendi, et al. 'Ecosystem-Based Water Security and the Sustainable Development Goals (Sdgs)'. *Ecohydrology & Hydrobiology* 18, no. 4 (2018/12/01/ 2018): 317–33.

WaCCLim. 'The Roadmap to a Low-Carbon Urban Water Utility' (2018). http://wacclim.org/wp-content/uploads/2018/12/2018_WaCCliM_Roadmap_EN_SCREEN.pdf.

Water Supply and Sanitation Collaborative Council. 'Public Funding for Sanitation—the Many Faces of Sanitation Subsidies' (2009). https://www.susana.org/en/knowledge-hub/resources-and-publications/library/details/2010.

Wehn, Uta, and Carlos Montalvo. 'Exploring the Dynamics of Water Innovation: Foundations for Water Innovation Studies'. *Journal of Cleaner Production* 171 (2018/01/10/ 2018): S1–S19.

Wendland, Kelly J., Miroslav Honzák, Rosimeiry Portela, Benjamin Vitale, Samuel Rubinoff, and Jeannicq Randrianarisoa. 'Targeting and Implementing Payments for Ecosystem Services: Opportunities for Bundling Biodiversity Conservation with Carbon and Water Services in Madagascar'. *Ecological Economics* 69, no. 11 (2010/09/15/ 2010): 2093–107.

Western Governors' Association. 'Water Transfers in the West: Projects, Trends, and Leading Practices in Voluntary Water Trading' (2012). http://www.westernstateswater.org/wp-content/uploads/2012/12/Water_Transfers_in_the_West_2012.pdf.

Wheatley Solutions. 'Water Trade Pilot Launches' (2022), accessed 6 January 2022, https://www.wheatleysolutions.co.uk/2020/12/01/water-catchment-data-hub-for-sharing-and-brokering-water-ready-to-pilot-in-the-east-anglia/.

Wheeler, Sarah Ann, Karina Schoengold, and Henning Bjornlund. 'Lessons to Be Learned from Groundwater Trading in Australia and the United States'. 493–517: Springer International Publishing, 2016.

WHO. 'Heatwaves'. https://www.who.int/health-topics/heatwaves#tab=tab_1.

WHO Europe. 'Water and Sanitation' (2022). https://www.euro.who.int/en/health-topics/environment-and-health/water-and-sanitation

Wisconsin Department of Natural Resources. 'Wetland Compensatory Mitigation' (2022), accessed 7 January 2022, https://dnr.wisconsin.gov/topic/Wetlands/mitigation.

World Bank. 'Tradablewater Rights: A Property Rights Approach to Resolving Water Shortages and Promoting Investment' (1996). https://documents1.worldbank.org/curated/en/941411468761706580/pdf/multi-page.pdf.

World Bank. 'Economic Impacts of Inadequate Sanitation in India' (2011). https://documents.worldbank.org/en/publication/documents-reports/documentdetail/820131468041640929/economic-impacts-of-inadequate-sanitation-in-india.

World Bank. 'Structuring Private-Sector Participation (Psp) Contracts for Small Scale Water Projects' (2014). https://library.pppknowledgelab.org/documents/4129/download.

World Bank. 'Innovative Finance for Development Solutions' (2015). https://olc.worldbank.org/system/files/Innovative_Finance_for_Development_Solutions.pdf.

World Bank. 'What Are Green Bonds?' (2015). https://documents.worldbank.org/en/publication/documents-reports/documentdetail/400251468187810398/what-are-green-bonds.

World Bank. 'Biodiversity Offsets: A User Guide' (2016). https://openknowledge.worldbank.org/handle/10986/25758.

World Bank. 'Financing Options for the 2030 Water Agenda' (2016). https://openknowledge.worldbank.org/handle/10986/25495.

World Bank. 'High and Dry: Climate Change, Water, and the Economy' (2016). https://openknowledge.worldbank.org/handle/10986/23665?utm_source=Global+Waters+%2B+Water+Currents&utm_campaign=9905bbdc1e-Water_Currents_Water+Utiliti_12_dec_2018&utm_medium=email&utm_term=0_fae9f9ae2b-9905bbdc1e-25803553.

World Bank. 'The Costs of Meeting the 2030 Sustainable Development Goal Targets on Drinking Water, Sanitation, and Hygiene' (2016). https://openknowledge.worldbank.org/handle/10986/23681

World Bank. 'Doing More with Less—Smarter Subsidies for Water Supply and Sanitation' (2019). https://www.worldbank.org/en/topic/water/publication/smarter-subsidies-for-water-supply-and-sanitation.

World Bank. 'Mobilising Private Finance for Nature' (2020). http://pubdocs.worldbank.org/en/916781601304630850/Finance-for-Nature-28-Sep-web-version.pdf.

World Bank. 'Municipal Public-Private Partnership Framework' (2020). https://openknowledge.worldbank.org/handle/10986/33572.

World Bank. 'Pontal - Public-Private Partnership Irrigation Project' 2021, accessed 6 January 2022, https://ppp.worldbank.org/public-private-partnership/library/pontal-public-private-partnership-irrigation-project.

World Bank. 'Ppps in Irrigation' (2022), accessed 6 January 2022, https://ppp.worldbank.org/public-private-partnership/ppp-sector/water-sanitation/ppps-irrigation.

World Bank. 'Stakeholder Communication and Engagement' (2022), accessed 6 January 2022, https://pppknowledgelab.org/guide/sections/39-stakeholder-communication-and-engagement.

World Bank. 'Water and Sanitation Agreements' (2022), https://ppp.worldbank.org/public-private-partnership/sector/water-sanitation/water-agreements.

Wunder, S. 'Are Direct Payments for Environmental Services Spelling Doom for Sustainable Forest Management in the Tropics?'. *Ecology and Society* 11 (2006).

Yang, Tong, Ruyin Long, Xiaotong Cui, Dandan Zhu, and Hong Chen. 'Application of the Public–Private Partnership Model to Urban Sewage Treatment'. *Journal of Cleaner Production* 142 (2017/01/20/ 2017): 1065–74. https://doi.org/https://doi.org/10.1016/j.jclepro.2016.04.152. https://www.sciencedirect.com/science/article/pii/S0959652616304413.

Zhang, Qian, Jun Nakatani, Tao Wang, Chunyan Chai, and Yuichi Moriguchi. 'Hidden Greenhouse Gas Emissions for Water Utilities in China's Cities'. *Journal of Cleaner Production* 162 (2017/09/20/ 2017): 665–77.

zu Ermgassen, Sophus Olav Sven Emil, Pratiwi Utamiputri, Leon Bennun, Stephen Edwards, and Joseph William Bull. 'The Role of 'No Net Loss' Policies in Conserving Biodiversity Threatened by the Global Infrastructure Boom'. *One Earth* 1, no. 3 (2019/11/22/ 2019): 305–15. https://doi.org/https://doi.org/10.1016/j.oneear.2019.10.019. http://www.sciencedirect.com/science/article/pii/S2590332219301332.

Index

Tables are indicated by an italic *t* following the page number.

adaptive management 101
ADB *see* Asian Development Bank
additionality 45–6, 46*t*, 47, 90, 99, 149*t*
affermage contract 135–6
ageing infrastructure 14–15, 37–9
aggregated biodiversity offsets 150–2, 151*t*
agriculture
  and alternative water sources 28
  and irrigation PPPs 139–40
  and nature-based solutions 29*t*
  and subsidies 194
  and water-food nexus 16
  and water pollution 16–17, 107–8
air pollution 33*t*
allowances 116–18, 166–7, 166*t*, 171
alternative water sources 1, 26–8, 174–5
anaerobic co-digestion 33
anaerobic digestion 32
Anglian Water 63–4, 170
aquifers 23*t*, 62, 179–81
artificial intelligence (AI) 25
Asian Development Bank 8, 43, 64, 131
Asia Pacific region 38–9
Atlanta 66
atmospheric water generation technology 28
Auckland Council 159–60
auctions 91, 180*t*
Australia 69, 111, 170, 171*t*

Baltimore City 115
banks 43, 78, 83, 84–5, 92, 131, 189
best management practices 118, 121–2, 173,
    174*t*, 194
best practices 187
BGI *see* blue-green infrastructure
bilateral agreements 92–3
bilateral contracts 180*t*
bilateral debt swaps 76–7
biodiversity loss 13–14, 145, 196
biodiversity offsets
  aggregated 150–2, 151*t*

bank programmes 196
  case studies 159–62
  definition 145–6
  financial sustainability 153, 154*t*
  as financing instruments 48, 196
  framework 154–9
  implementation 152, 157–9
  metrics 148, 150*t*
  mitigation hierarchy 147–8, 156
  performance and success 153
  principles 149*t*
  for renewable energy projects 197
  selecting sites 148
  types of 146–7
  use of 145
  and wetland mitigation 197
biodiversity protection 90, 91*t*
biogas 32
biomethane 32
bioplastic 35
blackwater 26–7 *see also* sewage
blended finance 44–7, 45*t*, 46*t*
blowdown water 28
blue-green infrastructure 176–8
BMPs *see* best management practices
Bolivia 74
bonds 53, 131 *see also* green bonds
Border Bank 69
Brazil 140
British Standards Institute 64
Build-Operate-Transfer contract 138
bundling 94
buyers of PWS schemes 94–5

Canada 122–4
capacity building 153
Capacity Buyback Program 123–4
cap-and-trade schemes 97, 166*t*, 199
capital shares 131
captured condensate 28
carbon offset payments 154*t*

carbon sequestration and storage 89
CBI *see* Climate Bonds Initiative
CBP3 *see* community-based public-private
    partnerships
cellulose 35
central banks 83
certification schemes 60–3, 95, 97,
    177–8, 198
Certified Climate Bond 60
charges *see* environmental charges
Chester 142–3
children 190
China 175
clearinghouses 92, 180*t*
Climate Bonds Initiative 60
climate change 11–12, 13
climate change adaptation 41, 57, 60, 68*t*
climate change mitigation 1–2, 10*t*, 32, 60,
    65, 201
collaboration 40, 40*t*, 100
Colorado Water Conservation Board 182
combined heat and power 32–3
combined sewer systems 15
commercial banks 189
commercial debt swaps 76
commercial sustainability 47
community-based public-private
    partnerships 141–3, 142*t*, 196
community engagement 178
concession agreements 138
conditionality 90
conservation banks 92, 152
Conservation International 74, 85
conservation investors 75, 84–5
conservation tillage 29*t*
conservation trust funds 154*t*
contracts *see also* public-private partnerships
    affermage 135–6
    bilateral 180*t*
    Build-Operate-Transfer 138
    Design-Build-Lease 138
    Design-Build-Operate 138
    lease 137–8
    management 135
    operation, management and
        maintenance 135, 139–40
corporate bonds 54*t*, 63–4
corporate social responsibility 44, 44*t*
Costa Rica 85–7
cost-sharing 97

cover crops 29*t*, 191
creditors 75, 76*t*, 84–5
credits 123*t*, 152, 166*t*, 175–8, 194, 196–9
credit trading 104, 166*t*, 175–8, 196–9
criteria aggregation 100
crowding-in 47

deaths 12
debt 73, 131, 189
debt-forgiveness 77, 77*t*
debt-for-nature swaps
    actors and motivations 75
    administering of funds 79–82
    benefits 76, 76*t*
    best practices 82–5, 189–91
    case study 85–7
    concept 73–5
    and environmental awareness 190
    as financing instruments 47
    and freshwater ecosystems 190
    general elements 77*t*
    operationalizing 78–9
    scheduling revenue flows 79
    types 76–7, 77*t*
    and water resources 190
    and water treatment systems 191
debtors 75, 76*t*, 82–3
debt swaps 73–5 *see also* debt-for-nature
    swaps
demand 12, 13, 16, 41
demand management 1, 22–3, 23*t*, 200–1
Denmark 108
desalination 15–16, 28, 61
Design-Build-Lease contract 138
Design-Build-Operate contract 138
developing countries 43, 73–5
development additionality 45
development finance institutions 46
development partners 40*t*
development rights purchase 97
DFIs *see* development finance institutions
DFNs *see* debt-for-nature swaps
disasters 8, 12
domestic financial facility 80–2, 82*t*
donor-funded projects 154*t*
donors 75, 76*t*
drinking water 15, 37, 38, 58*t*, 95–6
drought defence 62
droughts 12, 16

earmarked charges 106
eco-certification 95
eco-labelling schemes 97
ecological restoration 63
economic growth 14
economic losses 12, 37
economic water security 8
ecosystems 9, 10*t*
ecosystem services 89–90, 98, 100, 197 *see also* Payments for Ecosystem Services
education 23*t*, 32, 190
EIBs *see* environmental impact bonds
electricity consumption 15–16, 17, 33*t*
eligible green projects 56–7, 68*t*, 187
end-users 130
energy 15–16, 33, 34 *see also* renewable energy; water-energy nexus
energy consumption 17
energy efficiency 56, 61, 68*t*, 175
EnTrade 101–2
environment, social, and governance 65, 67–8
Environmental and Social Impact Assessment 155–6
environmental awareness 190
environmental charges
    benefits 107*t*
    case studies 111–12, 113, 115
    concept 106
    definition 105–6
    irrigation water pricing 112–13
    stormwater fees 113–15, 114*t*
    water pollution taxes 105–8, 192
    water pricing 108–11
environmental flows 182, 200
Environmental Impact Assessment 155–6
environmental impact bonds 64–6, 187, 188–9
Environmental Investment Allowance 116–18
Environmental Protection Agency 142
environmental taxes 105–15, 107*t*
environmental water buyback 182
environmental water security 8
equity 131
equity investment 45*t*
equivalence 149*t*
Essex & Suffolk Water 170
Europe 12, 15
European Union 16

ex-ante monitoring 172
exchanges 92
ex-post monitoring 172

facility-owned buildings 34
farm service agreement 140
Farm Stewardship Program 118
fee discounts 119, 122–3, 123*t*
fees
    irrigation 112–13, 140
    in-lieu 152, 177, 197
    and public finance 42
    stormwater 113–15, 114*t*, 193
    user 132
    and water service PPPs 132–8
filtration avoidance programmes 95–6
finance/financing
    barriers to 39*t*
    blended 44–7, 45*t*, 46*t*
    collaboration 40*t*
    and corporate social responsibility 44*t*
    innovative 38–42
    instruments 3, 45*t*, 47–8, 201
    international public 43
    lack of understanding 2
    of PPPs 131
    principles 49*t*
    private 43–4
    public 42
    sources 42–7
financial additionality 45
financial sustainability 153, 154*t*
fiscal environmental taxes 106
floating PV installations 34
flood defences 62
floodplains 29*t*, 194
floods 12, 14*t*, 29*t*, 44*t*, 58*t*, 62
fog harvesting 28
food demand 16
forests 29*t*
Fox Canyon Water Market 181
freshwater ecosystems 9, 11, 16, 190

GBPs *see* Green Bond Principles
GDP 13, 14, 37
general obligation bonds 54
global material usage 13–14
global warming 11
Global Water Partnership 7
goals 98, 99, 142*t*

government agencies 189
government bonds 54t, 63
governments
  and biodiversity offsets 153
  and collaboration 40t
  and PPPs 128–9, 131–4
  and water investment 41
grants 45t, 81, 118–19, 121–2, 194
Gray Water Rebate 122
Greater Western Water 111–12, 112t
Green Bond Principles 56–60, 58t
green bonds
  benefits 55
  best practices 187–8
  case studies 63–4
  certification 60–3
  as financing instruments 47
  and green infrastructure projects 187–8
  issuing process 55–6
  market 54
  and multilateral agencies 188
  pricing 54–5
  principles 56–60, 58t
  and renewable energy 61
  supply 54
  types of 54t
  use of 53–4
  and water utilities 188
green buildings 29t
Green Construction Board 64
green economy 7, 8
green funds 85
green growth 1, 8–9, 9t, 11–17
greenhouse gas emissions 12, 14–15, 17
green infrastructure
  and community-based PPPs 141–3
  and EIBs 188–9
  and green bonds 187
  investment growth in 37
  and nature-based solutions 32, 37
  for water management 29t
Green Infrastructure Grant Opportunities
    Program 121–2
Green Loan Principles 67–8
green loans
  benefits 66–7
  best practices 187
  case studies 69–70, 70t
  commercial 189
  as financing instruments 47

government guarantees 189
  principles 67–8
  use of 66–7, 187
  and water technologies 189
green parking lots 29t
green parks 29t
green projects 67–8, 68t
green roofs 29t
green stormwater infrastructure
    142–3
green streets 29t
Green Technology Financing
    Scheme 69–70, 70t
grey infrastructure 1–2, 32
greywater 26, 194
groundwater recharge 11, 29t, 62
groundwater trading 179–82, 180t, 199
Guelph 122–3, 123t

Healthy Waters Biodiversity Offset
    Bank 159–60
High Level Panel on Water 40–1
hub farm agreement 140
hydropower energy recovery 34

Illinois 121–2
incentives 91t, 107t, 118–24
India 37
Industrial Water Rate Program 123–4
Information and Communication
    Technology 24
infrastructure concession 140
in lieu fees 152, 161, 177, 197
innovative financing 38–42
intermediaries 46, 93, 93t, 100
International Capital Market Association 56
International Finance Corporation 146
international public finance 43
inventive taxes 106
inventory development 41
investment 40–1, 48, 49t
irrigation projects 195
irrigation public-private
    partnerships 139–40
irrigation systems 193
irrigation water pricing 112–13

Japan Bank for International
    Cooperation 43
junior debt 131

KfW Bankengruppe 43
knowledge gaps 39t

landowners 95
land purchases 97
landscape beauty 89
landscape plans 99
layering 94
leadership 33t
lease contract 138
lenders 130
loan guarantees 45t, 120, 189
Loan Market Association 67
loans 81, 131 see also green loans
local governments 141
local management authorities 83
local residents and interest groups 83

machine learning 25
Malaysia 69–70, 70t
managed aquifer recharge 23t
management contract 135
market-based instruments 47, 105, 107, 192
market development 46t, 120–1
market mechanisms 152
Maryland 173–4, 174t
material usage 13–14
MBIs see market-based instruments
MDBs see multilateral development banks
megacities 13
Melbourne 111–12
metals 35
mezzanine debt 131
micro-trading 175
mitigation banking 19, 92, 161
mitigation hierarchy 147–8, 156
multilateral agencies 188
multilateral development bank bonds 54t, 64
multilateral development banks 43, 46, 131
Murray-Darling Basin 170, 171t

natural resource extraction 13–14
natural water retention measures 29t
nature-based solutions
    benefits 32, 37
    concept 2, 200–1
    and green bond certification 62–3
    types of 29t
    underinvestment in 37, 38

for water management 28–32
and water utilities PWS 191–2
Nature Conservancy see The Nature
    Conservancy
Net Gain 146, 148, 155, 156
Netherlands 116–18
New Jersey Infrastructure Bank 63
New Zealand 159–60
nitrogen 34
No Net Loss 146, 148, 155, 156, 158, 159
nutrients 27t, 191
NWRM see natural water retention
    measures

OECD 8, 44, 82
onsite non-potable reuse systems 26
operating costs 48
operation, management and maintenance
    contracts 135, 139–40
operational (institutional) additionality 45
outcome-based payments 92

Paris Club 74, 76
partnerships
    community-based public-private 141–3,
        196
    irrigation public-private 139–40, 195
    public-private 47, 127–35, 195
    water service public-private 135–9, 195
Payments for Ecosystem Services
    additionality and conditionality 90
    auctions or performance payments 92–3
    benefits 91t
    bundling and layering 94
    concept 89–90
    intermediaries 93, 93t
    market type 92–3
    targeting 99
Payments for Watershed Services
    best practices 191–2
    buyers and sellers 94–5
    case study 101–2
    concept 89, 94
    as financing instruments 47
    guideline framework for effective
        targeting 98–101
    payment mechanisms 97–8
    and source water protection 95–6
    and utilities 96
    and water utilities 191–2

performance-based payments 64–6, 91–2, 119, 123–4, 135, 137*t*
performance measurement 132–3
permanence, and biodiversity offsets 149*t*
permits, tradable *see* tradable permits
permittee responsible mitigation 161–2, 197
perpetual funds 80–1
PES schemes *see* Payments for Ecosystem Services
pesticides taxes 107–8, 192
philanthropy 43, 95, 154
Philippines 77*t*
phosphorous 34
planning permission 44*t*
pollution
  air 33*t*
  and environmental charges 105–8, 192
  water 12, 16–17, 107–8, 171, 192, 198
Pontal–Public-Private Partnership Irrigation Project 140
population growth 12, 13
PPPs *see* public-private partnerships
preservation offsets 149*t*
prior rights 168*t*
private finance 43–4, 120
private payment schemes 97
private sector 40*t*, 95, 128–32, 139–40
procurement and award 134
programme costs 44*t*
project bonds 54, 131
projects for PPPs 135–8
project-specific revenue transfers 154*t*
public allocation 168*t*
public education 23*t*, 32, 83
public finance 38, 42, 43
public health 32, 33*t*
public payment schemes 97–8
public-private partnerships
  best practices 195–6
  community 141–3, 196
  compensation 132
  concept 127–9
  as financing instruments 47
  financing of 131
  irrigation 139–40, 195
  lifecycle 133–4
  measuring performance 132–3
  roles of parties 129–30
  special purpose vehicles 131–2
  stakeholder communication 130–1

  for traditional water infrastructure 195
  use of 127, 129, 195
  water service 134–9, 195
public sector 94, 130
PWS schemes *see* Payments for Watershed Services

quality of life 65

rain gardens 29*t*
rainwater harvesting 27, 118, 175, 199
rebates 119, 122
renewable energy
  benefits 33*t*
  and biodiversity offsets 197
  as eligible green projects 56, 68*t*
  on facility-owned buildings 34
  and green bonds 61
  opportunities 2
  from wastewater 32–3
  for water management 32–4
research and development 153
resource extraction 13–14
resource recovery 34–5
restoration offsets 149*t*
retention ponds 29*t*
retrofits 194
revenue obligation bonds 54
reverse auctions 180*t*
revolving funds 81
riparian buffers 29*t*
riparian rights 168*t*
risk mitigation 46*t*

sanitation 12, 15, 37, 38, 58*t*
Saskatchewan 118
Saudi Arabia 138–9
Saudi Water Partnership Company 138–9
scheduling revenue flows 79
Scottish Borders Council 160–1
securitized bonds 54
self-generated revenues 154*t*
sellers 94–5
service provider 130
service provision thresholds 99
sewage 12, 14*t*, 15, 26–7, 32–5, 58*t*
sinking funds 81
site selection 148, 155–6
smart digital water management 23*t*, 24–6, 25*t*, 200

smart water grids 24–5, 175
smart water meters 1, 23t, 24–5
soil 29t
solar energy 34
Somerset Catchment Market 101–2
source water protection 23t, 95–6
South San Joaquin Irrigation District 113
spatial demand and distribution 98
spatial synergy 98–9
special purpose vehicles 131–2
stakeholder communication 130–1
stormwater
    credits 122–3, 123t, 194, 198–9
    fees 113–15, 114t, 115, 193
    harvesting 27–8
    management 62–3
    quality 193
    runoff 32
Stormwater Authority of Chester 142–3
Stormwater Retention Credit 178
stormwater volume credit trading 175–8,
    178
strategic planning 41
structured finance 45t
struvite 35
subordinated debt 131
subsidies 23t, 115–18, 194
surface water 23t
sustainability 47, 142t
sustainable development 12
Sustainable Development Goals 9, 10t, 37
sustainable land and water resources
    management 58t
sustainable water and wastewater
    management 57
systemic additionality 45

targeting 99, 100
tariffs 42
taxation
    environmental 105–15, 107t
    for investments in water technologies 193
    and public finance 42
    water pollution 105–8, 192
    and water technologies 193
technical assistance 45t
technologies 22, 24–6, 32–5, 69–70, 70t,
    102, 189, 193
The Nature Conservancy 74, 85, 181, 182
thermal energy 15, 33

thermal oxidation 33
TMDL see Total Maximum Daily Load
TNC see The Nature Conservancy
Toronto Water 123–4
Total Maximum Daily Load 171
tradable permits 48, 165, 197
tradable permit schemes 165–7, 166t,
    197–200
tradable water rights 167–71, 168t, 169t
trading boundaries 177
transfer payments 97
Tucson Water 122

unaccounted-for-water 23t
undervaluing of water 39t
United Kingdom 63–4, 101–2, 160–1,
    170
United Nations
    Environment Programme 8
    UN-Water 7
United States
    ageing infrastructure 15
    community-based public-private
        partnerships 142–3
    debt-for-nature swaps 74, 77t, 85–7
    environmental impact bonds 66
    grants 121–2
    green bonds 63
    green loans 69
    groundwater trading 181–2
    irrigation water pricing 113
    likelihood of a megadrought 12
    and PWS schemes 96
    rebates 122
    spending on water infrastructure 37
    stormwater fees 115
    stormwater volume credit trading 178
    utilities 96
    and water pollution 17
    water quality trading 173–4
    wetland mitigation 161–2
unsafe sources 12
untreated sewage 12
urban forests 29t
urbanization 8, 13, 14t, 17
urban rainwater trading schemes 199
urban water trading 174–5
user charges 106
user fees 114, 132

valuation services 98
vanilla bonds 53
Ventura County, California 194
volumetric water charges 110, 193

Washington DC 178
wastewater
 as alternative water source 26–7
 and energy consumption 15–16, 17
 and facility-owned buildings 34
 and renewable energy 2, 32–3, 33t, 201
 and resource recovery 34–5
 treatment plants 2, 191
 and urbanization 14t
 and water infrastructure criteria 61
water allocations 13, 23, 23t, 199
water augmentation 23t
water bodies 29t
water conservation 22–3, 119–21, 195
water efficiency 23t, 119–21
water-energy nexus 15–16, 33t
water-food nexus 16–17
water infrastructure
 ageing 14–15, 37–9
 and biodiversity offsets 154t
 capital intensive 39t
 criteria 60–3
 and environmental impact bonds 188–9
 and GBP 61–2
 and grants 121–2
 green 2, 29t, 37, 65, 121–2, 200–1
 and green bonds 187–8
 grey 1–2
 optimizing 42
 and PPPs 127, 138–43, 195–6
 underinvestment in 38
Water Infrastructure Criteria 60–3
water metering 23t, 24–5
water pollution 12, 16–17, 107–8, 171,
  192, 198

water pricing 23t, 108–13, 169, 169t, 193
water purification systems 28
water quality 11, 13, 14t, 29t, 62–3, 65, 194
water quality trading 171–4, 172t, 198
water recycling 26–8, 27t, 28
water-related disasters 8, 12
water reporting metrics 57–60
water reuse 1, 26–8, 27t, 58t
water rights 168–9, 182, 198, 200 *see also*
  tradable water rights
water-scarce areas 7
water security 1, 7–9, 9t, 11–17, 33t, 201
water service public-private
  partnerships 134–9, 136t, 137t
watershed protection programmes 89, 96
water sources, alternative 1, 26–8, 174–5
water storage 61, 62
water stress 13, 27t
water trading *see* tradable permits
water utilities
 and barriers to financing 39t
 and discounted rates 195
 and EIBs 188
 and energy consumption 17
 and green bonds 188
 and greywater rebates 194
 and incentives 118–19
 and PPPs 195
 and PWS schemes 96, 191–2
 and renewable energy 2, 34
 and resource recovery 34–5
 and stormwater credits 194
 and water pricing 109–12, 193
Wessex Water 101–2
wetlands 62, 161–2, 197
Wheatley Watersource 170
wind energy 34
Wisconsin 161–2
World Bank 43, 140
World Wildlife Fund 74